Library of Southern Civilization

The NEW ORLEANS of LAFCADIO HEARN

ILLUSTRATED SKETCHES FROM THE

Daily City Item

EDITED, WITH AN INTRODUCTION, BY
DELIA LaBARRE

LOUISIANA STATE UNIVERSITY PRESS
BATON ROUGE

Published by Louisiana State University Press
www.lsupress.org

Copyright © 2007 by Louisiana State University Press
All rights reserved. Except in the case of brief quotations used in articles or reviews, no part of this publication may be reproduced or transmitted in any format or by any means without written permission of Louisiana State University Press.

Louisiana Paperback Edition, 2021

Designer: Michelle A. Neustrom
Typefaces: Century Schoolbook, Vineta, News Gothic

Frontispiece: Engraving of Lafcadio Hearn from *Harper's Illustrated Weekly*, ca. 1885, courtesy of Tulane University Special Collections.
Cover illustration: "A Day Among a Pile of Bones Found on the Lake Coast" (Hearn self-portrait).

Library of Congress Cataloging-in-Publication Data

The New Orleans of Lafcadio Hearn : illustrated sketches from the Daily city item / edited, with an introduction, by Delia LaBarre.
     p. cm. — (Library of southern civilization)
  Includes bibliographical references.
  ISBN 978-0-8071-3243-2 (cloth : alk. paper)
1. New Orleans (La.)—Social life and customs—19th century—Anecdotes. 2. New Orleans (La.)—Social life and customs—19th century—Pictorial works. 3. City and town life—Louisiana—New Orleans—History—19th century—Anecdotes. 4. City and town life—Louisiana—New Orleans—History—19th century—Pictorial works. I. LaBarre, Delia. II. Daily item (New Orleans, La.)
  F379.N55N48 2007
  976.3'3505—dc22

                                                  2006035068

ISBN 978-0-8071-7694-8 (paperback) | ISBN 978-0-8071-3571-6 (pdf) | ISBN 978-0-8071-4827-3 (epub)

CONTENTS

Acknowledgments	xi
Introduction: *The Vitriol and Balm of a Nineteenth-Century Prophet*	xiii
Editorial Note	lii

The Haunted and the Haunters	1
Free Board and Lodging for Thieves	2
The Delivering Angel	3
The Ideal Commissioner	4
The Opium Vice	4
Frank J. Mumford	5
Mumford of Ours	6
"This Way? Or This?"	6
Dog Days	7
Police Board	7
The Devil on Carondelet Street	8
The Oarsmen	8
Exthract from the Spach ov Paddy Whack	9
The Tropical Palm	10
(Away, Away)	11
The Smile That Johnson Smole	12
Crushing out the Vipers	12
Military Salutes	13
Boom-Boom	13
Illustrated Letters from the People (June 24)	15
Illustrated Letters from the People: "Boots!"	16
The Amateur Musician	16
The Last of Tilden and the Last of Grant	17
Illustrated Letters from the People (June 28)	17
The Unspeakable Velocipede	18
The Bicycle Fiend's Defense	20
The Organ Grinder	21
Illustrated Letters from the People: "I Know YOU'LL Give Me One"	22
The Nurse Maid	23
Illustrated Letters from the People: My Office in My Hat	24
Feminine Intolerance	25

CONTENTS

Hancock and English	27
Morning Calls—Very Early	28
The Go-at	29
Oakland Park Scenery	30
"Forty Fights to a Dance"	31
Citizen-Executioner Sherman	32
In the Vise	33
Illustrated Letters from the People (July 12)	34
The Last Shake of the Bloody Shirt	35
How They Do It	36
The Wolfish Dog	37
Illustrated Letters from the People: Street Car Nuisances	38
Ultra-Canal	38
Dr. Tanner (July 18)	39
"Shine?"	40
Dr. Tanner (July 20)	40
Illustrated Letters from the People: Mischievous Boys	41
Illustrated Letters from the People (July 22)	42
Illustrated Letters from the People: The Banana Curse	43
Dr. Tanner (July 24)	44
The Knife-Grinder	44
Dr. Tanner's Present Aspect	45
"The Direful Boost"	46
——! ——!! Mosquitoes!!!	47
Illustrated Letters from the People: House Hunting Nuisance	48
Attention, Rowdies!	49
Taxpayers' Catechism	50
Ah Sin on the Situation	50
The Fatal Plunge	51
Illustrated Letters from the People (August 4)	52
Ins and Outs	53
Under the Electric Light	54
Dr. Tanner: Slams the Door on the Undertaker's Nose	55
Scat!	55
Seeking a Sensation	56
Lake-Side Lickings	58
Sarah Bernhardt	59
Illustrated Letters from the People (August 12)	59

CONTENTS

Voluntary Contributions	60
Jewell's Defence of Garfield	61
By the Murmuring Waves	61
Hunting for the Honest Eight	62
Naughty Boys	62
Ghosteses	63
Coming Events Cast Their Shadows Before	64
Quack! Quack!	64
The Chinese Vice	65
Cat-ankarous	66
Go-it	66
Murder and Violence	67
Char-coal	67
Rowdyism Suppressed	68
Not a Dream at All	69
Our Ghouls	69
The Witch	70
Des Perches	71
Washerwomen	72
Sons of the Sea	73
A Small Nuisance	74
The Milkman	75
Prickly Heat	76
The Hand-Maiden	77
Dandy-Traps	78
Contraband	79
The Indignant Dead	79
Whited Sepulchres	80
Dead Sea Fruit	81
The Flower-Sellers	82
The Man with the Small Electric Machine	83
The Alligators	83
The Police Board	84
The Vendor of Wisdom	86
The Curse of the Newspaper Vendor	87
At the Photographer's	88
Cakes and Candy	89
The Puller of Noses	90
Ye Pilot	91
Awful Consequences of Poor Shooting	91

CONTENTS

A Warning to Advertisers	91
Frantic Appeals for Help	92
Police Efficiency	93
The Master Spirit	94
The Police Mutual Aid Society	95
Illustrated Letters from the People: Another Chance for Reform	95
You Pays Your Money, and You Takes Your Choice	97
The *Great Eastern*	98
The Wages of Sin	98
That Verdict	99
Poney Up!	100
329	100
Want to Investigate	100
Statement of a Victim	101
That Villainous Broker	102
Improved Police Ideas	103
Blackmailing	103
Nothing like Self-Esteem	104
Scourged to the Ballot	105
The Smokers of Pipes	105
The Festive	106
Aïda	107
How History Is Written	107
Not 329 but 350	109
And He Spake to Them Another Parable	109
Dreams of the Elector—Before and After	109
Journalistic Dissection	109
Youthful Smokers	110
Commercial Statuary	110
Spanish Moss	111
Fire!	112
All Saints!	113
The Chinese Poison	113
Dreams of the Ballet	114
A Day of Reckoning	114
Gladness in the Granite Building	114
French Opera	115
The Shooting Season	116
That Piano Organ	116

CONTENTS

Une Première Danseuse	117
The French Opera: Madame Emilie Ambre	117
Recollections of the Theatrical Season	118
Dissatisfied	118
The French Opera House: Jourdan	119
Those Furniture Men	119
The French Opera House: Mauge	119
The Bone of Contention	120
The French Opera House (Enrico Utto)	120
The French Opera: Gossi	121
The Pelican's Ghost	121
Something to Be Proud Of	122
Thanksgiving	122
British Recollections of New Orleans	123
The Man Socially Loved	123
Curious!	123
An Artful Dodger	124
After Thanksgiving	124
Our Model Police Force	124
"Oft in the Stilly Night," Etc.	125
Ugh!!	126
The French Opera: Mr. Momas, Leader of the Orchestra	126
Moral Edification	127
"Wet Enough for You?"	127
Web-Footed	127
Taxes	127
Tantalizing	128
Officers of the Law	128
Significant Paragraphs from the President's Message	128
Won't Wait Till the Holidays	129
A Miller Who Couldn't Mill	129
The Sanitary Conference	129
The Inundations	130
Notes on Columns	131
Bibliography	171

ACKNOWLEDGMENTS

This volume would not have been possible without a Publishing Initiative Grant from the Louisiana Endowment for the Humanities (LEH), state affiliate of the National Endowment for the Humanities, which supported the editing of the texts and the work of collecting, scanning, and cleaning the woodcut images, most of which were drawn from microfilm copies, since the originals have been lost. LEH, under the leadership of President and Executive Director Michael Sartisky, continues to be a heroic organization vital to the cultural conservation and preservation of New Orleans and Louisiana. I would also like to express my appreciation to Deputy Director John R. Kemp and Associate Director Jennifer Mitchel.

Thanks to S. Frederick Starr, who has long held that Lafcadio Hearn's Louisiana works deserve more attention, I was introduced to Hearn's work almost a decade ago. While assisting Dr. Starr on his collection *Inventing New Orleans: Writings of Lafcadio Hearn* (University Press of Mississippi, 2001), I learned about the large body of illustrated columns Hearn had created, most of which had never been republished. Dr. Starr's advice and support during various phases of this project have been invaluable. I am also especially indebted to John Maxwell Hamilton, Dean of the Manship School of Mass Communication at Louisiana State University and author of *Casanova Was a Book Lover* (Louisiana State University Press, 2000), for his interest in Hearn and his advice and encouragement in seeking a publisher. William D. Reeves, author of *Historic Louisiana: An Illustrated History* (Louisiana Historical Society, 2003), read an early draft of the manuscript and made valuable comments. The linguist Tom Klingler, author of *If I Could Turn My Tongue Like That: The Creole Language of Pointe Coupée Parish, Louisiana* (Louisiana State University Press, 2003), generously contributed a translation of the Creole song illustrated by Lafcadio Hearn, "Morning Calls—Very Early."

Sylvia Metzinger—formerly with Tulane Special Collections and now head of Rare Books, Cincinnati–Hamilton County Public Library—was helpful in tracking down the few remaining original newspapers containing Hearn's woodcuts, which are housed at Tulane University. I wish to express my appreciation to Tulane University's Lance Query, Dean of Libraries; Wilbur Meneray, Director of Special Collections; and Leon Miller, Manuscript Archivist. I am also grateful to Louisiana State University's Hill Memorial Library and the Mississippi Valley Newspaper Project, funded by the National Endowment for the Humanities, without which all trace of most of Hearn's illustrated columns might have been lost. Thanks are also due to the facilities, holdings, and staffs of the New Orleans Public Library, especially to Irene Wainwright, Archivist, Louisiana Division; Special Collections of Loyola University New Orleans, especially Arthur E. Carpenter, University Archivist; the Williams Research Center of the Historic New Orleans Collection; and the Maselli Museum and Library of New Orleans. I am also particularly grateful to Grant Dupré of Dupré's Printing and Copying in Baton Rouge, whose consultation on the scanning and cleaning of the images was vital, and to the Lafcadio Hearn/Koizumi Yakumo Center for the use of its computer, generously donated by Russell S. Clark of Baton Rouge.

Not least among the individuals who have made this volume possible are members of the staff of Louisiana State University Press, especially MaryKatherine Callaway, Director; Rand Dotson, History Editor; Catherine L. Kadair, Senior Editor; Barbara Outland, Marketing Manager; and Michelle A. Garrod, Designer. Many thanks also to freelance copyeditor Julia Ridley Smith.

INTRODUCTION
The Vitriol and Balm of a Nineteenth-Century Prophet

Historians have called the last few decades of the nineteenth century in the United States the Gilded Age, a period of technological progress and opulent wealth. But New Orleans was left far behind after the Civil War, showing few signs of renewed prosperity until the 1880s.[1] Even after Reconstruction ended in 1877, reform was haltingly slow in the city, and it never recovered its former status as Queen of the South.

By 1880, some New Orleanians (those with interests in the Louisiana Lottery Company, for example) had been swept into easy times. In sharp contrast, however, the city was drowning in debt and often literally in floodwaters. Despite the end of Reconstruction's carpetbag rule, graft and corruption continued under new Democratic administrators. The criminal justice system was ineffectual. For months, public school teachers and other city employees went unpaid. Adding to the general malaise, a yellow fever epidemic in 1878 crippled commerce and left behind a bereaved population.

Despite these conditions and Sabbatarians' disapproval of Creoles' Sunday recreations, the city still emanated its inherent joie de vivre. The 1880–81 season of the French Opera House was one of the most brilliant. Even though the majority of citizens would never see, let alone receive, an ornate invitation to an extravagant Carnival ball, they could attend the spectacular parades. They could also watch W. C. Coup's circus parade, and many could afford a ticket to one of his Monster Shows, where "That Grand Electric Light . . . turns darkness into noonday sunlight! Floods the earth with fairy tints! Gilds with eternal grandeur every mortal object!"[2] It was the age of the electric light—in 1880 a novel attraction but for many a hopeful sign of a brighter future. That year lamplighters of various nationalities still made the rounds at dusk to light the city's gas lamps, but throughout the summer, West-End Garden, the popular resort on Lake Pontchartrain, advertised "Beautiful Electric Lights."[3] At that time only exterior electric lamps were available, but newspapers reported that an interior incandescent light bulb was just around the corner. Yet not everyone was optimistic about New Orleans' future, electrified or not.

Diogenes is said to have wandered in the daylight with a lighted lamp searching for an honest man. Lafcadio Hearn depicted him in a woodcut (August 16, 1880) as hunting in complete darkness for honest men to serve as city administrators. For realists, dispelling the moral darkness of New Orleans was more daunting than illuminating the physical world. Earlier that same year, Hearn wrote of the city's hard times in a letter. "Times are not good here. The city is crumbling into ashes. It has been buried under a lava-flood of taxes and frauds and maladministrations so that it has become only a study for archaeologists. Its condition is so bad that when I write about it, as I intend to do soon, nobody will believe I am telling the truth."[4] To these complaints, which seem to echo the Hebrew prophets, he added, "But it is better to live here in sackcloth and ashes, than to own the whole State of Ohio." This thorough disillusionment following idealization—Hearn would later shake off the ashes of New Orleans as he had the dust of Cincinnati—colored a misanthropic streak that contributed to his soon becoming a superb satirist.

Since the summer of 1878, Hearn had been assistant editor of the *Daily City Item,* a four-page reformer-Democratic daily founded in 1877, whose success was largely due to innovation and old-fashioned legwork— it had neither telephone nor telegraphic service—in filling the afternoon niche of the local newspaper market.[5] It had survived the short-lived *Evening News* of the year before; it was holding its own against the other English-language dailies—the *Daily Picayune,* the *New Orleans Democrat,* and the *New Orleans Times*—and their afternoon editions; and it was compatible with the two surviving foreign-language dailies, *L'Abeille* and *Deutsche Zeitung.*[6] But now the little paper had a formidable new competitor, a daily evening paper with a familiar publisher and editor which debuted early in 1880. Circulation of H. J. Hearsey's *Daily States* climbed as that of the *City Item* declined, causing consternation among the latter's publishers and staff.[7]

Hearn, of all people, knew that creating sensations increased sales. He had built his reputation in Cincinnati as a sensational journalist.[8] Although he had won praise for his translations of French literature and his series "Fantastics," which had begun in the *City Item* the previous year, something else extraordinary was needed to lure back their fickle audience, and expand it.[9] Less than two years earlier, in his editorial "Illustrated Newspapers," Hearn had written the axiom that would inspire a solution: "Merit is developed by rivalry, as invention by necessity." Competition would bring improved quality to U.S. illustrated journals, most of which he thought were inferior to their European models.[10] New Orleans did not then have an illustrated journal of any kind; moreover, daily newspapers with regular illustrations were rare in the United States.

On May 21, 1880, Hearn praised Joseph Keppler's illustrated periodical, which was "now beyond all question one of the ablest journals in the world devoted to political satire." *Puck,* he said, "will do more public good by its cartoons than a hundred editorials alone could accomplish even in the most influential newspaper in the country. But one person will comprehend and digest an exhaustive editorial upon some vital question where a hundred will study and comprehend a good cartoon."[11] The following afternoon the front page of the *City Item* featured a curious miniature woodcut of bats flying over a turret of Orleans Parish Prison, which was located on Rampart Street—one of the original boundaries of the colonial city. The title above the picture, "The Haunted and the Haunters," is borrowed from an eerie Edward Bulwer-Lytton story published twenty years earlier.[12] The text beneath the illustration complains about the subjection of prisoners, and neighbors of the prison, to the stench of bat guano. Moving from Old Testament allusions, the author invokes the spirit of François Rabelais by a hilarious philosophical argument in which the offensive odor is compared to decaying shoe-leather, miscarried eggs, and dead cats—suggesting a litany typical of the sixteenth-century French comic genius. The narrator of the unsigned column then refers to Jeremiah's despair at the depravity of his people, expanding the prophet's famous rhetorical question as he asks readers: "Is there no sulphur, no carbolic acid, no gunpowder, no vitriol, no dynamite in Louisiana? Is there no balm in Gilead?" The image is complete. The narrator, like Jeremiah at the gates of Jerusalem, is at the outskirts of New Orleans lamenting the corruption of the city.[13]

The origin of Hearn's association of the stench of bat guano with Gilead was an exposé from his Cincinnati days. Employing his prodigious powers of description and wry wit, Hearn wrote in his sketch "The Balm of Gilead, an Afternoon in the Stink Factory" that "some railroad official blessed with a fine sense of irony and who had, no doubt, heard much in early Sunday-school days regarding the virtues of the Balm of Gilead," had called a little railroad station outside of Cincinnati—where the nearby Cincinnati Fertilizer Manufacturing Company announced itself with an overpowering offensive odor—Gilead.[14] In the fall of 1879, Hearn had written an editorial on a bat infestation in a New Orleans schoolhouse which may have caused a child's death, with a quote from Jeremiah as its epigraph: "I will make this city an Astonishment and a Hissing; every one that shall pass by it shall be astonished, and shall hiss, because of all the plagues thereof—Jeremiah, XIX, 8." At the end of the piece, he adds that the inhabitants of the schoolhouse were squeaking rather than hissing.[15]

In New Orleans, Hearn continued to show his skill of tickling the public with allusions to the prophet Jeremiah while addressing most unpleasant subjects, thereby responding to the philosophical question posed by Rabelais's Epistemon: "how [is it that] a man might be ready to bepiss himself with laughter, when he has no heart to be merry?"[16] Having written sketches in a variety of styles and genres since his Cincinnati days (1869–77), Hearn was no stranger to satire, but his illustrated columns of 1880 prove that he had become a master of the art form and suggest that he understood satire's ancient origins—points that have not been recognized in past assessments of this body of work.

In a cursory reading of Hearn's illustrated series for the *City Item*, it seems a curious parade of vignettes depicting New Orleans. Over the past century the impression has been maintained that they are but farragoes on various subjects in numerous styles, with little if anything binding them into a conceptual whole. That Hearn created both pictures and text has further complicated comparisons to other bodies of work. Some of the pictures are cartoons, some are portraits, and some illustrate texts greatly varied in structure, style, and tone. Their subjects seem to have little unity other than describing and commenting on New Orleans' social and political life, as well as the national political scene.

But in a closer study of the first week's columns—these few fairly represent the whole—we find evidence supporting a more concise description of the series. This set is, according to the definition Hearn appears to have followed, satire in the original Latin sense: *satura*, which means "medley" or "full of variety." The satire of ancient Rome included praise of virtue and encomiums as exemplary alternatives to the vice and folly under attack elsewhere.[17]

The dramatic quality of the texts and pictures in Hearn's series and their parallels to ancient satire should also be considered. Roman satire, drawn from the plays of Greek Old Comedy, began on the stage and eventually became wholly textual, intended to be read rather than performed.[18] The earliest stage performances in Rome were presented during a plague, with the purpose of appeasing angry gods. Dramatized fables with severe morals included interludes performed by *exodiarii*, singers and dancers "who accompanied the flute with all sorts of mountebank tricks, gestures, dances, gesticulations, and the like, mixed with satirical songs, and sometimes with the performance of coarse farces." These light interludes were intended both to give the gods pleasure and to entertain the audience so that it "might not go away oppressed with melancholy from those serious pieces of the theatre."[19]

Framed by allusions to Jeremiah and, by extension, to the displeasure of the Hebrew god, Hearn's illustrated satire appeared amid the threat of another yellow fever epidemic. Several of Hearn's illustrated columns—for example, "Exthract from the Spach ov Paddy Whack" (June 4) and "Sons of the Sea" (September 1)—are correlations of *exodiarii;* others are reminiscent of antimasque characters of the Renaissance stage. The figure in "The Master Spirit" (September 26) evokes the title character of *Mephistopheles,* which had been performed in New Orleans months earlier by the Strakosch Italian Opera Company.[20] Positioned in the upper right column of the first page of the newspaper, the figures in Hearn's illustrations can easily be imagined as characters in a variety show. "Ultra-Canal" (July 17), in which a Creole servant explains that the man with the habit of losing everything has finally lost himself, would have been as much at home on the vaudeville stage of 1880 as on the printed page. Hearn's literary sketches are also in voices of various personae. Only one—"Spanish Moss" (October 28)—bears Hearn's signature and is intended to be in the poet's own voice. Some pieces are written in an anonymous editorial voice, others in the voices of various citizens who write "letters to the editor" about pet peeves; one is a dialogue between a ward boss and a subpoenaed witness, and another the song of a Creole vendor.

When viewing this entire "show," we can discern in its great variety a thematic unity: the presentation of various vices and virtues of 1880 New Orleans, framed by a modern Jeremiah's prophecy that divine retributions will be suffered if reforms are not made. Hearn's entire series is indeed a large work of illustrated satire intended to arraign corruptions and vices, to praise virtues, and to entertain. Throughout its history satire has been intended primarily as a corrective to society's vices and follies, but no less has it aimed to tickle the audience, perhaps even to convulse it with laughter.

LAUGHTER AND WOE

In 1866 the *Nation* said virtuous indignation was not usually humorous, that treating great immoralities with levity was inappropriate because to ridicule them "diminished the abhorrence with which they should be regarded."[21] This argument runs contrary to the premise that satire "heals with morals what it hurts with wit," and it goes back to a centuries-old debate over whether satire is related to tragedy or comedy. The public has generally agreed that vice and folly deserve to be and should be laughed at. However, in response to such criticisms as the *Nation*'s, satirists have traditionally written an *apologia*. They often sum up their reasons for writing satire in the *"facit indignatio versum"* of Juvenal, in whose time the corruption in Rome was so extreme that it was difficult *not* to write satire.[22]

In Alexander Pope's apologia, "Epistle to Dr. Arbuthnot," he asks, "What *Drop* or *Nostrum* can this plague remove?"[23] The plague of vices against which Pope wages war can only be cured with harsh medicine. The preferred treatment of many satirists for social ills has been to cauterize corruption with vitriolic wit, then to apply a balm of morals. "Satire is of the nature of moral philosophy, as being instructive," wrote John Dryden.[24] Comparisons of satirists' tones have largely been based on the proportions of vitriol and balm they have administered, which have depended as much on the conditions of the times in which a satirist lived as on his or her personality. The gentle touch of William Makepeace Thackeray in his works for *Punch* (or, the *London Charivari*) has been attributed to his jovial nature and the relatively trouble-free political era in which he lived.[25] Comparing the two main satirists of classical Rome, Dryden said Horace wrote during a less corrupt era of Rome's history, whereas "Juvenal's times required a more painful kind of operation."[26]

The practice of satire is often implied to be analogous to the medical profession. Jeremiah follows "Is there no balm in Gilead?" with "Is there no physician there?" When the twentieth-century New Orleans cartoonist John Churchill Chase was called the "Gentle Surgeon," he objected, not because he thought the comparison less than apropos but because "cartoonists aren't *supposed* to be gentle," likening a gentle cartoonist to "the old-time 'painless' dentist."[27] The most forceful Civil War cartoonist of the Southern viewpoint actually was a dentist, with the strength to yank out a jaw tooth quickly if not painlessly.[28] Whether employing pictorial or textual means, satirists have historically seen themselves as providing remedies for social ills which usually require cutting and extraction.

Throughout the centuries many physicians have written satire, and many a satirist who was not a medical professional formed a close bond with one. Pope addressed his "bill of complaint," as he called his apologia, to Dr. John Arbuthnot—physician to Queen Anne, distinguished wit, and supporter of Pope's attack on the prevalent vices at that time. Hearn's father was a surgeon in the British army and nephew to Dr. Arbuthnot.[29]

It is unsurprising, then, that Hearn took an interest in medical topics and that he may have identified with the great satirist almost as if he were a blood relation. While in New Orleans, Hearn also developed a close friendship with Rudolph Matas, a neurological surgeon involved in public health issues, particularly efforts to prevent another yellow fever epidemic in the city.[30]

It is well known that Hearn identified with Edgar Allan Poe, particularly with his famous poem "The Raven." Hearn had adopted the title as his own moniker while in Cincinnati, where he was particularly influenced by Poe in his writings on gruesome topics.[31] Hearn nods to Poe in the beginning of his illustrated series, for the allusion in "The Haunted and the Haunters" to Jeremiah's "balm of Gilead" also echoes a passage from "The Raven":

> "Prophet!" said I, "thing of evil!—prophet still, if bird or devil!—
> Whether Tempter sent, or whether tempest tossed thee here ashore,
> Desolate yet all undaunted, on this desert land enchanted—
> On this home by Horror haunted—tell me truly, I implore—
> Is there—*is* there balm in Gilead?—tell me—tell me, I implore!"
> Quoth the Raven "Nevermore."[32]

The narrator of "The Haunted and the Haunters" can be interpreted as a loquacious raven, reinforcing the idea that in Hearn's series—this Book of the Raven, if you will—the curative balm of Gilead does not exist unless it is accompanied by sulfur, carbolic acid, gunpowder, vitriol, and dynamite.

The prophet Jeremiah is not a physician, nor has he faith in a remedy for the depravity of his people other than punishment. What he does have is a talent for raillery. In many ancient cultures, the poet, satirist, prophet, teacher, and encomiast were one and the same. This individual was also considered a warrior whose weapon, satire, was believed to be fatal.[33] (A striking recent example of this belief, however unintentional, is the deadly result of the publication of a cartoon by a Danish artist depicting the prophet Mohammed.) The *filid*, or poet satirist, of pre-Christian Ireland was also medicine man, historian, genealogist, lawyer, and so on. Poet satirists were believed to possess magical powers, and the public feared them: "blessed is he who is praised, woe is him who is satirized."[34] The fury of the ancient Greek satirist Archilocus was believed to possess power to raise blisters on the skin of his victims, and, similarly, the Irish satirist was believed capable of rhyming rats to death.

Voudouism, which in some ways resembles the pre-Christian practices of satirists, was among the interests of Hearn, who was a folklorist.[35]

Like satire in its earliest times, *voudou* spells were feared by the superstitious to be efficacious, and Hearn, as well as others, thought there was merit in this fear. Hearn wrote that a dread of contracting fever had the power of making the immune system susceptible to a disease; thus, the imagination of a superstitious person could cause the fulfillment of a fortune-teller's prediction.[36] Bulwer-Lytton pondered in his story "The Haunted and the Haunters"—subtitled "The House and the Brain"—the potentially fatal effects of unmitigated fear.[37] Although belief that satirists actually possess magical powers faded centuries ago in Western civilization, opinions that written and pictorial satires can cause adverse health effects in their targets have lingered.[38] The savagery of Thomas Nast's cartoons on Horace Greeley during the presidential race of 1872 was believed by many to have hastened Greeley's death.[39]

Hearn appears to have been familiar with the history of satire—to have consciously drawn from its various stages and respected its potential as a harmful as well as a healing agent. It is no stretch to consider that he saw himself as somewhat of a medicine man/prophet/poet, engaging at times in "magical satire," not through spells and incantations but by instilling fear in certain subjects through the use of images and warnings. In his satire he seems to have played the roles of a prophet warning of coming events; a teacher instructing with parables; a historian recording events for future generations; an encomiast praising virtue; a warrior raising sharp points of satire; and a medicine man cutting and cauterizing with some words, soothing with others. Hearn appears to have had equal appreciation for satire by Horace—said to be "commonly in jest, and laughs while he instructs"—and Juvenal, specialist in a censorious, searingly witty style. At times, he applies the light Horatian touch as a corrective, as in "The Organ Grinder" (June 30), "Washerwomen" (August 31), and "The Hand-Maiden" (September 5). At other times, he uses a heavier hand, as in "That Villainous Broker" (October 7) and "Cat-ankarous" (August 22), which may not have raised blisters or drowned rats (or cats) but were nonetheless powerful.

Besides these variations of "vitriol and balm," Hearn uses an array of structural and stylistic devices, also found in classical Roman formal verse satire, including miniature dramas, proverbs and maxims, fables, sermons, debates, vignettes, brief fictions, visions, and so on.[40] Likewise, Hearn employs an assortment of rhetorical devices, including absurd exaggeration, allusion, repetition, simile, burlesque, parody, irony, and inversion of irony—all traditional tools of the satirist. Hearn did not follow in his series the tradition of offering a formal apologia, an appropriate omission considering the raison d'être of the *City Item* was municipal and social reform. Its charter stated that its objects were "to promote the commercial, industrial, social and political interests of the state and country, and to give tone, vigor, point and effect to everything calculated to elevate, refine and ennoble public sentiment and feeling; and to that end . . . without fear or favor, decry and condemn all frauds, peculation, corruption and crime wherever found."[41]

We find nonetheless something of an apologia in Hearn's essay "Laughter and Woe," which ponders the "satanic and sardonic character" of American humor developed by "the diabolical ingenuity of about half-a-dozen ungodly newspapers which devote much talent and exceedingly great pains to the art of titillating the risibles of people by depicting human misery and misfortune in a ludicrous guise." Thousands of other papers, including the *City Item*, copy these jokes and lampoons, he writes, because they and all their readers have become corrupt. Each generation, blasé about the humor of the one before, demands something increasingly devilish; therefore only imaginary misfortunes—no real ones are awful enough—can do the trick.

> We must be getting very wicked, very wicked indeed; and before long we may be laughing at things we should tremble at hearing of. What will become of this country? Will our descendants begin to laugh at everything like certain wicked French journals that make sport of things heavenly or of things infernal and crack jokes about the patriarchs and prophets and cherubim and seraphim and the saints and angels? There is an English author who holds that all laughter is either wicked or foolish, and he argues his point well;—asking among other questions what rational sequence is there between a smutty story and a burst of uproarious laughter, and why people should see anything to giggle over while a person falls down and hurts himself? We can not answer these questions, but we know that it is awfully funny to see somebody come down on the sidewalk with a paddy sort of noise and a sorrowful and surprised expression of countenance. And when we see such things we could not help laughing, even to save our lives.[42]

Throughout his writings for the *City Item*, Hearn had been emulating "wicked French journals" in his satire and making sport of religious themes and figures, especially the prophets. But it is not until the last line that he pivots his argument and lifts his mask to reveal that he has been grinning the entire time. The inverted irony of the piece is typical of essays by Jonathan Swift and other satirists, who have often used a guise of conservative values as a rhetorical device.[43]

Hearn published this essay several weeks after one of his "Illustrated Letters from the People," subtitled "The Banana Curse" (July 23), appeared, accompanied by a picture of a man slipping on a banana peel and falling. (Although Hearn wrote these pieces, he may have based some on actual letters.) "An Enraged Citizen" invokes the proverbially patient but cranky prophet Job in his letter as he calls for extreme punishments—"All the worldly goods and possessions of a man who throws a banana peel on the sidewalk should be confiscated"—which escalate in absurdity. The offender should be whipped repeatedly and revived with ice water. "After this he ought to be kept in prison for twenty-five years and whipped twice a month with piano wire." Hearn, in the editorial voice, replies, *"It seems to us that our correspondent is a little too severe. Perhaps he is at present taking his meals off the mantel-piece."* The cartoon and the text satirizing the enraged citizen's raillery are enough to make one smile to see a banana peel on a sidewalk rather than feel sympathetic indignation.

But the next day Hearn reported in his brief editorial "Good!" on a New York ordinance that established fines for tossing on sidewalks "banana-peels . . . or anything else which may cause people to slip and hurt themselves." New Orleans, he says, should pass a similar law but with higher fines, for nowhere else in the United States are so many bananas eaten and thrown on the streets. "This law is really a necessity of civilizations," he concludes. "London and Paris long since adopted police regulations to prevent this lazy, filthy, and criminal practice." Here the moral purpose of the previous day's satire is clarified, even though the tone and content—a banana peel could cause an entire civilization to slip and fall—smack of mock seriousness. Nevertheless, Hearn, following the principle that satire "heals with morals what it hurts with wit," shows that human woe can be made the object of laughter to serve as entertainment and corrective (in this case, of extremism), while at the same time illustrating the need for social reform.

On the other hand, the parody of the famous satirical passage of the Book of Job in "Prickly Heat" (September 4) recommends nothing more than laughter, prayers to cool breezes, and patience. "Extracht from the Spach ov Paddy Whack" (June 4) involves another railer who is portrayed simply to provoke laughter and represent one of the characters typical of New Orleans streets.

Despite individual works recommending patience or good reason in place of irrational reactions, and those that only mildly admonish or even praise, the majority of Hearn's pieces are bleak representations of the city's crime and corruption. The police ring, the defalcation by the civil sheriff, greedy brokers, quacks, gamblers, rowdies, hoodlums, opium den keepers, and so on, permeate the rest of the series with grim prophesy. According to Alvin B. Kernan, author of *The Cankered Muse,* this pessimism, too, is characteristic of traditional satire. "Although there is always at least a suggestion of some kind of humane ideal in satire—it may in the blackest type of satire exist only as the unnamed opposite of the idiocy and villainy portrayed—this ideal is never heavily stressed, for in the satirist's vision of the world decency is forever in a precarious position near the edge of extinction, and the world is about to pass into eternal darkness. Consequently, every effort is made to emphasize the destroying ugliness and power of vice."[44] The allusion to Jeremiah at the beginning sets the tone of impending doom throughout Hearn's series.

A prelude to the bleak vision of the series was Hearn's earlier satire in which the devil visits the city. Satisfied that the city was thoroughly corrupt, he "departed elsewhere in search of employment. 'They have no need of me,' said the Devil, in the State of Louisiana.'"[45] Published months before Hearn's letter about the city's "lava-flood of taxes and frauds and maladministrations," this sketch indicates that when Hearn decided to write about those times, as he said he intended to do soon, it would be in stinging satire.

Even though the victory of reform mayoral candidate Joseph Shakspeare in November 1880 gave reason for optimism, it by no means represented to Hearn a panacea. The penultimate illustrated column, which appeared in early December, depicts the specter of another yellow fever epidemic. After a two-month hiatus, Hearn added one last woodcut of the deluge of the city after a tempest. *La fin couronne les œuvres.* The scene fulfills the jeremiad prophecy suggested in the first illustrated column and completes Hearn's comic vision for the series. "The Inundations" shows a black porter carrying Mayor Shakspeare through the water on his back (a motif appearing earlier in the political cartoon of August 14, "Jewell's Defence of Garfield"). In early 1881 Shakspeare faced numerous problems, not least of which were the flood and the city's debts. He had been elected by a narrow margin. The demands for reforms in Hearn's illustrated series no doubt helped, as did the black vote. When Shakspeare ran again eight years later, the black vote definitely carried him to victory.[46]

The caption refers to the fine work of the relief committee; the text speaks of "negroes that play the part of St. Christopher." But Hearn has also circled back to his initial allusion to Rabelais's *Gargantua and Pantagruel,* in which a flood occurred when Pantagruel

> pissed amidst the camp so well and so copiously, that he drowned them all, and there was a particular deluge, ten leagues round about . . . The enemies, after that they were awaked, seeing on one side of the fire in the camp, and on the other the inundation of the urinal deluge, could not tell what to say, nor what to think. Some said, that it was the end of the world, and the final judgment which ought to be by fire. Others, again thought that the sea gods, Neptune, Proteus, Triton, and the rest of them, did persecute them, for that indeed they found it to be like sea-water and salt . . . The giants seeing all their camp drowned, carried away their King Anarchus upon their backs, as well as they could.[47]

The suggestion of a flood of urine is not so far from the reality of New Orleans in 1880–81, for it did not yet have a sewerage system, and leaky privies were a constant problem.[48]

It no doubt delighted Hearn to be able to close his series with a reference to a great flood, the most severe in living memory.[49] In one of his columns, he had written of insects as "a veritable realization of the swarm of flies that afflicted the land of Egypt" ("Under the Electric Light" of August 6), and elsewhere he had mentioned that a plague of locusts visited the United States every seventeen years, the last time having been in 1863.[50] In "'Oft in the Stilly Night,' Etc." (November 28), he writes: "These black and dismal nights recall the Plague of Egyptian darkness." And in "Wet Enough for You?" (December 1), he says that when the sun suddenly appeared after days of rain, "the people of New Orleans began to think that the world was coming to an end." After months of inclement weather and overcast skies, he writes that hopefully there would be "some lifting of the Egyptian darkness. If we are being afflicted for our hardness of heart, this punishment is too long continued to effect any great moral benefit."[51]

From beginning to end, Hearn's series fits Michael Seidel's description of satire: "a grinning tragedy, the relentless pursuit by the satirist of negative incidentals, a ritualized articulation of damaging facts, nervous impulses in the face of civilized breakdowns."[52] But even though there is a moral basis for Hearn's arguments, they are not moralistic. Reforms should be enacted because they are good and right for a civilized society, not because they conform to religious doctrine based on narrow interpretations of religious texts. He advised Sabbatarians who objected to the

Sunday recreational activities in New Orleans to remember the "teachings of the Divine Master who said, 'The Sabbath was made for man; not man for the Sabbath,'" and to recognize that New Orleans was "not a Puritanical community. It is a Catholic community; it is a Latin city still, and remains largely faithful to its Latin father."[53] In response to an astrologer's prediction that the end of the world would occur in 1881, Hearn wrote an editorial called "An Astrological Ass." For him, apocalyptic visions were best suited to playful art that would not frighten "good simple folk."[54]

That Hearn was an irreverent and mischievous skeptic is further evident in an epilogue to his two illustrated columns on the bicycle: "The Unspeakable Velocipede" (June 29) and "The Bicycle Fiend's Defense" (July 21). In January 1881, he wrote a sententious story on the subject—it also seems inspired by Rabelais's chronicles of giants—in which "a horrid, horrid boy rushing madly along the sidewalk upon a vile velocipede" collided with a barrel being rolled along on the street by a gigantic man. "'So you wouldn't get out of the way of it?' grimly observed the gigantic man. 'Ah, ha!—so you wouldn't get out of the way of it!' And the boy wept. And each of his tears was to us more precious than the balm of Gilead or the roses of Gulistan."[55] The world Hearn created was not drawn from an overly virtuous perspective. "The whirligig of time is bringing in his revenges" begins one of his columns ("Citizen-Executioner Sherman," July 10). Revenge, though not a virtue, was also a balm to the sufferer.

"Those Furniture Men" (November 14) begins with another Shakespeare quote, this one from a tragedy, and several times Hearn drops one of his favorite phrases, "in the dead waste and middle of the night," from *Hamlet*. It no doubt gave Hearn great joy to end his "grinning tragedy" with a poignant woodcut of the mayor who shared the great bard's surname. Years later in his lectures to Japanese students, Hearn referred to "the divine Shakespeare," whose perfect imagination allowed him, like the gods, to create a world and people it.[56]

"A SORT OF ILLUSTRATED JOURNAL"

In his illustrated series, Hearn drew from a staggering number of pictorial and textual sources. His primary models were the satirical journals of Europe, especially *Le Charivari,* the illustrated comic daily founded by Louis Phillipon in 1832 which featured engravings by Honoré Daumier, among other artists.[57] The Paris paper took its name from the ancient Roman custom, a form of social satire that had survived for many centuries in France and was transported to its colonies, including New Orleans. *Charivari* "means and conveys the derisive noise made at night with pans, cauldrons, basins, etc., in front of the houses of people who are marrying for the second or third time or are marrying someone of a very different age from themselves."[58] The custom changed over the years, largely due to laws attempting to prohibit or at least curb the practice.

A spectacular charivari took place in New Orleans in 1805, on the occasion of the widow Madame Don André Almonaster's marriage, when thousands of costumed and masked people converged outside her home on the Place d'Armes, making "discordant and noisy music, such as old kettles, and shovels, and tongs, and clanging metals can strike out."[59] Seventy-five years later Hearn reported on a tamer charivari:

> The residents of the neighborhood of the Ninth Street Market were awakened from their slumber last night by an accumulation of noises that would have done credit to the ancients at the Tower of Babel. At first one would imagine that all the amateur musicians in town had congregated at the corner to take their first lesson, but on arriving our reporter learned that a popular merchant on the shady side of life, after sixty years of bachelorhood, had taken unto himself a charming widow . . . All the available hand organs in the neighborhood were hired at an immense expense, and the assortment of tin pans and horns would have done credit to our largest hardware establishment.

The crowd "retired on the approach of a detachment of peelers."[60] Since 1867, it had been illegal "to make charivari."[61] This sketch, called "A Musical Compliment," was published on the first page, just right of the illustrated column "The Nurse Maid" (July 2), which ridicules "naughty" nannies who neglect the children in their care while being wooed by "bad young men."

The description of a charivari adjacent to the satire on nursemaids hints at Hearn's concept of his illustrated columns as *Le Charivari* of New Orleans. His series is also a tribute to the recently deceased illustrator of *Le Charivari* and *Le Monde Illustré*—Cham, whom Hearn eulogized as "the most celebrated of the French comic artists." His death was a serious blow to *Le Monde Illustré*, which he had built up with his graceful and ludicrous caricatures. Hearn wondered if the journal could survive the loss. "Paris is too giddy, too artistic, too fond of pleasures to care for the digestion of dry facts. Paris pays the man best who can make her laugh or weep better than others. She pays for the pleasure of emotions; and leaves the record of hard facts for the digestion of her business men and politicians. Thus a journal dies with the genius which created its success by tickling the risibilities or provoking the tears of fickle, passionate Paris."[62]

Hearn's own temperament and aesthetic preferences were best suited for the audience and journalism of Paris, which was "purely a literary feature."[63] If there was anywhere in the United States he could have found such an audience for what he most wanted to create, it was New Orleans, the Paris of America, as the city once had been known.[64] Hearn seemed to be trying to lead the *City Item* and its readers as far in the direction of a Parisian journal as they would tolerate. The first of his series of fanciful sketches and "Fantastics," influenced by the writings of French romantics such as Théophile Gautier and Gustave Flaubert, began appearing in the *City Item* the same day as his eulogy of Cham, and most were published during his cycle of illustrated satire.[65]

All these works by Hearn indicate the extraordinary freedom he exercised in writing for the *City Item*. In a letter to his Cincinnati friend Henry Watkin, Hearn said he wrote whatever he pleased, which was the opposite of some of his experiences in Ohio, particularly his collaboration in 1874 with the French-born artist Henry Farny on a publication they called *Ye Giglampz: A Weekly Illustrated Journal Devoted to Art, Literature and Satire*.[66] In his series for the *City Item*, Hearn satisfied some of the creative vision he had had for *Ye Giglampz*, which had been sadly frustrated by Farny's overweening editorial control.[67] Lasting only nine issues, *Ye Giglampz* was another of the country's many failed comic journals of that period.[68] The artwork is unmemorable; the writings, even Hearn's, are for the most part unremarkable. Much of it consisted of reprints from *Punch,* and its title and logo are confusing. The title *Ye Giglampz* refers to large, owlish spectacles such as Hearn wore but also—along with the masthead symbol of an owl superimposed over a sun—likely alludes to Diogenes' search for an honest man.[69] *The Lantern,* an illustrated satirical paper that had appeared twenty years earlier, also had on its cover an owl surrounded by sun rays.[70] But the intended meanings of the title and masthead image of *Ye Giglampz* have to this day eluded understanding.

Even though Hearn was invited and paid to be the journal's editor, Farny insisted on superseding Hearn's editorial decisions and censoring his writings—they were probably not so different from much of what he later published in the *City Item*—causing Hearn to resign more than once. Finally, acting as editor and illustrator, Farny committed a fatal blunder in what was consequently the penultimate issue. Without considering their incongruence with the paper's usual satiric tone, he published sketches of current recovery efforts following a steamboat conflagration. To make matters worse, Farny referred to the illustrations as "cartoons," which, being a painter, he probably used in the sense of a sketch as a plan for a work of art.[71] But since 1843, in the English-speaking world, the word *cartoon* had come to mean primarily a satirical drawing.[72] Hence, public reaction ranged from confusion to outrage. The small staff quit in disgust—it was Hearn's fifth resignation—and the already financially troubled paper died from self-inflicted embarrassment.[73]

Subsequently, in the pages of the *Cincinnati Enquirer,* Hearn described the follies of the journal from its beginning, poking fun at himself but perhaps also having his revenge against Farny in light satire.[74] Years later, in his analysis of illustrated journals, Hearn commented that recent works by Matt Morgan, "a skillful and ingenious cartoonist" for *Leslie's Illustrated Monthly,* were inferior to those the artist had executed for the *London Tomahawk.* Hearn speculated, "Perhaps he was obliged to work 'under instruction,' and prohibited from exercising his own taste and fancy."[75]

Several factors were key to the popular and artistic success of Hearn's illustrated satire for the *City Item* of 1880. He was a more mature writer and editor than he had been when involved in *Ye Giglampz,* he was for the most part allowed to exercise his own "taste and fancy," and he expressed himself deftly in comedy or tragedy. No one interpreted pieces like "Cakes and Candy" (September 18) and "Fire!" (October 29) as anything but works full of pathos.

The political satire he employs is probably the most surprising aspect of the series. Hearn has been represented as having an aversion to writing on Louisiana politics because of his *Cincinnati Commercial* "Ozias Midwinter" letters, which were supposed to comment on the aftermath of the disputed national and state election of 1876 but instead mostly described some of the unique social and cultural characteristics that he found in New Orleans.[76] A more plausible explanation may be that it was personally risky for him to write about politics. The Republican party had lost control of the local government, and the Democratic party was splintered into factions. To write anything favorable to one faction would alienate another, possibly preventing his chances of getting hired by a newspaper.

Most of the political editorials for the *City Item* were written by the managing editor, Mark Bigney, or its publisher, Col. John Fairfax.[77] The paper was reformer-Democratic and a fervent supporter of Gen. Winfield S. Hancock for president. (It often boasted of originating the idea of Hancock's candidacy.)[78] Hearn did not mind having to follow a newspaper's editorial policy, but he resented the unstated policies that resulted in arbitrary alteration of his texts and outright censorship, as he had experienced in Cincinnati. Hearn hinted that American newspapers should model their newspapers after the French. "The manager of the daily guides the policy of the paper. When a certain policy is determined upon, probably a hundred different writers, regular and irregular, will all direct their articles (no matter on what subject) to one point of view. Every department, every page, every line of the paper will reflect the same policy; correspondents, leader-writers, critics, feuilletonists, all alike will converge upon one point. The least dissonance is never perceptible."[79] While Thomas Nast made no secret of his allegiance to the Republican party, Hearn's political sympathies at that time are unknown. They are also irrelevant. Satires on Garfield and the Republican party were easily folded into his satirical mix without departing from his creative vision. Hearn was capable of incorporating political content into his art, but it was artistic, not political, impulses that motivated him.

Even though Hearn had invested tremendous creativity in his illustrated cycle of columns and his fantastics during 1880, the only known written reference he made to his woodcuts is in a letter. "I made them turn it [the *City Item*] into a sort of illustrated journal about five months ago. The pictures are not magnificent, but the experiment paid well, for the adoption of my suggestion put the journal on its feet at a time when it was on the verge of dissolution."[80] Although the illustrations were only part of what pulled the paper out of its crisis, it was a modest claim. Hearn was among the pioneers of the daily newspaper editorial cartoon. The *New York Daily Graphic,* the first fully illustrated newspaper, began in 1873, but the *New York World* did not carry a daily editorial cartoon until Joseph Pulitzer acquired it from Jay Gould in 1883.[81] Hearn's illustrations ran for less than seven months, but at the end of 1880 the *City Item* was among the relatively few U.S. newspapers that had run a daily editorial illustration for such a long period.

In 1880 most newspapers were printed on letterpresses. Copperplate engravings and lithographic images required separate presses to print the art, while the text was printed on the letterpress. However, a woodcut, like the movable type of the letterpress, is printed by relief, so text and illustration could be printed simultaneously. Although less costly than other means of printing artwork, the woodcut was still prohibitively expensive for the five-cent daily newspaper. Therefore, if original portraits, cartoons, or illustrations appeared at all in a daily, they did so only sporadically or in an occasional brief series. Daily illustrations were generally limited to thumbnail decorative art and display advertisement cuts. Some of the latter were often quite elaborate, but advertisers paid for them, and the same cut might be used for months or even years. Electrotype reproductions made it possible for product advertisements to be printed simultaneously in multiple journals and to endure more wear.

The vibrant color cartoons of *Puck* were printed by the latest innovations of lithography. However, the first journal in the United States printed entirely by lithography was in New Orleans: *Le Charivari Louisianais,* a short-lived illustrated weekly published in 1846, was written in longhand to avoid the cost of printing the text in a separate run on a letterpress.[82] During its first year, the *New York Daily Graphic* printed the first halftone by lithographic process to appear in a newspaper.[83] New York journals, of course, were the leaders in the technological advances made in newspaper printing. Papers elsewhere lagged far behind, making do with the equipment they had. Many newspapers, for instance, continued to use letterpresses long after their contemporaries converted to drum presses that printed from photolithographic plates, allowing photographs and line drawings to be copied. The greatest technological advance for the *City Item* in 1880 was the Waterworks Company's new machinery, which began furnishing power through its water lines in June, allowing newspapers to use hydraulic motors for their presses rather than steam-powered engines, thereby saving on insurance premiums.[84]

Instead of looking forward to widespread use of lithographic printing, which would allow art to flourish in daily newspapers, Hearn found it disappointing that fine wood engravings "refused to become popular in the East" outside of magazine illustration. For news journals he predicted technological advancements in the science of telegraphy which would not come about for another century: "photographs of important events in Europe might be yet transmitted by cable, and published in New York within a few hours after their occurrence."[85] But he remained partial to the woodcut for art journals. It was a typical Hearn position. He was not antimodernist, as many have portrayed him, but was in some respects an Emersonian cultural conservative: "The arts and inventions of each period are only its costume, and do not invigorate men. The harm of the improved machinery may compensate its good."[86]

So Hearn praised the "dainty marvels" of *Scribner's Monthly* "that surprise those who place a limit to the capacity of wood engraving." Noting a particular drawing style with which he later experimented in some of his own woodcuts (such as "Military Salutes," June 10), he said, "A taste is also being developed for that delightful and dreamy style of outline caricature—that whimsical and fantastic spirit of etching, which constitutes the great charm of the *Journal Amusant, Charivari, London Fun* and other comic papers."[87]

In an 1877 dispatch from New Orleans, Hearn had described the weekly journal *Le Carillon* but did not speak of its illustrations. He was also probably aware of the illustrated *Le Charivari Louisianais*; *La Revue Louisianaise,* which had included caricatures of New Orleans personages; and the 1876 weekly political cartoon series of the *Democrat*.[88] But his praise for American journals was reserved for *Puck,* which he said was "now the leading illustrated periodical of this country, and worthy to vie with the best European journals of caricature."[89] According to Hearn, the rest of the illustrated papers in the United States were inferior to the European journals from which they borrowed—the *Illustrated London News,* the *London Graphic,* the *London Illustrated Times, Le Monde Illustré, L'Illustration,* and *Deutsche Illustrierte Zeitung*.[90] These papers, in addition to the comic papers named above, indicate the wide range of journals Hearn regularly perused, his aesthetic preferences, and the illustrations from which he might have drawn inspiration for his own ideas and designs.

That Hearn was intrigued by wood engravings was not all that motivated him to create nearly two hundred of his own images. Compliments no doubt encouraged him as well. Hearn's series won the paper merit, even from its latest rival. After the first week of illustrations, the *States* paid its compliments: "The New Orleans *Graphic,* late *Item,* is attracting attention by its daily issue of sterling etchings and line engravings. We can cordially congratulate our neighbor upon its enterprise. While upon the subject, we may as well mention that, sitting where we are, we can hear the click of the rapid little press over the way, turning out its twenty-eight to thirty copies per minute, and are glad to know that the inauguration of the *States* has in no wise impaired the large circulation of the sterling little paper." It was a cordial and perhaps conciliatory note from the paper's intemperate editor, H. J. Hearsey, who had, two years earlier, while editor of the *Democrat,* challenged *City Item* managing editor Mark Bigney to a duel after an exchange of cutting remarks about the contents of their respective papers.[91]

Other compliments were reprinted from regional papers. "The daily New Orleans *City Item* has brought out a number of apt illustrations recently, a new idea with this paper, but an excellent one," wrote the *Advertiser* of Hansboro, Mississippi. "*The City Item* has just completed the third year of its existence, and enters volume four a permanent and paying institution," said the *Donaldsonville Chief,* adding, "The *Item* has recently begun the pictorial illustration of local matters and events, and some extremely happy hits have been made by the humorous representations which daily appear in its columns."[92]

The *City Item,* of course, never indicated to its readers or advertisers that it had been having financial difficulties. Instead, the paper mentioned that it "carries upon its front such evidences of growing prosperity that we have no need to 'blow a horn.' We thank our friends, and shall continue to deserve their growing favors." The illustrations, which continued for the next six and a half months, helped the paper through a difficult financial period, but they were only part of the paper's strategy. In early September, several months after the illustrated columns commenced, the paper announced that advertising demands made it necessary to expand its format from six to seven columns and to add more than two inches in length. "In view of the gratifying additions to our subscription list and the assured favor of *The Item* in domestic and business circles, its proprietors have determined not only to increase its size, but to add to its attractions in every respect. This is done for the double purpose of successfully meeting the pressure of competition and of keeping up with the demands of progress." It never altered its daily boast that its was "The Largest City Circulation of any Paper in New Orleans." Promoting the spin that the paper was thriving was vital to its success. Only a prosperous paper could afford an original daily woodcut.[93]

Hearn's illustrations contributed greatly to the paper's success, but he never received the attention such work deserved. The year 1880 was particularly productive for Hearn. He designed and engraved the woodblocks and wrote the accompanying texts, wrote other essays and fictional pieces, contributed translations to the *Democrat,* and performed his other editorial tasks for the *City Item.* Few other writers were also cartoonists or illustrators, and few cartoonists were also writers. With his wood engravings Hearn became a member of a small class, which includes Benjamin Franklin, creator of the first political cartoon published in the United States, and Frank Bellew, a prolific Anglo-Irish cartoonist and author of numerous short works for magazines and newspapers. Hearn might also be compared to Thackeray, although the latter had formal art training, began his career as an illustrator before abandoning it completely for writing, and made his own etchings but not his wood engravings.[94]

Hearn likely hoped his illustrated series would be appreciated as a work of visual and literary art, but he knew that at least posterity would appreciate it as a documentary of 1880 life. "Nothing is really more important as a historical record than a first-class illustrated journal," he wrote two years before he began his series. "They reflect the habits, customs, fashions, prejudices, hopes, delusions, vices and virtues of a generation better than the most ingenious description of the most scrupulous historian. Examining the old files of *Punch* or the *London News* gives one a clearer idea of the spirit of society and the color of events half a century ago than all their contemporary history."[95]

The same year he wrote in a letter that the "modest 'Item'" was "a poor little sheet" that went "no farther north than Saint Louis."[96] Perhaps he had greater ambitions for the paper after he began his illustration project, for when a Mexican newspaper described the *City Item* as "an obscure paper in New York," Hearn responded indignantly in his illustrated "How History is Written" (October 15): "In the first place *The Daily City Item* is not 'an obscure paper published in New York,' but a very popular illustrated daily published in New Orleans." Nonetheless, the illustrations ended two months later, and it was over a decade before the paper again published regular original illustrations pertaining to the local social and political scene. It was the *Mascot,* a weekly established in 1882, that took over as the lead illustrated journal in the city. But Hearn's series was a precursor of that journal and the editorial cartoons in today's sole daily of New Orleans, the *Times-Picayune,* as well as many other city newspapers.

THE PENKNIFE, MIGHTIER THAN THE PEN

It was unusual for a writer to not only illustrate his own work but also produce his own woodcuts, which is perhaps partly why in later years there was confusion over who had actually made the engravings for Hearn's series. Apparently relying on oral historical accounts, Edward Larocque Tinker published in *Lafcadio Hearn's American Days* (1924) that the firm Bennett and Zenneck made the woodcuts from Hearn's sketches. Based on what was, in fact, a false premise, Tinker speculated that the illustrations ended when Zenneck, while visiting the editor of the *Mascot,* was shot dead by a disgruntled reader.[97]

Bennett and Zenneck may have provided advertising engravings for the *City Item,* but it is unlikely that a paper in financial difficulties could pay professionals for daily engravings, something even prosperous newspapers could not justify. In an interview in *Creole Sketches,* published the same year as Tinker's book, Col. John Fairfax, owner of the *City Item* in 1880, stated that he and the editor, Mark Bigney, generally wrote the political articles. "But I'll tell you what he [Hearn] did write—those verses illustrated with woodcuts. They were all Hearn's—his ideas, his verses, his drawings. He drew those cartoons . . . and he cut them with his penknife on wood-blocks—on the backs of old wooden types, which had been used for advertisements. They were just the right height, you see, to fit into the bed—we used the old-fashioned flat-bed press, of course—and every day he would whittle out one of those drawings." According to Fairfax, Hearn carved his woodcuts in the manner of previous centuries, not with a graver or burin, but "a penknife that had two blades, using first the large and then the small one, to get the effect he wanted on the block." If Hearn was paid extra for his labor-intense endeavor, it could not have been much. His beginning salary of ten dollars a week had been increased to twenty by the time he left the paper in late 1881 for a position paying thirty dollars as literary editor of the newly merged *Times-Democrat*.[98]

Casual observation reinforces Fairfax's claim. The woodcuts lack the skill and precision evident in the portraits of Hancock and English, which were by a professional engraver. Yet Hearn's cuts are not without compositional and technical competence, and he had no assistance in his sketches, something even some professional cartoonists were known to have relied on. For example, the wife of *New York Herald* cartoonist Charles Nelan drew female figures for him. Other cartoonists, such as one who drew two bones in the upper arm of a skeleton, were less familiar with bone structure than Hearn, whose interest in anatomy during his Cincinnati days paid off when it came to drawing the human form, as did his notorious visits to New Orleans brothels.[99]

Although his paternal uncle, whom Hearn had met as a child, was a popular painter in France, Hearn never received formal art training. However, as a young boy in Dublin, he had accidentally discovered in his Aunt Sarah Brenane's library "several beautiful books about art—great folio books containing figures of gods and of demigods, athletes and heroes, nymphs and fauns and nereids, and all the charming monsters—half-man, half-animal—of Greek mythology." These mesmerizing images were also a link in his imagination to his Greek heritage, distant since he had been abandoned by his Cytheran mother among his father's relations in Ireland. But the innocent joy of the encounter was short-lived. The book disappeared for a while, and when it was returned the boy found the naked breasts and limbs "erased with a penknife" and baggy drawers drawn onto gods. In retrospect, he was philosophic, even appreciative, writing that "this barbarism proved of some educational value. It furnished me with many problems of restoration; and I often tried very hard to reproduce in pencil-drawing the obliterated or the hidden line." While he labored over his woodcuts, Hearn must have recalled that early childhood experience of censorship and the art training it had provided, and he must have appreciated the irony of his using a penknife to create illustrations rather than destroy them as his prudish relative had done.[100]

As a schoolboy he illustrated his poems and notebooks with drawings, and as an adult he occasionally sprinkled his correspondence with humorous sketches. However, there is no indication that he ever intended to be a graphic rather than literary artist, or that he planned to illustrate his own texts for an extended length of time.[101] It is not surprising that he became intrigued with creating his own cartoons when he believed they could be more powerful than a hundred written editorials. But what did Hearn mean by *cartoon*? The only time he used the word was to describe editorial art as published in *Puck*. A cartoon in this sense is a pictorial commentary—social or political criticism expressed in drawing with little more text than tags and a caption—which needs no further explanation. As Hearn comments in "And He Spake to Them Another Parable" (October 18), "The above will be comprehended by all intelligent, and even by a large number of non-intelligent, minds."

A great cartoon is said to be a memorable image resulting from the marriage of art and idea in a union of mutual support, but many brilliant cartoons are the result of a potent idea expressed with mediocre artistic skill.[102] In "This Way? Or This?" (May 30), Hearn effectively satirized duelists and the intrigue they inspired by representing them with little more sophistication than stick figures. Yet, by simply reversing in the second panel the figures and props marked "blood" and "gore," he expressed with great efficiency that the sad results were the same whether rapiers or Colts were used (although the latter was more likely to be lethal). And the simple gesture—figures with one wrist on the hip and the other hand aiming a pistol at close range while they both gaze out at the public—emphasized the absurdity of the chivalrous code of the *duello*. This cartoon was among the first woodcuts Hearn executed. From the beginning he could with a few crude lines thoroughly and succinctly provide a full commentary on a subject on which hundreds of exhaustive editorials had been written.

According to Hearn's own definition, roughly half of his woodcuts are cartoons. Most of these are political, in that they seek to establish greater order through governmental action.[103] A few of the illustrations could be considered of equal importance to their respective texts, for instance, the burlesqued profile "The Ideal Commissioner" (May 26). The other half of the images are not cartoons but illustrations of texts not dependent on the visual component for their meaning. Images such as those accompanying the "Illustrated Letters from the People" are memorable but secondary enhancements. In some columns the text might lend a different meaning than the image by itself. For instance, the explanation in "Cakes and Candy" (September 18) of the precarious nature of the vendor's income and attachment to her customers, many of whom died during the yellow fever epidemic of 1878, tinges with tragedy an otherwise pleasant scene of children buying sweets. Only *Bon Dieu* knows the whereabouts of her absent little customers.

Hearn also experimented with caricatures of personages, as in his depiction of Capt. Anthony Sambola of "Military Salutes" (June 10). In the background the men of Fifth Company Orleans Artillery are represented by silhouettes of stick figures that resemble ancient graffiti. The caricature "Dissatisfied" (November 12) of a glowering man was apparently inspired by a *Puck* cartoon published two weeks earlier, for Hearn described it in the same issue of the *City Item* as "a very curious political study of faces, which appear in every imaginable phase of grotesqueness."

The series on Dr. Tanner, the fanatical physician whose forty-day fast attracted national media attention, begins with an engraving made from a photograph taken on the seventeenth day of the physician's fast and a pledge "to continue to publish portraits of him at intervals of two or three days, until the fast is over." The subsequent woodcuts show a man degenerating into a caricature of himself. "That Villainous Broker" (October 7) is a sportive grotesque of gleeful horror, phantasmagorical imagery from popular demonology that Hearn also uses in several other woodcuts.[104]

Inspirations for Hearn's designs came from New Orleans life and a multitude of other sources. His woodcuts of local characters and hucksters seem to be after the school of the seventeenth-century artist Jacques Callot. There are interesting similarities between a Callot woodcut called *A Mediaeval Death-bed* and Hearn's "The Wages of Sin" (October 1). "The Nurse Maid" (July 2) may be partly inspired by Thackeray's etching from *Our Street* (1847), the caption of which is "Why our Nursemaids like Kensington Gardens." However, Thackeray's image only hints at impropriety while Hearn's scene depicts the disastrous results of a nursemaid's preoccupation with her suitor and neglect of the child in her care.[105]

Hearn also experimented with various visual styles and techniques. The chiaroscuro of "Coming Events Cast Their Shadows Before" (August 19) is after Gustave Doré, Hearn's favorite artist. Several woodcuts—for example, "The Police Board" (September 14) and "Won't Wait Till the Holidays" (December 7)—are variations of a style first used in fifteenth-century etchings and revived in the early 1800s.[106] Dramatic effects are achieved with minimal carving: sparse white lines appear in stark contrast to the black background. Hearn used this graphic "reversal" technique more and more as the series drew to its close.

Obviously, Tinker's speculation that the illustrations may have ceased due to the untimely death of the engraver Adolph Zenneck is baseless because Hearn engraved the woodblocks himself. Furthermore, the *Mascot* did not exist until 1882. It was in 1886 that Zenneck was "winged" in the office of the *Mascot*'s editor, while someone else died of a gunshot wound. Tinker's confused attribution of Hearn's woodcuts to Bennett and Zenneck had some basis in fact, however, for it was they who produced the series of weekly (signed) political cartoons that appeared in the *Democrat* in 1876.[107]

The cartoon series in the *City Item* had begun for three reasons: the paper was in financial trouble, due in part to new rivals in the afternoon newspaper market; the *City Item*'s managers wanted to boost support for the slate of municipal reform candidates and for Hancock's presidential bid; and Hearn had the creative impulses and talent to produce a series of illustrated satire. By mid-December declining circulation had apparently been turned around, a reversal that Hearn's illustrations undoubtedly helped, and the paper's finances improved through increased circulation and additional advertising. With the election of the reformer candidate, Shakspeare, the satirical series lost what had been its primary direct and indirect target, the administration of the Democratic Regulars.

Also, there may have been intelligence that the *New Orleans Times* would soon discontinue its afternoon edition. On January 15, 1881, the *City Item* gloated over its demise, for which it took credit. "We observe this morning that the *Daily City Item* has finally compelled the New Orleans *Times* to suppress its evening edition,—a fact which the *Times* naturally dislikes to acknowledge and vainly attempts to explain in another way. Among other things the *Times* observes that it prefers no longer 'to stand in the way of' a certain evening daily. We never heard of anything more disinterested than this:—the suppression of an evening edition through pure good will to a rival. Well, well, well!" In the same issue, the *City Item* published a doggerel (probably penned by Hearn) called "Funeral of the *Evening Times*," which begins: "Who killed the *Evening Times*? / 'I,' said *The Item,* / 'With my little fight-em / I killed the *Times.*'" One less competitor for advertising and consumer sales certainly eased the *City Item*'s financial worries, but there was more to this unsympathetic reaction to the death of an edition of a rival paper.

After the *New Orleans Crescent* was censored during federal occupation, the *Times* had supplanted it and survived by being sympathetic to the Union; therefore many New Orleanians thought the failure of the paper would be good riddance. Hearn's "Journalistic Dissection" (October 21) shows E. A. Burke performing surgery on a patient represented as the *Times* with a broadsword labeled "Democrat." Within a year the *Times* was purchased by the *Democrat,* which became the *Times-Democrat.*

Burke wielded great political power. Ever since he and Charles T. Howard separated the *Democrat* from H. J. Hearsey (because of the latter's antilottery stance), Burke as managing editor set out to outdo every other paper. When Hearn's translations of French literature in the *City Item* were well received by readers, the *Democrat* made an offer to publish future ones, a proposal Hearn was permitted to accept.[108] Naturally, the *Democrat* eventually began publishing illustrations—extravagant ones that were much larger than Hearn's. The first appeared on October 30, followed by another on November 7.[109] On December 17, less than three weeks after the last of Hearn's competent but rather crude "French Opera" portraits, the *Democrat* published a stunning half-page (sixteen times the size of Hearn's woodcuts) professional engraving of a scene from *Aïda,* which had opened at the French Opera House. Although Hearn's series had ended, this ostentatious display implied that it was out of generosity that Burke had allowed the *City Item* to publish its illustrated series, and for that matter to survive at all, without showing it up months earlier with such grand pictures.

As his biographer Jonathan Cott points out in *Wandering Ghost,* Hearn by this time was probably suffering from severe eye strain, which was likely the main reason he abruptly ended his series in December. Being blind in his left eye (since a boyhood accident) and severely myopic in his right, Hearn frequently complained in his letters about his poor eyesight. He found it impossible to work by gaslight, and by December 10, the date of the second-to-last illustration—only one more appeared, two months later—the daylight hours had diminished considerably. In an 1881 letter, probably written early in the year, he complained, "My visual misfortune has reduced my hours of work to one third. I only work from 10 A.M. to 2 P.M. You will see, therefore, that my work must be rapid. At 2 P.M. my eyes are usually worn out." No doubt using a magnifying glass for long hours on his nearly two hundred woodcuts had further damaged his eyes.[110]

Hearn's blindness might tempt some who have not fully appreciated his genius and his technical adeptness as an amateur engraver to paraphrase Samuel Johnson's comparison of a woman's preaching to a dog dancing on his hind legs: what is remarkable is not that he has done it well but that he has done it at all. But Hearn *did* do it well, even dogs dancing—or, rather, fighting, as in "The Bone of Contention" (November 16)—on their hind legs. Regardless of their technical and artistic deficiencies, Hearn's images are memorable. The vigor, grace, and liveliness of the forms and the dynamic cohesiveness of composition in Hearn's images are lacking in the cartoons and illustrations of many professionals. In spite of their great variety, Hearn developed from his first woodcut to the last a unique style in which the full range of his wit, from razor-sharp condemnation to tender affection, is expressed. Like a singer whose success is due not to a perfect but to a singular voice, Hearn composed visual images that are compelling and enduring. These miniature graphic documentaries of a past era are worth innumerable words.

CONCLUSION

At the turn of the twentieth century, many U.S. journalists believed their practice to be more art than trade.[111] But they were among those who had enjoyed the luxury of working for journals large and solvent enough to insulate them from the regular business affairs of their papers, and they made no comparisons between themselves and their European counterparts. Hearn had no such illusions in 1880. He saw the U.S. newspaper as primarily a business that would become more so, and it was partly for that reason that he was always a reluctant journalist who maintained a European perspective.

He was, after all, foreign born, and his education was European. His Jesuit training provided him with skills of rhetoric lacking in most American educations.[112] Gore Vidal has said that "although every American has a sense of humor . . . few Americans have ever been able to cope with wit or irony, and even the simplest jokes often cause unease, especially today, when every phrase must be examined for covert sexism, racism, ageism."[113] This growing deficiency in the understanding and tolerance of various forms of wit decreases the number of people in a population who are literate, for no one is really literate who does not understand irony. Daumier was sentenced to five months' imprisonment in France because his satiric cartoons on Louis Philippe were well understood.[114] In recent years a story by Flannery O'Connor was removed from a mandatory reading list by a Louisiana parochial school district after parents and students took umbrage because they were unable to grasp the irony of its title, which contains the "*N*-word."

During Hearn's time in New Orleans the *N*-word was used liberally, and he uses it ironically in his illustrated columns. "One of the vilest nuisances in the way of toys invented to amuse the mischievous boys of this country at the expense of quiet people is the thing commonly termed a 'nigger-shooter.' Why it should be called nigger-shooter I do not know, for it is not exclusively used to shoot at Ethiopians with" ("Illustrated Letters from the People: Mischievous Boys," July 21). But call it that many New Orleanians did, well into the twentieth century, in spite of Hearn's musing. When the toy was finally banned by a city ordinance, it was referred to by its popular name.[115]

Unfortunately, many marginally literate people and school administrators who are not committed to raising literacy levels in students and their parents will not understand or appreciate Hearn's tongue-in-cheek humor any more than that of Flannery O'Connor. A Creole proverb of Trinidad which Hearn included in his collection *Gombo Zhèbes* is *Faut páoûoles môr poumoune pè vivre* ("Words must die that people may live"). "Ironical," Hearn adds, not wishing to risk literal interpretation by his American readers.[116]

Words must live that people may live, and laugh. Hearn upheld the French tradition of making sport of heavenly and infernal things and cracking jokes about patriarchs and prophets. To the satirist nothing is sacred. Former schoolmates from St. Cuthbert's at Ushaw in Great Britain recalled "Paddy" Hearn as the school clown, whose pranks earned him numerous floggings, but he laughed and "wrote poetry about them and the Virgin birth."[117] He alarmed a "ghostly father" by making what appeared to be a sincere confession that he "had been guilty of desiring with unspeakable desire that the devil would come to me in the shapes he came to those anchorites of the desert." To Hearn's regret, "the merciless succubi all continued to remain in hell!"[118] However, he summoned them quite successfully in creations such as "That Villainous Broker" (October 7).

Traditions of irreverent playfulness in art date back to ancient times, but to appreciate them requires an understanding beyond literal interpretation of art and literature, including religious texts. When Hearn wrote of the New Orleans Sabbatarians (which included his friend George Washington Cable), he said, "We have a better opinion of God. We do not believe that the All-father rejoices in the misery of his children."[119] By the same token, such a being would have to have an intelligent sense of humor to approve of satirists' making sport of things heavenly and infernal.

Hearn was remembered by his schoolmates as a merry prankster—full of mischief, but also kind and good-humored. According to his Irish friend of New Orleans and occasional bodyguard, Denny Corcoran, Hearn "loved books, and pictures, and statuary and birds, and flowers, and animals, and the wilderness . . . but he did not care for people."[120] Without this misanthropic facet of his character, Hearn's satire undoubtedly would have been different. The occasional harsh tone and exuberance of his expressions had as much to do with his personality as the corruption of his day. At times he exhibited fierce indignation, on one occasion irrevocably altering his career and life.

After arriving in Japan on a *Harper's* commission, Hearn learned that the illustrator who had accompanied him was being paid more per page for his sketches than Hearn was for his text. Naturally, writers have always believed that, since book and journal illustrations are subservient to the written word, illustrators and photographers should work for the writer, not vice versa. The full-page engravings for *Harper's Illustrated Weekly* always upstaged Hearn's articles, which were published unobtrusively on a separate page of dense text. But that the artist was to be paid more was for Hearn beyond the pale. He sent to *Harper's* editor Allen Alden an epistle complaining about "the power of your brutal firm, which deals in books precisely as they might deal in pork or hay. I could have forgiven all that;—but your desire to utilize me simply to illustrate the idiocies of a sign-painter, rather overreaches the plan." When the offended Alden responded, Hearn dramatically ended the relationship (and his source of income) with the overloaded exuberance of a Rabelaisian-Irish curse: "Please to understand that your resentment has for me less than the value of a bottled fart, and your bank-account less consequence than a wooden shithouse struck by lightning."[121] He was on his own in a country that could not have been more foreign.

Much of what was said in a eulogy of Thackeray could as easily apply to Hearn and his illustrated series—"that large, acute, and fine understanding; that searching inevitable inner and outer eye; that keen and yet kindly satiric touch; that wonderful humor and play of soul!" "A savage touch" would have to be added, however, because Hearn's satire ranges from the gentle to the savage. Hearn probably found his most sympathetic audience in his friend from Cincinnati days, Charley Johnson, whose "Rabelaisian mirth, and his Gargantuesque laughter" Hearn enjoyed because they mirrored his own.[122]

Hearn had a sense for absurdities and amusing qualities in his environment, and he had an extraordinary ability to modulate his criticism and praise along a continuum between cauterizing vitriol and medicinal balm. It is easy, as Juvenal said, to write satire. But it is not easy to range from the heavy-handedness of Juvenal to the light touch of Horace. Hearn exercised great restraint as well as uninhibited extravagance in his personal life, but if he had misanthropic tendencies, his humanitarian impulses were stronger.

The effect of satire on society is usually not easily measured, but it should not be discounted. Hearn and other satirists throughout the centuries have usually hoped to play a part in molding the events and conditions they address in verse, prose, or pictures. Sometimes they have, perhaps none as dramatically as Thomas Nast, who published a cartoon resulting in the arrest of "Boss" Tweed in Spain.[123] More often, satires are but one of a number of influences. Sometimes they have articulated seeds of discontent, encouraging further germination in the public mind, or they have nourished the frustrations of the public, prompting it, if not the government, to take action. The city council of New Orleans appears to have responded quickly to Hearn's "Illustrated Letters from the People: My Office in My Hat" (July 3) by passing ordinances authorizing the Administrator of Commerce to keep the river bank and wharves clear of wares and to confiscate the goods of violators. "The Organ Grinder" (June 30) likely helped persuade the city council to restrict organ grinders' hours. However, levee retailers and organ grinders were small and powerless classes. It was not until 1885 that tossing fruit peelings on sidewalks became illegal, and not until 1884 that ordinances outlawing the sale of opium and keeping "opium joints" were passed.[124] It took entirely new slates of city administrators and councilmen to establish many of the city's reforms. But Hearn's illustrated columns on Orleans Parish Prison, along with other editorials he published in the *City Item,* were early outcries of a prison reform movement, which George Washington Cable joined the following year.[125]

If they have not always succeeded in directly effecting reform, there is abundant evidence that satirists have at least managed to ruffle feathers. It might be said that if a satirist, whether cartoonist or writer, does not do that at least occasionally, he or she should take up producing nothing but panegyrics. Some of Hearn's illustrated columns were cause for complaints among readers. Yet his representations of negative ethnic stereotypes, however offensive they may strike some people today, were in keeping with the prevailing attitudes of the time. The Chinese laundryman who "no speakee Ginglish" was actually a sympathetic portrayal compared with the increasingly anti-Chinese sentiment among the public at that time. Hearn's representation in "Paddy Whack" of a drunken Irishman was attacked for representing a common negative stereotype. However, the *City Item*'s editor defended the piece while heaping praise on the local Irish community which had made many contributions to the city. (Hearn, whose first name was Patrick, was half Irish and throughout his youth was called "Paddy.") The police commissioner targeted in one of the first illustrated columns immediately wrote to defend himself against accusations of hiring superannuated men to serve as policemen. Those most offended by the columns were the police sergeants and captains, who were identified as the culprits mainly responsible for blackmailing the city's prostitutes. The police were a formidable foe. But it was not as suicidal for the paper to target Crescent City police as it would have been to challenge, say, the Louisiana Lottery Company.[126]

Politicians have had mixed reactions to satires directed at them. There is no record of what Mayor Shakspeare thought of his portrayal in Hearn's last woodcut, but there is little reason for him to have been offended. Hearn's illustrated satire had played a role in his election and in the reform movement he led. As the Haitian Creole proverb goes, "Conspiracy is stronger than witchcraft."[127] Hearn's series was part of a conspiracy of reformers.

Even though the *City Item* did not continue as the leader of illustrated newspapers in New Orleans, Hearn's series was a prelude to the *Mascot* and herald of the daily editorial cartoon, which became more feasible as newspapers converted from the letterpress, which required illustrations in relief, like the woodcut or electrotype, to presses that used photolithographic processes, which allowed papers to also publish photographs. As the letterpress was abandoned, woodcuts faded from newspapers. Hearn's production of a daily illustration was phenomenal, even by present standards. Most newspapers today run syndicated editorial cartoons and require only a few cartoons a week from their own artist, and those are in a medium far less demanding than the woodcut.

During the time Hearn created his illustrated series, he lived on Bourbon Street, less than a block from the French Opera House. His quarters were above those of a fortune-teller, likely the same depicted in "The Witch" (August 29).[128] It was she, the activities at the opera house, the beggars, the hucksters, and the sights in the squares, among other things, that made up the dreamlike atmosphere Hearn recorded in his illustrated series. In a letter of 1880 he wrote: "And it may come to pass that I shall have stranger things to tell you; for this is a land of magical moons and of witches and of warlocks; and were I to tell you all that I have seen and heard in these years in this enchanted City of Dreams you would verily deem me mad rather than morbid."[129] Through his illustrated series we enter his enchanted dream of the city of New Orleans, which is full of surprises, strange characters, unfamiliar sounds, odors, voices, and phantasmagorical images. The ancient and the modern are blended. Hearn saw the distant past in the present and the possibilities of a far-off future in new discoveries and inventions. In Hearn's imaginative presentation, all is like a dream of another time and place, and yet not unlike our own.

The perfect imagination, Hearn told his Japanese students, is "the power of creating complete images in the mind . . . an imagination that, in the time of wakefulness, operates with all the distinctness and truth of imagination in dreams." Like gods, a genius "makes a world, and peoples it."[130] Hearn neither suggested that his was a perfect imagination nor claimed to be a genius. But if it was not out of the genius of a perfect imagination that this "City of Dreams" comes to us in images and texts, we can be grateful for the creative genius of *imperfect* imaginations. We can also be glad we are a little less wicked than he prophesized. A century and a quarter later, his satire can make his posterity laugh, even when it has no heart to be merry. We have as many reasons to exclaim, like Jeremiah, our forebears, and our nineteenth-century prophet Lafcadio Hearn: "Is there no balm in Gilead?!"

NOTES

1. Joy Jackson, *New Orleans in the Gilded Age: Politics and Urban Progress, 1880–1896* (Baton Rouge: Louisiana State University Press, 1969), viii.

2. *New Orleans Democrat*, full page display advertisement, October 10, 1880.

3. Tenth U.S. Census, 1880. A daily advertisement in the *City Item* promoted "Professor Sporer's world-wide renowned military band, composed of twenty-five of the leading artists of the country, together with the beautiful electric lights."

4. Lafcadio Hearn to Henry E. Krehbiel, in *Life and Letters of Lafcadio Hearn: The Writings of Lafcadio Hearn in Sixteen Volumes,* ed. Elizabeth Bisland (Boston: Houghton Mifflin, 1923), 1:205. Although the month and day of the letter is unknown, mention is made of Carnival parades.

5. The name of the newspaper during the time Hearn was on its staff was the *Daily City Item*. The name *City Item* is used throughout the introduction and notes on columns so as not to confuse the paper with its later periods. The *City Item* installed its first telephone in early 1881. See Hearn, "Our Telephone," *City Item* (hereafter cited as *CI*), November 16, 1881.

6. The names *New Orleans Times* and *New Orleans Democrat* are hereafter abbreviated to the *Times* and *Democrat*. Both of these papers, as well as the *City Item* and the *Daily States*, were eventually merged with the *Picayune* to become the present-day *Times-Picayune*. John Wilds, *Afternoon Story: A Century of the "New Orleans States-Item"* (Baton Rouge: Louisiana State University Press, 1976), 65–69.

7. The *Daily States* (hereafter referred to as the *States*) was later renamed the *New Orleans States*. After merging with the *New Orleans Item*, the paper was called the *New Orleans States and New Orleans Item*, and eventually renamed the *States-Item* (Wilds, *Afternoon Story*, 2). Elizabeth Stevenson, *Lafcadio Hearn* (New York: Macmillan, 1961), 100. Stevenson describes the newspaper's financial troubles. The theory that Hearsey's successful new evening paper the *States* was a cause of declining circulation of the *City Item* is presented here for the first time.

8. Jonathan Cott, *Wandering Ghost: The Odyssey of Lafcadio Hearn* (New York: Knopf, 1991), 39–54.

9. "We do not remember to have ever read a series of more brilliant articles," wrote the *Claiborne Guardian*, "than those which appear under the . . . heading [Fantastics] in that bright little paper, THE CITY ITEM." Reprinted in *CI*, September 19, 1880.

10. "Illustrated Newspapers," *CI*, September 13, 1878.

11. *CI*, May 21, 1880.

12. *Harper's New Monthly Magazine* 22, no. 129 (February 1861): 365–79. Six years earlier Hearn had named another article for the *Cincinnati Enquirer* "The Haunted and The Haunters"; see Jon Christopher Hughes, ed., *Period of the Gruesome: Selected Cincinnati Journalism of Lafcadio Hearn* (Lanham, MD: University Press of America, 1990), 38–42.

13. Later, in "A Day of Reckoning" (November 4), Hearn depicts a lamenting figure in "sackcloth and ashes," who represents "Democracy of the North."

14. "Balm of Gilead," *Cincinnati Commercial*, October 3, 1875; Lafcadio Hearn, *Occidental Gleanings of Lafcadio Hearn: Sketches and Essays Now First Collected*, 2 vols., ed. Albert Mordell (New York: Dodd, Mead, and Co., 1925), 1:102 (also collected in Hughes, *Period of the Gruesome*). See also a discussion on this article in Cott, *Wandering Ghost*, 60–61.

15. "The Most Remarkable Schoolhouse in the World," *CI*, October 20, 1879.

16. François Rabelais, *Gargantua and Pantagruel*, trans. Sir Thomas Urquhart and Peter Le Motteaux (London: D. Nutt, 1900), chap. 43.

17. John Dryden, "A Discourse Concerning the Origin and Progress of Satire," *Essays of John Dryden*, ed. W. P. Ker (New York: Russell and Russell, 1961), 2:54–59.

18. Ibid.

19. Thomas Wright, *A History of Caricature and Grotesque in Literature and Art* (1865; reprint, New York: Frederick Ungar, 1968), 23; Dryden, *Essays*, 2:59.

20. See "Mephistopheles," *CI*, January 22, 1881; collected in Hearn, *Occidental Gleanings*, vol. 2.

21. "The Limits of Caricature," *Nation* 55 (July 19, 1866). Quoted in Stephen Hess and Milton Kaplan, *The Ungentlemanly Art: A History of American Political Cartoons* (New York: Macmillan, 1968), 168.

22. Robert C. Elliott, *Satire: Magic, Ritual, Art* (Princeton, 1960), 111, 107.

23. Alexander Pope, "Epistle to Dr. Arbuthnot, Being the Prologue to the Satires," *Alexander Pope: Selected Works*, ed. Louis Kronenberger (New York: Random House, 1948), 177.

24. Dryden, *Essays*, 2:75.

25. John Buchanan-Brown, ed., *The Illustrations of William Makepeace Thackeray* (London: David and Charles, 1979), 24.

26. Dryden, *Essays*, 2:94.

27. Edison B. Allen, ed., *Of Time and Chase* (New Orleans: Habersham Corporation, 1969), 11. John Churchill Chase was editorial cartoonist for the *Morning Tribune, Item, Times-Picayune, New Orleans States, States-Item*, and WDSU-TV.

28. Hess and Kaplan, *The Ungentlemanly Art*, 87–88.

29. Stevenson, *Lafcadio Hearn*, 3, 7.

30. Cott, *Wandering Ghost*, 162–65.

31. Milton Bronner, ed., *Letters from the Raven, Being the Correspondence of Lafcadio Hearn with Henry Watkin* (New York: Brentano's, 1907), 27–28.

32. Thomas Ollive Mabbott, ed., *Collected Works of Edgar Allan Poe* (Cambridge, MA: Belknap, 1969), 1:368.

33. Elliott, *Satire*, 3–48; see also Vivian Mercier, *The Irish Comic Tradition* (Oxford: Oxford University Press, 1962), 6–10.

34. Geoffrey Keating, *The History of Ireland*, trans. Rev. Patrick S. Dinneen et al. (Irish Texts Society, 1908), 3:79–95, quoted in Elliott, *Satire*, 24.

35. See, e.g., his articles "St. John's Eve—Voudouism" and "The Last of the Voudoos," collected in Lafcadio Hearn, *Inventing New Orleans: Writings of Lafcadio Hearn*, ed. S. Frederick Starr (Jackson: University Press of Mississippi, 2001).

36. Hearn, "Physiology of Fear," *CI*, August 28, 1878; collected in Hearn, *Occidental Gleanings*, vol. 2.

37. Edward Bulwer-Lytton, "The Haunted and the Haunters" in *A Strange Story and the Haunted and the Haunters* (Philadelphia: J. B. Lippincott and Co., 1881), 340–90, first published in *Harper's New Monthly Magazine* 22, no. 129 (February 1861).

38. Elliott, *Satire*, 13. See also Mercier, *The Irish Comic Tradition*, 7, who (in 1969) said superstitious belief in satire may not be entirely extinct in Ireland.

39. Hess and Kaplan, *The Ungentlemanly Art*, 100–101.

40. Mary Claire Randolph, "The Structural Design of the Formal Verse Satire," *Philological Quarterly* 21 (1942): 373, quoted in Elliott, *Satire*, 111.

41. Wilds, *Afternoon Story*, 7.

42. *CI*, August 17, 1880.

43. David Worcester, "Selections from *The Art of Satire*," in *Modern Satire*, ed. Alvin B. Kernan (New York: Harcourt Brace Jovanovich, 1962), 185.

44. Alvin B. Kernan, *The Cankered Muse: Satire of the English Renaissance* (New Haven: Yale University Press, 1959), 11.

45. "A Visit to New Orleans," in Lafcadio Hearn, *Creole Sketches*, ed. Charles Woodward Hutson (Boston: Houghton Mifflin, 1924), 38–44; Hearn, *Inventing New Orleans*, 173–74.

46. Jackson, *New Orleans in the Gilded Age*, 33.

47. Rabelais, *Gargantua and Pantagruel*, chaps. 28–29.

48. George E. Waring and George W. Cable, *History and Present Condition of New Orleans, Louisiana, from Report on Social Statistics of Cities, 10th Census of the U.S.* (Washington, D.C.: U.S. Department of the Interior, 1881), 272.

49. *Democrat*, February 18, 1881. "The winter of 1880–81 will be known in this country as 'the winter of deluges.'"

50. "The seventeen-year locust has begun its pilgrimage . . . " (*CI*, June 7, 1880).

51. "The Weather," *CI*, March 18, 1881.

52. Michael Seidel, *Satiric Inheritance* (Princeton: Princeton University Press, 1979), 3.

53. Lafcadio Hearn, "Sunday Recreations," *CI*, July 17, 1880; also "Sunday Amusements," *CI*, October 19, 1880.

54. Hearn, "An Astrological Ass," *CI*, February 19, 1881.

55. Hearn, [untitled], *CI*, January 18, 1881.

56. Lafcadio Hearn, *Lectures on Shakespeare by Lafcadio Hearn*, ed. Iwao Inagaki (Tokyo: Hokuseido, 1928), 11–14.

57. Hess and Kaplan, *The Ungentlemanly Art*, 81.

58. Claude Lévi-Strauss, *The Raw and the Cooked*, trans. John Weightman and Doreen Weightman (Chicago: University of Chicago Press, 1964), 1:286.

59. John F. Watson, "Notitia of Incidents at New Orleans in 1804 and 1805," *American Pioneer: A Monthly Periodical Devoted to the Object of the Logan Historical Society* (Chillicothe, Ohio: Jno. S. Williams), 2 (1842): 229.

60. Hearn, "A Musical Compliment," *CI*, July 2, 1880.

61. N.S. 427; Art. 172 (Edwin L. Jewell, *Jewell's Digest*, 1882 ed., 340).

62. Hearn, "Odds and Ends," *CI*, September 14, 1879.

63. Ibid.

64. "New Orleans was formerly known as the Paris of America; and with favorable circumstances we believe she might again earn that enviable distinction" (Lafcadio Hearn, [untitled], *CI*, October 3, 1879).

65. The first was "All in White," *CI*, September 14, 1879, which is technically not a fantastic sketch, as are those which Hearn published under the title "Fantastics." For a discussion of literature of the fantastic, see Richard Grant, *Théophile Gautier* (Boston: Twayne, 1975), 118–32.

66. Lafcadio Hearn to Henry Watkin, in Bronner, *Letters*, 57.

67. Jon Christopher Hughes, introduction to Lafcadio Hearn and Henry Farny, *Ye Giglampz: A Weekly Illustrated Journal Devoted to Art, Literature, and Satire* (Cincinnati: Crossroads Books, with the Public Library of Cincinnati and Hamilton County, 1983), 10–18.

68. See Hess and Kaplan, *The Ungentlemanly Art*, 81–82.

69. Hearn, "Giglampz!" *Cincinnati Enquirer*, October 4, 1874, collected in Albert Mordell, *An American Miscellany*, 2 vols. (New York: Dodd, Mead, and Co., 1924), 1:13–28.

70. Ibid., 1:83.

71. *Ye Giglampz*, vol. 1, no. 8 (August 4, 1874).

72. Hess and Kaplan, *The Ungentlemanly Art*, 16–17.

73. Hughes, introduction to *Ye Giglampz*, 17.

74. Hearn, "Giglampz!"

75. "Balm of Gilead," *Cincinnati Commercial*, October 3, 1875; Hearn, *Occidental Gleanings*, 1:102 (also collected in Hughes, *Period of the Gruesome*). See also a discussion on this article in Cott, *Wandering Ghost*, 60–61.

76. McWilliams, *Lafcadio Hearn*, 101–2; Bronner, *Letters*, 191. Stevenson differs in her account (*Lafcadio Hearn*, 79–83) of Hearn's "Ozias Midwinter" letters. She attributes the cessation of these articles to the absence of a contract and Hearn's frustration with the paper's slowness to pay him. The *Commercial* was, unbeknownst to Hearn, having financial difficulties.

77. Hearn, *Creole Sketches*, xx.

78. See, e.g., "Wayside Notes," *CI,* June 24, 1880.

79. Hearn, "French Journalism," *CI,* September 16, 1880, collected in Hearn, *Editorials by Lafcadio Hearn,* ed. Charles Woodward Hutson (Boston: Houghton Mifflin, 1926), 99–104.

80. Hearn to H. E. Krehbiel (exact date unknown). Quoted in Edward Larocque Tinker, *Lafcadio Hearn's American Days* (New York: Dodd, Mead and Co., 1924), 88.

81. Hess and Kaplan, *The Ungentlemanly Art,* 120, 119–22; Charles Press, *The Political Cartoon* (London, 1981), 263.

82. Edward Larocque Tinker, *Bibliography of the French Newspapers and Periodicals of Louisiana* (Worcester, MA: American Antiquarian Society, 1933), 14, 43–44; original editions in the Manuscript Division, Special Collections, Howard-Tilton Library, Tulane University.

83. John Clyde Oswald, *A History of Printing: Its Development Through Five Hundred Years* (New York: Appleton and Co., 1928), 324.

84. "Wayside Notes," *CI,* April 25, 1880.

85. "Illustrated Newspapers," *CI,* September 13, 1878.

86. Ralph Waldo Emerson, "Self-Reliance," in *Ralph Waldo Emerson: Essays and Lectures* (New York: Library of America, 1983), 280.

87. "Illustrated Newspapers," *CI,* September 13, 1878.

88. "The City of the South," *Cincinnati Commercial,* December 10, 1877; Hearn, *Occidental Gleanings,* 1:188–90. *Le Carillon: Journal peu politique et litterature, encore moins pas du tout serieux* was published between the years 1869 and 1875. See Tinker, *Bibliography,* 10, 25, 30, and 34, for reproductions of the masthead and cartoons. *La Revue Louisianaise* (1846–48) featured caricatures by the artist Garbeille. See Tinker, *Bibliography,* 14, 73. Although a number of issues of the *Democrat* are missing in the microfilm record, it appears that these ran from early May through December 1876.

89. Hearn, "A Study of Cartoons," *CI,* November 18, 1878.

90. "Illustrated Newspapers," *CI,* September 13, 1878.

91. Wilds, *Afternoon Story,* 7–9.

92. *CI,* June 3, 1880, June 24, 1880.

93. *CI,* May 27, 1880, September 6, 1880.

94. Hess and Kaplan, *The Ungentlemanly Art,* 85; Buchanan-Brown, *The Illustrations of William Makepeace Thackeray,* 10–12, 18.

95. "Illustrated Newspapers," *CI,* September 13, 1878.

96. Hearn to H. E. Krehbiel, 1878, in Bisland, *Life and Letters,* 177.

97. Tinker, *Lafcadio Hearn's American Days,* 86, 89.

98. Ethel Hutson, "Lafcadio Hearn's Cartoons," in Hearn, *Creole Sketches,* xxii; Oswald, *A History of Printing,* 322; Wilds, *Afternoon Story,* 14–15.

99. Hess and Kaplan, *The Ungentlemanly Art,* 19, 180; Cott, *Wandering Ghost,* 174–81.

100. Stevenson, *Lafcadio Hearn,* 5, 7. Richard Holmes Hearn made arrangements for the child Lafcadio, his mother, and an English interpreter to travel from Greece to Dublin in 1852. "Idolatry," in Bisland, *Life and Letters,* 24–27.

101. Stevenson, *Lafcadio Hearn,* 23. For examples of drawings in his letters, see Hearn to Henry Watkin, in Bronner, *Letters,* 29, 30, 36a, 40a, 42, 44, 70a, 73; and Hearn to H. E. Krehbiel in Bisland, *Life and Letters,* 81, 84–88.

102. Hess and Kaplan, *The Ungentlemanly Art,* 21–22.

103. Charles Press, *The Political Cartoon* (London: Associated University Presses, 1981), 11.

104. Thomas Wright, *A History of Caricature and Grotesque in Literature and Art* (1865; reprint, New York: Frederick Ungar, 1968), lvi.

105. See the entries on Jacques Callot (1593–1635) in Wright, *A History,* 296–98, 300–310; see also *A Mediaeval Death-bed* (from a block-book, *Ars Moriendi, De Tentationibus Morientium*), 68. Buchanan-Brown, *The Illustrations of William Makepeace Thackeray,* plate 82.

106. Oswald, *A History of Printing,* 322. Unfortunately, due to inferior archival preservation, much detail in some of Hearn's woodcuts, especially these, has been lost.

107. "A Terrible Affray," *Times-Democrat,* January 13, 1885. Tinker may have later realized his error, for he does not mention this incident in his book *Two-Gun Journalism in New Orleans* (Worcester, MA: American Antiquarian Society, 1952). It appears that S. W. Bennett executed most of the *Democrat* series of cartoons, which usually ran in weekend editions from May through December, often with the same cartoon printed on Saturday and Sunday.

108. According to P. D. Perkins and Ione Perkins, *Lafcadio Hearn: A Bibliography* (Boston: Houghton Mifflin, 1934), the *Democrat* first published Hearn's translations from the foreign press on May 16, 1880.

109. "Under Garfield's Chinese Cheap Labor Plan," *Democrat,* October 30, 1880; and "Mr. Eads' Great Ship Railway for the American Isthmus," November 7, 1800. Prior to this, the *Democrat* had published an occasional smaller illustration, e.g., on June 25 a portrait of Hancock, and on July 11 a small reproduction from Puck on an inside page.

110. Cott, *Wandering Ghost,* 131, 28–29; Bisland, *Life and Letters,* 153, 155, 158, 172, 222; Bronner, *Letters,* 51, 54, 70–70a.

111. John Smith Kendall, "New Orleans Newspapermen of Yesterday," *Louisiana Historical Quarterly* 29, no. 3 (July 1946): 771; H. L. Mencken, "Reflections on Journalism: Reminiscence," in *The Impossible H. L. Mencken,* ed. Marion Elizabeth Rodgers (New York, 1991), 1–2.

112. Maurice DuQuesnay, professor of English literature, University of Louisiana at Lafayette, offered me this insight on Hearn's Jesuit education.

113. Gore Vidal, foreword to Mencken, *The Impossible H. L. Mencken,* xix.

114. Hess and Kaplan, *The Ungentlemanly Art,* 80.

115. Ordinance 6865, in Edwin L. Jewell, comp., *Jewell's Digest of the City Ordinances, Together with the Constitutional Provisions and Acts of the General Assembly, Relative to the Government of the City of New Orleans* (1882; rev. ed. New Orleans: Edwin L. Jewell, 1887), 541–42.

116. Lafcadio Hearn, *Gombo Zhèbes: Little Dictionary of Creole Proverbs in Six Dialects* (New York: W. H. Coleman, 1885), proverb no. 135.

117. Nina H. Kennard, *Lafcadio Hearn* (New York: Appleton and Co., 1912), 44.

118. Stevenson, *Lafcadio Hearn,* 21.

119. See Arlin Turner, *George W. Cable: A Biography* (Baton Rouge: Louisiana State University Press, 1966), 277. According to Turner, Cable was not intolerant of others who did not strictly observe Sunday exclusively as a day of rest and worship. See Lafcadio Hearn, "Sunday Amusements," *CI,* July 17, 1880.

120. "Lafcadio Hearn" (unsigned manuscript), folder 63, Lafcadio Hearn Correspondence, Special Collections and Archives, Monroe Library, Loyola University, New Orleans.

121. Stevenson, *Lafcadio Hearn,* 204–5.

122. Bisland, *Life and Letters,* 301.

123. Hess and Kaplan, *The Ungentlemanly Art*, 13–14.

124. See A.S. 6572, Arts. 146–50, A.S. 6677, and Ordinance 750 in *Jewell's Digest* (1887 ed.), 146–47, 339, 75–76, 539.

125. "The Prison and Asylum Commission," *CI*, November 6, 1881. See also Turner, *George W. Cable*, 124–26.

126. H. J. Hearsey took an antilottery position while publisher and editor of the *Democrat*, and as a result, lottery company operator Charles T. Howard and state treasurer E. A. Burke cheated him out of ownership of the paper through shrewd political maneuverings (see Wilds, *Afternoon Story*, 21–40).

127. From Hearn, *Gombo Zhèbes;* also see Hearn, *Inventing New Orleans*, 209.

128. According to city directories, the house in which Hearn lived from 1879 through 1880 is now 508 Bourbon Street, one house up from the place popularly believed to be his residence. The office of the *City Item* was at what is now 530 Natchez Street. See Hearn to H. E. Krehbiel, February 1881, in Bisland, *Life and Letters*, 213.

129. Bisland, *Life and Letters*, 209.

130. Hearn, *Lectures*, 11–14.

THE NEW ORLEANS OF LAFCADIO HEARN

EDITORIAL NOTE

The reproductions herein of Lafcadio Hearn's woodcuts are generally approximately 75% of their original size. The works for which additional information is provided in the Notes on Columns are indicated with a plus sign (⁺) after the title. Dates placed above the title in brackets are unascertainable and therefore estimated. Sometimes two of Hearn's woodcuts appeared in the same issue, the second one on an inside page and often a re-run of a woodcut previously published; therefore, the same date occasionally appears above two sequential columns. Columns that originally appeared beneath a republished woodcut have been pulled out of chronological sequence and paired with the earlier one. Approximately twenty-five illustrations and accompanying texts are missing from archival and microfilm records.

Saturday, May 22, 1880
THE HAUNTED AND THE HAUNTERS+

In ancient times criminals were delivered to wild beasts, who tortured and devoured them.

In modern Louisiana criminals are delivered not to lions, tigers, or panthers to be devoured; but to certain fiendish winged things, which were anciently termed flitter-mice, and which possess, like certain monsters described by Rabelais, the power of stinking people to death.

The building chosen for the infliction of this dreadful punishment is an antiquated structure modelled after the Spanish prisons of Colonial time, crowned with turrets from which vigilant sentries, armed with rifles, may slug those who strive vainly to escape from the silent fury of the odoriferous monsters.

Any wayfarer who lingers in the neighbourhood of Congo Square about sundown may behold the weird prison, and a vast flock of winged demons hovering above it, preparing to hold their ghastly revels under a gibbous moon.

He may also smell the ghoulish odour outshaken from the wings of the innumerable host of imps. The odour is never to be forgotten. It contains suggestions of many odours—decaying shoe-leather, miscarried eggs, and dead cats—and yet is unlike any of these. It is an original and astonishing odour which inspires fantastic visions of death and dissolution.

There are many people who hold that criminals should not be tortured. Humanitarians have declared that the object of capital punishment is not punishment in reality, but only a necessary means of protecting society against crime. In order to save ourselves from being bitten by snakes we must kill the snakes; but we cannot blame the reptile for using its fangs according to the dictates of its ophidian proclivities.

We feel inclined to this belief ourselves. We do not consider that the cause of morality is aided in the least by delivering unhappy criminals to the bats. Better, we think, that the wicked be favoured with a speedy death than that they be slowly driven out of the world by the most indescribable of stinks.

But even granting, for the sake of argument, that it is right and proper that evil-doers be delivered up to the bats;—granting even that they ought to be smeared all over with bat guano seven times a day—let us ask why should the innocent be made to suffer with the guilty?

Why should property be depreciated in the immediate neighbourhood of the prison and beyond it by the wild and savage violence of the stink?—

why should unoffending and law-abiding citizens be compelled to bear the punishment of convicts?—why should no efforts be made to prevent the stench from extending over a square mile of peaceable neighbourhood?—why in short should not the bat-torture be inflicted only without the corporate limits of the city?

Why? Oh! Why?

Is there no sulphur, no carbolic acid, no gunpowder, no vitriol, no dynamite in Louisiana? Is there no balm in Gilead?

Thursday, June 3, 1880
FREE BOARD AND LODGING FOR THIEVES[†]

It is a curious and shameful fact that we have no efficacious system of punishment for small offenses against the law. All petty crimes are indexed off with penalties of fine or imprisonment in the Paris Prison; but the fines are not paid in nine cases out of ten, and the Parish Prison has no terrors for the evil-doer except its remarkable stink. We have no doubt the latter is injurious to human life in the long run, but after a few days the nostrils of a prisoner are numbed, and he ceases to distinguish the smell. The smell, in fact, is "nothing when you get used to it."

The expense of maintaining the grotesque and bat-haunted institution is, by no means light; and the people have a right to complain of a burthen which they support without the least advantage to themselves. The Parish Prison is a white elephant and consumes much of our substance without producing aught in return.

In return for acts of ruffianism, theft, and many other things, loafers are pensioned off by the city for various periods of time. They violate the law, and are terribly punished by having free board and lodging at the public expense, and nothing whatever to do. A confirmed loafer could desire nothing better, and but for the smell of the bats, we have no doubt he would gladly spend a great part of his time in prison upon such easy terms.

It was different in the old days here; and it is at this very moment very different indeed in all other large cities in the United States. There are workhouses in the neighborhood of most metropolitan cities where convicts are compelled to make themselves useful; or there are chain-gang systems which enable the loafers and thieves of a community to make themselves generally useful at intervals.

It is lamentable at this time when the city is almost bankrupt;—when private citizens have to raise subscriptions to pay school teachers;—when the police are receiving a shamefully small stipend (and are nevertheless discharged for not paying their debts);—when money is needed as it was never needed before for sanitary purposes,—it is lamentable, we repeat, under such circumstances to find New Orleans obliged to pay out larger sums for labor which the inhabitants of the Parish Prison could be made to do for nothing.

There certainly ought to be some reform in this matter. The city would be less distressed if she ceased to pay salaries of four or five thousand dollars a year to politicians for doing nothing; and if she compelled her criminals to earn their board and lodging. But sinecures and mal-administration of law are doing more to impoverish her than aught else.

Monday, May 24, 1880
THE DELIVERING ANGEL+

Leave the beautiful gates ajar;
  O, Turnkey, open the door,
    And we'll carve his name,
    On the scroll of Fame,
  When we reach the shining shore,
  With a Bowie knife, deep in gore!

From his pardoning shoulders spring,
  Already, sweet angel wings;
    For he is our pard,
    And it shall go hard
  If we do not, grateful, sing,
  When saved from the hempen swing!

We dance to express our joy,—
  We three and the rest of the ten:—
    Our garb is quaint
    But that's no restraint
  When we rise from the felon's den,
  For are we not pardoned men?

What though we riot in crime,
  In rape, in murder, and all
    Of the deadly deeds
    Which the Devil breeds,—

How blest is the pardoning scrawl
Which frees us whene'er we fall!

Wednesday, May 26, 1880
THE IDEAL COMMISSIONER+

We have the pleasure, ladies and gentlemen, to introduce to you the Ideal Police Commissioner (I.P.C.).

You will perceive in the intellectuality of his beetling brow, the noble curves of his cranial dome, and the stunning solidity of his cheek,— the man of all others best fitted by nature and art to animate the hearts of the police force with lofty sentiments of patriotism and courage.

With this I.P.C. originated the idea of converting police stations into infirmaries, and the pensioning off of decrepit and maimed beings therein.

In return these beings are expected to patrol the streets, clothed in police garb, as scarecrows for robbers. It often happens that the robbers are not very much frightened; and it may also seem that the decrepit persons thus pensioned off upon the police force are obliged to work too hard;— but nevertheless the charity of the I.P.C. must be duly recognized. His thought was noble, though the result proved unsatisfactory. It is, however, by the intent, not the result, that the Ideal Commissioner is to be judged.

Friday, May 28, 1880
THE OPIUM VICE+

The subtle and pernicious influence of the Chinese opium vice is spreading rapidly through the city.

We spoke yesterday of a den on Dauphine street; but the public must not suppose that this is the only one.

There are also public smoking dens on St. Peter street and on Royal street, and on other streets where the vice is less publicly indulged in, the *clientele* being chiefly composed of Mongolians.

At these public dens numbers of degraded women and men assemble nightly to drown thought and stifle memory with the fumes of opium. For those who once acquire this fatal vice, all hope is dead. The motto which Dante inscribes above the gates of hell should be inscribed above the doors of opium dens.

It is curious that the authorities, who are well aware of the prevalence of this vice, have not yet taken measures against its further extension.

We recommend the matter to the attention of the State Board of Health, the Sanitary Association, and the City Council. The latter can crush these infamous places out of existence by the passage of a much needed law upon the subject.

Saturday, May 29, 1880
FRANK J. MUMFORD[+]

Amateur Champion of the United States.

Frank J. Mumford, the young gentleman whose picture heads this column, was born in this city on the twenty-fifth day of December, 1856, and is, consequently, twenty-three years and five months old. He is rather slightly built, but well proportioned, and possesses considerable strength.

In June, 1877, he became connected with the Magnolia Rowing Club, with which organization he remained without attracting any particular attention as an oarsman until June, 1878, when he joined the Perseverance Club. On the 15th of July, in the same year, he made his first appearance in public, rowing against Crotty in the State regatta at the New Lake End. On this occasion he was defeated by the plucky boy from Galveston, but made a good second.

On August 20, 1878, he visited Newark, N.J., and took part in the national amateur regatta, winning a heat, and gaining a position in the race by defeating Julien Kennedy, of Yale. When the men were placed for the final heat, however, Mumford was in shoal water, and as his contestants got the lead, it is claimed by starting at the word ready, he withdrew from the race.

On Monday, June 16, 1879, Mumford entered in the Hope regatta, under most favorable auspices; he was in splendid condition and entertained bright hopes of victory. From the start Musgrove had the lead, which he kept, closely followed by Crotty and Mumford, who was pulling a stiff oar. As the three boats neared the goal, however, Mumford lost his head and upset his boat, leaving the race to Musgrove, who came in an easy winner, making the two miles, with a turn, in 14:25½.

On Friday, July 11, 1879, Mumford recorded his first victory, and won the amateur championship of the United States, at the National regatta at Saratoga. The course was one mile and a half straight away, and on the first heat for positions, he came in second, thereby gaining a place in the race. From the start, the boy pulled his best, and came in winner in 9:50.

This race proved to be the turning in the tide of defeat, which for so long a time had beset him.

Saturday, July 10, 1880
MUMFORD OF OURS+
He Comes to the Front Again as Amateur Champion of America.

The news of Frank J. Mumford's victory at Philadelphia was received here last evening and created considerable excitement among oarsmen. Of course the "I told you so's" were plentiful and expressed their joy in their usual shallow way, but it was among the young oarsman's personal friends, the members of the Perseverance Club and our good citizens, who are always desirous of seeing a New Orleans boy victorious, that the news was received with real pleasure.

Mumford, since he left us some weeks ago, has been very successful, and his trip may be set down as one round of victories. This makes the second time that Mumford has won the senior single scull prize of the National Amateur Oarsman's Association. It is suggested by many that a grand reception be tendered Mumford upon his return to this city and the suggestion will no doubt be adopted.

Sunday, May 30, 1880
"THIS WAY? OR THIS?"+

And Midsummer Night Doings.

[Monday, May 31, 1880]
DOG DAYS+

O, days when the sun rays fiercely burn;
   O nights when the wild dogs whine;
When rabies the sweetest waters spurn
   And howl for the strong strychnine!
Yield, gentle guardian of the peace;
Deal out the sausage which gives surcease!

See, See, the froth of the canine's mouth,
   The foam of his fevered tongue,
And hear the gnash of his madd'ning teeth,
   Like steel-trap fiercely sprung:—
The stiffening strychnine alone can save
Your gentle ones from the maniac's grave.

Hear, hear the wildcat's hideous screech,
   As he maddens the noon of night,
With the mimic tones of an infant's speech,
   And voices of fierce affright,
While the gun explodes and the bootjack's hurled
To drive him "anywhere out of the world."

O stiffening strychnine, your magic power
   Is certain to bring relief;
'Tis the vital need of the dog's mad hour,—
   Of a time when the cat like a thief
Fills the night with a fierce and a savage yell
That would drive the fiends from the gates of hell.

How Patrolmen Slumber on Their Beats.
While the Lives and Property of the Community are in Danger.

Tuesday, June 1, 1880
POLICE BOARD+
The Usual Number of Cases of Neglect of Duty

Murder and Robbery walk the street,
   Armed with the weapons of deadly strife;
While the mild policeman sleeps on his beat,
   Caring for naught save his precious life.

See how the weird procession moves;
   All unopposed to its bloody goal;
While the sleeping Peeler calmly proves
How much he values his little soul.

Wednesday, June 2, 1880
THE DEVIL ON CARONDELET STREET[+]

"Here we go up, up, up,
And here we go down, down, downy."

Knights of the Flags, bring hither your rags—
    Your stocks, your warrants—I'll hold them all.
Of his ample margin your Master brags:
    Come, lover of lucre, now heed my call.
Up, Up, with the bulls, my gentle sonny!
Down, down with the bears, if you want your
    money!

Up, up they go on the curbstone row,
    The premium bonds that so lately fell;
I manage it all in my court below
    And send my orders direct from hell!
The dealers I weigh in a way most funny,
And poise the scales with their own loved
    money.

Up, up, hurrah! for the changeful law!
    Hurrah for the victims that loudly squeal!
In my pleadings can never be found a flaw;
    In "spots" and "futures" I always deal.
Now up now down, it's truly funny,
How sharps and flats sell their souls for money.

Thursday, June 3, 1880
THE OARSMEN[+]

After two o'clock the trains of the New Orleans City railroad left Canal street packed with passengers for the New Lake End for the purpose of witnessing the first day's regatta of the St. John Rowing Club.

By four o'clock there were from five to seven thousand people at the Lake anxiously waiting for the signal for the race, but Boreas destined that they should be disappointed, for a northeast and east wind began blowing, accompanied by a few pellets of rain, which caused the immense concourse to several times seek shelter. The effect of the wind on the water can well be imagined; in a few moments the white caps, the dreaded enemy of the scullers, made their appearance and kept continually rolling in until after dark, when the wind died away, too late for the race.

At six o'clock Mr. J. Dens Huger, who had been selected as umpire, Col. Gus A. Breaux, the original umpire selected, having been called away from the city, announced to the spectators and crews that the races had been postponed—yesterday's to to-day and to-day's till tomorrow.

The persons present were not disappointed, however, for shortly after the announcement of the postponement the double-scull crews of the Pensacolas, Hillsdalce, Cohoce, St. John, and Riverside clubs took to the basin and pulled up and down. Several times two of the crews were side by side, when a lively spurt would be witnessed and cheered by the public along both sides of the canal.

The visiting oarsmen are enthusiastic in their praise of the members of the St. John Club and of the New Orleans public in general for the reception accorded them. The "Shoes," who have traveled considerably, do not hesitate to state that their reception excelled any they have ever received.

Friday, June 4, 1880
EXTHRACT FROM THE SPACH OV PADDY WHACK+

"Gimme a nickel, Misther.

"Accordin' to the Jewdishery ov the United States, this is a free counthry; an' I'll spake all I want to, you ould divil-tailed omadhaun—

"Give us a nickel.

"I am Gineral Grant and Gineral Grant is me. Whin the King iv England said to Gineral Washington—May the Divil tear yer livers out, ye black son of a dirty mother—Dam yez all, I'll spake all I plaze; an' I'll plaze just what I plaze . . . As I was sayin',—Whin the King iv Italy said to Gineral Washington—

Exchange Alley—usually between the hours of 11 A.M. and 1 P.M. or any other hour.

"Give us a nickel, boss.

"Go to d—— ye ould yellow-livered jackass of a spalpeen;—may your money git blue-mowldy for want of surkilation! . . . As I was sayin', ladies and gintilmin an' fello-citizens of the You-nited States,—it is a dizzgrace to see, in this free counthry, a man wanting a bit to put betune his teeth. Yere not contint to starve the wurruking man,—but wid yer odorless machines yez spile his appetite. Whin the King iv Gomorrah said to Gineral Grant—

"Give us a nickel.

"Ye ould baldheaded double-gutted pot-iv-thripe, may all the divils bite yez. Iv yez think to dhrive me out iv the public streets, that yez can't pay for to kape from stinking, yez'll foind that this is a free country. I'll stand me ground, bi-the Hokey, like a Roosian—

"Give us a nickel.

"Yere a gintleman, divil take yez, an God forgive me for tellin' sich a lie . . .

Here a policeman took him by the ear and gently, but firmly, led him away.

Saturday, June 5, 1880
THE TROPICAL PALM[+]

Michel's Woodyard, Orleans street, near the corner of Dauphine.

Some whisper that it sprang from the heart of a young girl, who died dreaming of palm-fringed shores, and pining for the murmur of the sea.

Some aver that it was borne hither from the Orient by the swarthy crew of a Corsair, who landed one wild and stormy night, and slew a Turkish refugee who dwelt where the tree now stands. And having buried him, they planted the palm above his grave.

Others state that it stood three centuries ago where it stands today; that it was once blown down, and that the present graceful trunk has sprung up from the ruins of the ancient one.

And it is also said that a Spanish resident who loved palms, and who had long dwelt in tropical countries, sent for the palm over the seas, that its graceful presence might remind him of summer lands and the mystic chant of the Spanish main.

There is also a story to the effect that he who fells the tree must render up the land on which it grew to the city; but we, having conversed with the owner of the ground, were otherwise informed.

The tree keeps its secret.

Whether planted by nature or by the hand of man,—by Indian or Spaniard, or French colonist,—whether created by the sweet magic of a woman's heart, as some men say;—whether transplanted from the gardens of Constantinople, as the quaint tradition relates;—whether it has witnessed the birth of this mighty city, and waved its *cacique*'s-plume above houses that ceased to exist before we were born, through all the days of the old French and Spanish governors; whether its leaves were agitated by the distant thunder of the famous battle with English invaders,—

whether it looked down upon O'Reilly's Spanish infantry filing by;—whether it sometimes whispers its thoughts into the ear of the Night,—who shall say?

Perhaps it has a mysterious, sentient life,—and holds in the hidden recesses of its being, some strange memories of pre-existence,—of low reefs white with foam,—of untrodden forests of taller palms,—of the chatter of apes and the shrieks of rainbow-plumaged birds,—of purple mountain peaks,—of quaint galleons and the songs of Spanish mariners. And, perchance, while striving in the night to collect these memories—faint and ghostly as objects seen through a sea-fog—it wonders vaguely that it should be able to live through the centuries, in so strange a land as this; and its leaves nod and whisper to one another until the tapers of the stars die out, and the great light of dawn glows over the river, and the noise of hammer and saw and the rumble of wagons harshly dispel the thin fancies of its vegetable brain.

Sunday, June 6, 1880
(AWAY, AWAY)+

Away, away o'er the waters bright,
Away to the piney hills
Where the wild winds play on their harp of pines,
A vesper hymn as the sun declines—
Where the wine of life distils.

Away where the wild gull cleaves the air;
Where the steamer cleaves the waves;
To feel the thrill of a fresher life
With children, sweetheart, or loving wife,
And laugh when the fierce wind raves.

Away to the bowers where clusters cling,
And the luscious grapes invite;
Where birds of fairest plumage sing,
Where health flows forth from each crystal spring,
And hearts throb with delight.

Away, away, on this summer day,
O'er the waves of Pontchartrain,
To lave in the lake where the silver sand
Runs out from the forest-bordered strand—
Such pleasures are not in vain.

Tuesday, June 8, 1880
THE SMILE THAT JOHNSON SMOLE+

Many a wicked smile he smole,
And many a wink he wunk.

Charles Johnson, a comical fellow with a decided taste for fire works, is perhaps too well known to require an introduction. His name has been published in all the great papers and in this way he has attained a notoriety which in a manner rivals Grant's. Johnson, like the great chief, has very little to say; he also has a peculiar smile which, to a number of admirers, speaks volumes.

When he was convicted and remanded to the Parish Prison for sentence, his classic mouth was rippled by a smile which said plainly, "When I get ready I will bring a big batch of prominent citizens with me." Well, he got ready yesterday, and signified his intention of making a statement, whereupon he was taken from the bat-house, better known as the Parish Prison, and closeted with District Attorney Finney, Charles Luzenberg, W. L. Evans, Judge Southworth, and a short-hand reporter.

What Johnson said during this interview has not yet been made public, but from what can be learned he spoke at great length and said very little more than his statement, published by a contemporary yesterday morning. Johnson, at the end of the interview was sent back to the Parish Prison to await sentence.

Wednesday, June 9, 1880
CRUSHING OUT THE VIPERS+

Out from the Third term nest they came;
The vipers that dreamed of a kingly crown;
But Young America saw the game,
And at once determined to crush them down—
Down, down, to their dire affright—
Down, down, to the shades of night.

But one escaped from another nest;
De Golyer Garfield, that is his name;
He spread his wings like an angel drest,

With the shreds of Satan Sherman's fame;
But he too will go down, down,
Beneath the American people's frown.

Thursday, June 10, 1880
MILITARY SALUTES

The five members of the committee who subscribed for the salute of twenty-one guns, are dimly discernible in the upper right-hand corner. The cannon is small; but for a twenty-five gun salute, the committee can not expect to hire a seventy-two ton Krupp. The bigger the salute the bigger the cannon.

Sunday, August 29, 1880
BOOM-BOOM[+]
A Cannon Needed for Christening.
Sambola's Assault and Capture of a Spanish Gun.

Everybody in this great city, large and small, has either seen or heard of Capt. Anthony Sambola, of the Fifth Company Orleans Artillery, or if they have not seen him, they certainly must have heard the thundering echo of the reports of his guns as he fired them on certain occasions at $1 or $1.50 a boom.

Capt. Sambola, if rumors are to be believed, has gotten himself, and certain men of his command, in a sore pickle, and a criminal prosecution is even threatened.

As far as could be ascertained the Fifth Company had at some previous period purchased a six-pound Spanish gun from the Rock Island arsenal, Ill. This cannon was placed in the hands of W. F. Clark, carriage builder, on Rampart street to be mounted by him. He performed his part of the contract satisfactorily, as was certified to by the command when they tested the piece at Frogmoor on Friday.

The cannon was used by the company by kind permission of Mr. Clark, to whom it was returned after being tested. He had not been fully paid for his work, and would not surrender the field piece unless the company or Capt. Sambola came up with the shekels.

But this remarkable cannon was to be christened at Luling's plantation, in the parish of St. Charles, last night, as the regiment was on its way to Donaldsonville, and consequently, last evening, when the Fifth Company assembled at the arsenal, their cannon was not there, and what did Capt. Sambola do but proceed to Clark's establishment, have it broken open, take out the Rock island piece, and proceed with it triumphantly to the boat, which was to convey the military excursion.

An *Item* reporter being informed that there had been a riot near Congo Square last night, and hearing the story about the cannon, called Mr. John Muldoon, an employee at Clark's establishment.

Mr. Muldoon said he had no objections to tell all he knew about the matter and proceeded with his tale:

"You see, this cannon that the papers have been talking about as having just arrived, has been in our shop for about eight months, and was mounted by Mr. Clark. On Friday Mr. Clark let Capt. Sambola have the gun, and they went to Frogmoor to test it, and the gun was brought back to the shop. Yesterday, during the day, I understood that Mr. Clark met Capt. Sambola, who said he would send for the gun, and Mr. Clark reminded that a little money at the same time wouldn't hurt.

"Well, after we closed up the shop, Mr. Clark left and advised me to remain about in case the gun was sent for, but not to give it up unless the money was plunked down.

"At seven o'clock a lieutenant and ten or twelve men came up. The lieutenant asked for the key. I told him that I didn't have it. He said that it was a dirty trick. I told them that only by the payment of the money due for the work on the gun could they get it. They threatened to break in, one of them alleging that it was State property. But they did not do anything further and left.

"Shortly after their departure Capt. Sambola came with almost all his company. Capt. Sambola came up to me and asked: 'Have you got the key of this place?'

"'No,' I answered.

"Capt. S—— 'I'm going to get that cannon; I'm going to break in the door and get my property.'

"'Mr. Clark would like to have his money,' I suggested.

"Capt. S—— 'I'll pay. I'll give you five dollars to watch this place.'

"'No,' I replied.

"Then the men began yelling, the crowd increased, and in the fuss Capt. Sambola gave the order to break in. They tried three doors and could not burst them, so finally they got to the last door, towards Toulouse street, on Basin, and broke it open and took the cannon out."

"What did they do with it then?" asked the *Item* reporter.

"They hitched it to a dray and went off."

"Did they leave the place open?"

"Yes—but Capt. Sambola put two men to watch it."

From inquiry among the neighbors, it seems that the affair was a riotous one, and that they were fearful that Capt. Sambola's command might do damage to life and property.

It appears that at nine o'clock last night the broken door was closed and nailed up by Corporal Broadhead of the fourth precinct.

Capt. Sambola and the Orleans Artillery are now at Donaldsonville amusing themselves, and are oblivious that they are the subjects of the town talk.

Thursday, June 24, 1880

ILLUSTRATED LETTERS FROM THE PEOPLE⁺

Editor City Item—I was very glad to see that you published the communication signed "A Lady" about those wretched little snobs who monopolize the crossings and stick their canes in people's faces. I have often had my dress dirtied by these nasty canes.

But there is another matter which seems to me equally worthy of your attention,—the fact that the small portion of the sidewalks which loafers do not occupy are too often covered with bags, bales, furniture packages, and above all, dry goods boxes—nasty horrid dry goods boxes, with ragged nails sticking out of them in all directions!

One would almost imagine that the sidewalk had been constructed merely for exhibitions of this kind, instead of for people to walk on.

I have several young lady friends who have had their dresses torn by nails in those empty dry-goods boxes piled up upon the sidewalks; and I tell you, Mr. Editor, if you were a woman and had taken pains and time and expense to make a nice dress only to get it torn in this way, you would feel mad enough to wish that the dry-goods boxes were all made into pyres to roast the dry-goods merchants upon.

I thought there was an ordinance forbidding the piling of empty boxes and barrels on the sidewalk. Why is it not enforced? We are going to form a lady's society here for the purpose of mutual support in bringing suits against the owners of those dry goods boxes against which we tear our dresses.

Please publish these few lines.

—Another Lady.

Friday, June 25, 1880
ILLUSTRATED LETTERS FROM THE PEOPLE+

"Boots!"

Editor City Item—Can't illustrate—never learned how—but no doubt your inimitable artist can do it up brown. By "it," I mean that foot which the fellow in the car holds up for every passenger to admire and wipe his clothes upon. Come to think of it, I mean rather the dirty boot than the dirty foot inside of it. It may be seen, with variations, on every car in the city, and therefore can be easily photographed, and as it is a much greater nuisance than either umbrella, puppy-cane, or pet-poodle, I hope it will receive due attention from the proper authorities.

Order.

[Saturday, June 26, 1880]
THE AMATEUR MUSICIAN

"Every man his own musician!"
Let the notes discordant swell;
Strain your throat with vocal efforts,
Make the cat-gut strings rebel.

With shapes angular and horrent,
Let your pictured notes arise,
As when bombs are madly bursting
In their circuit through the skies.

Shriek! O, genius undeveloped!
Screech and crack, oh trembling strings!
Haply she may like the racket—
That poor angel without wings;—

But, Oh do not once imagine,
When you make that angel weep,
That your dismal noise is music:
Others curse you loud and deep;—

Curse you as a fiend from torment,
Come their tender nerves to shock,

Curse you as the evil genius
Of the babies in the block.

Sunday, June 27, 1880
THE LAST OF TILDEN AND THE LAST OF GRANT[+]

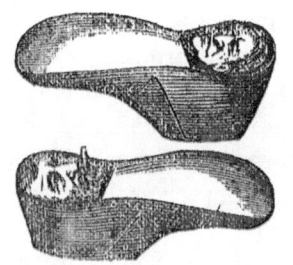

The lasts of which we obtained the correct designs as above reproduced, will never again serve for the making of presidential shoes. The new presidential last is large and roomy and high in the instep; and it will serve only for a man of larger growth than those who have so long sat in the White House.

Tilden has virtually become a political mummy,—so has Grant. And with them the party evils which they represented. Had the manufacturers of Presidential Shoes at Cincinnati modeled their last on the old pattern, the Grant last might at a later day have been called into requisition.

But the fashions change in presidential shoes as in other things when there are smart and shrewd manufacturers to make them. The new fashion will hereafter prevail. Sometimes old fashions are revived, but only at long intervals; and generally an ugly fashion has a poor chance of resurrection.

The Grant and Tilden lasts were ugly patterns; and we believe they have as little chance of being used again as the long-toed shoes of the sixteenth century. We reproduce the design, however, as a curiosity of obsolete fashion; and doubt if any of our readers will regret the condemnation of the originals to the lumber room of played-out political rubbish.

Monday, June 28, 1880
ILLUSTRATED LETTERS FROM THE PEOPLE

Editor City Item—There are several other nuisances which deserve to be classed in the same category with your dry goods boxes and canes. I may refer especially to the skipping rope nuisance.

I often find the sidewalk obstructed by children who are too ill-bred to make room for passersby. They stretch a rope across the way, and one is obliged to force his way through and spoil the game, or else go round in the mud.

If one has to push the children out of the way, then there is a howl from the parents about "people that are mean to little children." They do not appear to think it any annoyance for pedestrians to be struck in the face by a nasty, dirty rope.

I blame the parents more than the children. They sit out on their steps and watch the children annoying people, and never interfere. I think the children ought to be at school, instead of monopolizing the street.

Baseball playing in the public thoroughfare and ball throwing is even a worse nuisance. There is a law against it; but I never saw a policeman stop it. Sometimes I have had the windows of my store broken, and one day, when I slapped a boy who had struck me in the eye with a ball, his mother came to the store and told me that I was "a big cowardly brute," and that my heart "would rattle in a mustard seed."

Must I be always condemned to see customers driven away from my place of business because there are games of high cockalorum and base ball and skipping-rope exhibitions perpetually going on outside the door?

A Storekeeper.

For our part we have not been seldom turned out of the even tenor of our way by the skipping-rope. The ball-throwing nuisance is far worse.

But our friend has not hit upon the greatest and most grievous of all the street nuisances which are due to children. There is one which would try the patience of a saint, and which is so provoking, so outrageous, so inexpressibly annoying that words fail to describe its aggravation. We shall do it full justice to-morrow.

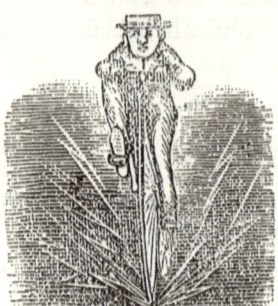

[Tuesday, June 29, 1880]
THE UNSPEAKABLE VELOCIPEDE[+]

A mad dog, a runaway horse, a drove of Texas steers on a stampede, a locomotive off the track, a hundred thousand firemen rushing to a fire, a drunken man reeling down the street with a fifty-pound can of nitroglycerine nicely balanced on his oscillating shoulder and liable to fall off without notice,—are things which may all be avoided by pedestrians possessing presence of mind and steady nerves. Because the bull, the locomotive, the mad dog, the nitroglycerine have all certain invariable and eternal rules of action, unchangeable as the laws of the Medes and Persians.

Given such and such conditions, we know how the terrible things above referred to will conduct themselves.

But no man ever lived—not even Moses or Solomon—who could discover any principle of action, any law governing movement, in the gyrations of the wild, treacherous, diabolical, and unspeakable velocipede. You might suppose on seeing a velocipede steering straight toward you that its furious charge might be escaped by a flank movement to right or left. But you are sadly mistaken.

You might escape an African lion or a Bengal tiger by a flank movement, but never a velocipede, which unites all the vices of ferocious beasts with none of their virtues.

The velocipede is like a vicious dog, because it always attacks any one who runs away from it; but it is also like a lion which attacks any one who dares to face it boldly. It is like a fox in treachery, like a panther in agility, like a tiger in cruelty, like a gorilla in ferocity, like a greyhound in speed, like a badger in taking a good hold of the calf of your leg, and like the Devil for impudence.

You cannot turn a corner so quickly that a velocipede cannot turn after you still quicker. There is but one possible means of escaping a velocipede. Velocipedes are like grizzly bears; they cannot climb trees.

You must, therefore, climb a tree when you see a velocipede; but if you are near-sighted it will do you no good; for in order to climb a tree quick enough to escape a velocipede, you must be able to see the velocipede coming at the distance of at least a mile. Greased lightning does not travel so quick as the most vicious and terrible of velocipedes, known as the Bicycle.

Happily the Bicycle is so vicious that few, even among the wickedest of New Orleans boys, dare to ride it.

A velocipede seems very light; but its weight increases according to the speed with which it is propelled. Sometimes it weighs several tons.

If you do not believe this, you have never been bitten in the calf of the leg by a furious velocipede.

The only way to attack the velocipede successfully is to attack their riders,—as the Romans learned to do in fighting against trained elephants. Trained elephants sometimes turned and trampled down their own supporters. So with velocipedes. If you stand your ground well and direct your just rage and wholly excusable indignation against the rider, you will find the velocipede treacherously abandon its owner and fling him in the dust and trample wildly upon him.

But we have nothing more to say on this subject. We can only hope that all who disagree with us may be made muddy victims of velocipede wrath, and have their legs smitten by bicycles running at the rate of one thousand miles per hour.

Wednesday, July 21, 1880
THE BICYCLE FIEND'S DEFENSE[+]

In response to an article published some time ago in *The Item*, and in which we publicly expressed our private opinion of velocipedes and bicycles, a bicycle fiend sends us the following. We are not responsible for the opinions of our correspondents, and our own opinion about the bicycle is not in sympathy with his'n; but we wish to do justice to all:

ILLUSTRATED LETTERS FROM THE PEOPLE

Editor City Item—The advantages of the modern bicycle over the old velocipede, which was used so extensively nine years ago, are: the placing of the seat almost directly over the centre of the front wheel, by which means a much larger wheel can be ridden, thus gaining in speed and making the act of propelling it more like walking, instead of pushing with the feet (as in the velocipede), which is so tiresome and injurious to the rider. Riding a bicycle is recommended by all physicians. It would be impossible to invent any exercise better calculated to call into play every muscle of the body than bicycling does.

The simple act of pointing the toes, as in standing on tip-toe, calls into play something like a dozen muscles of the foot and leg; then the leg can not be moved either backwards or forwards without using some powerful muscles which are attached to the trunk. The whole leg is at work propelling the bicycle, and every muscle of the arms and body is constantly at work in retaining the balance and guiding the machine. It strengthens the whole body, particularly the upper part, and in this respect is invaluable to men of sedentary occupations. It gives tone to the lungs and digestive organs. The exercise promotes steadiness of the hand and eye, and calls for quick and correct judgment. It affords pleasurable excitement, which is what most men drink liquor for, and it leaves no sting behind.

But little was known of the bicycle in this country until a year or so ago, when there were a few of them in use in Boston and vicinity; but as soon as the machine was found to be of practical use, and beneficial to health, the number rapidly increased, until now there are hundreds in daily use in the same locality, and horsemen are beginning to find out that it takes a fast horse to beat a bicycle for a mile, and for a day's ride, few would care to follow one, as it would tire the horse more than it would the bicyclist, provided the horse could keep up. We have many fine roads in this country, and as nearly every road is passable for a bicycle, it is very probable that where there are now hundreds, in another year there will be thousands.

The difficulties of learning are not so great as those of swimming, skating, or horse riding, a few hours being generally enough to learn each successive stage on the way to complete mastery over the machine.

As bicycle clubs are all the rage in our Northern and Eastern cities, it seems as if, with all the advantages afforded by our beautiful shell roads, our young men are slow to avail themselves of the pleasure to be derived from this healthful and really graceful exercise.

Wednesday, June 30, 1880
THE ORGAN GRINDER+

Where is the man with soul so dead as not to be moved by the music of the organ grinder well ground out?

Echoes of Verdi, of Gounod, of Lecocq, of Donizetti, of Meyerbeer;—memories of gorgeous gas-lit opera nights, of splendid scenery, and the white-limbed witches of the ballet;—fragments of mountain airs which recall blue peaks of the Tyrol or braes bathed in Scotch mists, or fair outlines of Irish hills,—all these and many other delightful things, are they not evoked from the magical heart of the organ?

Have not men thousands of leagues from their native land, wandering among the streets of a strange city where their own tongue was not spoken, often started and paused and listened with tears in their eyes to tunes which brought back visions of their native land again?

Are not these organ grinders, who voyage through all the cities of the civilized world, the Apostles of music,—preaching in all lands the universal religion of music, and the holy magic of expressing human passion in harmony?

For these and all other things must we not honor and bless the olivaceous complexioned organ grinder?

Yea, verily, but there are likewise Certain Things the Organ Grinder doth, which at times make men to wax wroth, and to pour out their souls in fierce malediction.

O reader, thou who lovest the music of the hand organ, has thou never in the solemn hours of the night been lying upon a sleepless bed,—

While the starry heaven flamed above thee, and the perfumed breath of the luke-warm night was about thee, and a most romantic and operatic-looking moon was gazing in upon thee through the window, with flitting mosquitoes sharply defined against its white face?

And while thus lying bathed in the moonlight and filled with a sense of contentment, thou wert suddenly startled by hearing an organ at the corner of the street.

A rich organ which began to play the very tune thou didst most desire to hear, not having heard it before for lo! these many years.

And having ground out several tantalizing notes suggestive of the exceeding beauty of the air in question, the organ grinder suddenly ceased to grind, and when thou didst seek to call him back, he had passed away and was not.

But upon retiring to thy couch in disappointment thou didst again hear the same cursed organ grinder grinding afar off—and suddenly ceasing to grind as before. Has it not often been so?—even so?

Ought there not to be a law to prohibit organ grinders from thus torturing expectation and enervating hope?

Forasmuch as they do these things we do abhor organ grinders.

Also we do abhor the organ grinder who for vile lucre doth consent to grind out everlastingly but one tune—and that a dancing tune—instead of the variety of tunes with which good organs are blessed. Surely this is a prostitution of the barrel organ.

Give the poor organ a show, oh lucre accumulating organ grinder!

Thursday, July 1, 1880

ILLUSTRATED LETTERS FROM THE PEOPLE

"I Know You'll Give Me One."

Editor City Item—Your illustrations of nuisances are forcible and to the point, and should be continued even though no good grow out of same at present. It is to be hoped that, like casting bread upon the waters, it may return in the near future a hundred fold and accrue to the honor of the *City Item* for the changes made and nuisances abated.

Can you not show us "The Slobbering Idiot" who rushes frantically up to the windows and steps off of the crowded cars, corner of Baronne and Canal street, scaring women and children almost to death?

Also the no-legged woman with her stumps tied up in old rags and sliding over the ground like some monster of departed days, forcing ladies to flee as though from the wrath to come.

Also the begging nuisances—those old termagants who "tackle" you at every corner and in low, whining tones insist on something to save a poor woman and her orphanless children from starvation, and on refusal cursing and abusing you for all they can lay their dirty tongues to.

Also the wide awake nigger who passes for blind, with his plaintive Mister,
> Please, sir,
>> Give a
>>> Poor
>>>> Blind
>>>>> Man
>>>>>> Five
>>>>>>> Cents,
>>>>>>>> Please, sir,

and who, when admonished to move on, beats the little cuffee, who plays the role of leader, because nothing is given.

Now these nuisances should be abated by the authorities at once. What harm and what injury they make can only be reported by family physicians. No other city on this continent would, or could, tolerate these intolerable and damnable nuisances, including "Paddy Whack" and all others of his ilk. Go on with the good work and may God reward you.

OLD SUBSCRIBER.

Friday, July 2, 1880
THE NURSE MAID

The pretty nurse maid who flirts with bad young men, ought to be considered as belonging to the category of public nuisances.

The flirting servant girl is the joy of well-dressed loafers, but the terror of staid and meditative people.

The naughty nurse maid hates quiet, respectable elderly looking people, and occasionally runs a perambulator over their toes just for the fun of "making them mad."

Sometimes, while looking over her shoulder at a naughty young man, instead of looking straight before her, she will propel her perambulator with such force that it will run half-way up the back of an unsuspecting pedestrian, who thinks he has been struck by a moving earthquake.

Then the wicked girl says, "Excuse me, sir!" and laughs at the naughty young man, and the naughty young man laughs back again.

What the naughty nurse maid best likes is to go to the parks with the children. In the parks one can have such a nice time.

The babies can yell as much as they please, but there is none to hear or succor them; while the nurse maid is being tickled under the chin by her nice young man.

Under such circumstances even if the earth were to open and swallow up baby-carriage, babies, and all, the nurse maid would not notice it.

While her young man is with her, her thoughts are not of this practical world; and certainly not of babies. It is only when the young man gets hard up for something to say, and has exhausted his stock of small talk that he occasionally calls his sweetheart's attention to the condition.

Then it is "Oh, gracious!"

And "Goodness alive!"

And "Oh, lordy!"

And, "I declare, Jim, you have no sense at all!—to keep me here like this!"

And "Oh goodness, Jim, I've got to go now, sure!"

And when the babies get home everybody says, "Did you ever see such mean, cross children in all your life?"

But nurse maids know that babies are practically deaf and dumb up to a certain age. So that they only smile and hold their peace, knowing that the babies can not give them away.

Saturday, July 3, 1880
ILLUSTRATED LETTERS FROM THE PEOPLE[+]

My Office in My Hat.

An' what are ye drivin' at?
I deals in corn, in hay an' oats,
An' all that, an' all that.
Nor care I how the people votes,
As I ride upon my tandem floats
With me office in me hat.

Editor City Item—I wish to say a word or two on the levee subject. Now, sir, if our City Fathers will only take the time and trouble to visit the levee, they will see for themselves the manner in which our river front is uselessly blockaded, especially at this season of the year.

Why, sir, a boat lands here and discharges her cargo, if she has room to do so; she starts back to St. Louis, and in two or three weeks returns, and frequently finds part of her previous cargo still on the landing, being peddled out by a few men who call themselves merchants; and who, if finally compelled to remove it by the wharfinger, only carries it to another part of the levee, and there peddles it out without expense, except tarpaulin hire, for they carry their office in their hat.

Why sir, you can see those men every morning come out, uncover their stuff, retail all day, cover up at night as snugly as a man would secure his store that he pays $150 or $200 a month for. Oh, shame! City Fathers, to allow such obstructions to commerce and allow those men to do as they please.

A few days ago a boat came from Cincinnati—the *Robert Mitchell*—there were only three or four boats at the wharf, but there was no room for her to discharge her cargo, so she had to go to the Vicksburg landing, or to Algiers, and that in the last week in June! Yet the City Fathers ask the merchants to give their opinion about it; and, as I said before, if they would only come out here, even this day, when there are only Western boats at the wharf, they can see the cause of it all.

A Merchant of the Levee.

Monday, July 5, 1880
FEMININE INTOLERANCE

"Phew!"

"Pah!"

"Ugh!"

"Horrid!"

"Oh, dear!"

Such expressions, uttered in a soft, sweet voice, accompanied by pretty looks of agonizing reproach are flying daily in our smoking cars at innocent smokers.

When the looks are very pretty and the angry eyes are very bright and the lips that reproach are very red, it is sometimes a little hard to preserve one's equanimity while indulging in the awful crime of smoking before Fair Women.

But when the physical aspect of the reproacher suggests hoary antiquity, the smoker smoketh with even greater nonchalance than before.

Unfortunately for our victimized smokers, however, old ladies seldom do such things. They have seen the world, and are too sensible to object because people choose to smoke in a smoking car—that is to say, a car specially devoted by the railroad company to the practice of smoking.

No, it is the young ladies who are the objectors, the "kickers," the plagues, and worries of our smoking cars.

"Faugh!"

"Phew!"

"Fee!"

"Pah!"

"Gracious!"

One would imagine that the young woman who utters such ejaculations, each time she takes her handkerchief away from her nose, is really laboring under terrible olfactory agony.

But this is a mistake.

The natural course for a woman to pursue who does not like smoke, is to seek a car in which smoking is not allowed.

But she does not always do so. On the contrary, she seeks the very car set aside for the benefit of smokers and of which the running expenses are paid by smokers.

Then she places herself beside or directly in front of the smokers, so that it is utterly impossible for them to prevent the smoke from blowing into her face; and then she begins:

"Pah!"

"Faugh!"

"Phew!"

"Oh my!"

She is seldom old or plain-featured, but usually young and pretty; and this fact leads us to infer that she does these naughty things merely in order to test her power over the sterner sex.

She says to herself, "I am young and pretty, and men ought not to smoke before young ladies. I shall tease them and make faces at them until they stop!"

She does tease and tantalize too; and the railroad companies ought to prohibit any lady under forty-five years of age from riding in smoking cars.

But when the girl who complains so terribly of tobacco smoke in a street car meets her lover Jack at home, she not only declares that she "loves the smell of tobacco," but brings him a light for his cigar with her own dainty fingers, and sometimes takes a little whiff just to please him, with—

"Oh, gracious!"

"Now!"

"My goodness, I will get all dizzy!"

But she doesn't get dizzy at all, not a bit of it. She has a strong little stomach and willful little disposition.

Tuesday, July 6, 1880

HANCOCK AND ENGLISH+

We present our readers to-day with the portraits of Hancock and English. The former has been exhibited by several of our contemporaries; the latter is now presented for the first time to the gaze of New Orleans readers through the enterprise of *The City Item*.

We have said so much to our readers about Gen. Hancock that it will hardly be necessary to say any more at present.

Of English it may be observed that he represents in a certain manner the interests of American capitalists and business men;—and that his own immense interests are knit irrevocably to those of the American public.

Yet Mr. English is not much of a politician. He is only a highly intelligent, and highly esteemed business man. His nomination was neither bought nor intrigued for. It was the spontaneous result of the great necessity to find a perfectly upright gentleman for the high office of Vice President. The same spirit of reform which called upon Hancock also called upon English.

Mr. English is only worth about ten millions of dollars; but he will not need to use his revenue in the campaign. His election is already as assured as that of Hancock.

English represents a type of American merchants, such as will sooner or later, it is to be hoped, form the municipal and State governments of all the country,—men who study politics only in their bearing upon national and local prosperity,—were too wealthy to be even suspected of selfish ends—men who care nothing for official salaries, but only for the honor of filling satisfactorily a position of trust,—men whose private interests depend upon public interests. To live by politics alone is almost to live by crime;—the people must learn this fact sooner or later and choose men to fill high offices and positions of trust who are not politicians, but only wise and good men like our future Vice President.

Wednesday, July 7, 1880
MORNING CALLS—VERY EARLY[+]

    Pitis sans papa, pitis sans maman!
    Qui ça ou z'aut fé pou gagnin l'arzan?
N'a couri l'aut bord, pou cerce pat sat,
N'a tournein bayou pou pece patassa,
    Et v'la comme ça n'a té fe pou l'arzan.

    Pitis sans papa, pitis sans maman,
    Qui ça ou z'aut fé pou gagnin l'arzan?
N'a couri dans bois fouille latanie,
N'a ven so racin pou fourbi planche,
    Et v'la comme ça n'a té fé pou l'arzan.

    Pitis sans papa, pitis sans maman,
    Qui ça vou z'aut' fé pou gagnin l'arzan?
Pou fé di té n'a a fouille sassafras,
Pou' fé li l'encr' n'a porte grain salgras (chou-gras),
    Et v'la comme ça na te fé pou' l'arzan.

    Pitis sans papa, pitis sans maman,
    Qui ça ou z'aut fé pou gagnin l'arzan?
N'a couri dans bois ramasse caucos,
Avé non la caze n'a trapé zozos,
    Et v'la comme ça n'a te fé pou l'arzan.

    Pitis sans papa, pitis sans maman,
    Qui ça ou z'aut' fé pou gagnin l'arzan?
N'a couri a soir chez Mamzell Maroto,
Dans la rie Ste. Anne, ou n'a té zoue loto,
    Et v'la comme ça n'a te fé pou l'arzan.

The above ancient Creole ditty contains some curious information about the occupations which some of our old-fashioned colored Creoles alone follow, and of which they alone know the secrets. We are indebted therefore to a gentleman of this city who has made a rich collection of these songs.

Thursday, July 8, 1880
THE GO-AT+

The go-at, like other quadrupeds of the domesticated kind, possess some vices and many virtues.

His name is derived from the former; his value from the latter. It is his habit to go-at unsuspicious people whose presence is distasteful to him; and his head, when used as a battering ram, is found to be extremely hard.

His virtues consist in the capacity of his stomach, in which he resembles the cassowary; and a nanny-goat has a peculiar power of extracting rich milk from brown paper, oyster cans, sawdust, old blacking-boxes, wearing apparel, straw hats, rags, garbage, old bonnets, and newspapers.

A nanny-goat well furnished with brown paper and oyster cans will give more milk than a creole cow.

Everybody that is poor has a goat because it costs nothing to keep them; and they pay well nevertheless for the privilege of being kept.

They represented in other days a peculiar New Orleans industry. There were goatherds here who used to make a good living by selling goats' milk.

Goats are usually good natured in this city, except toward wicked boys and wicked dogs. These do not like goats.

But they are not often troubled with scruples of conscience. They will eat up a thousand-dollar garden with as much ease and nonchalance as they would a roll of grocery wrapping paper.

Consequently goats are regarded by owners of luxuriant shrubberies and gardens with a sinister and suspicious eye.

Goats are valuable to a community in spite of certain odoriferous peculiarities; and it would be much better if there were fewer cats and dogs and more goats.

Cats pretend to catch mice and rats; but they sleep all day and scream like lost souls all night, and do other nasty things which goats never do, and it costs a great deal to keep them in beefsteak and other grub. They are, moreover, ridiculously fastidious about their provisions.

One good rat-trap is worth more than 100 cats.

Dogs are good sometimes; but they are more often bad. They get mad sometimes and bite people; and they go on sprees all night long, and get into disgraceful fights on the street corners.

Goats go at people only under certain justifiable circumstances, and the consequence is not hydrophobia, but merely an inability on the part of the victim to sit down with comfort for a few days.

They eat whatever they can get and are thankful for it, and they help poor people to live through hard times. They are not beautiful; but they are good, practical creatures, which only need a little mild discipline to keep them within the bounds of usefulness and virtue. They do not get fits, like cats, or diseases like dogs; for, living like anchorites, they are blessed with constitutions of advancement and the stomachs of ostriches.

God bless the go-at!

Friday, July 9, 1880
OAKLAND PARK SCENERY+

O, but it was a Bright idea,
    To drive the peelers away from the park,
For the roughs and rascals like to see a
    Little bit of a rowdy lark.

They like to play with the colt and bludgeon;
    They like to sport with the gentler sex;
To mildly frighten the timid gudgeon,
    And souls of the well-dressed gallants vex.

They like rough sport and bloody noses—
    To woo, as the lion woos his bride—
And when your well-dressed gallant shows his
    Head or heels, they go for his hide.

For every peeler they have a feeler,
    And when he's absent they like the fun
Of giving some other chap a reeler,
    And making the coward crowd to run.

Thus Bright they thank for his Bright idea
    Of keeping the peelers away from the park,
For they care but little who is to be a
    Bullseye for them when they're on a lark.

Monday, July 12, 1880
"FORTY FIGHTS TO A DANCE"
What Was Seen at the Oakland Park.
The Effect of Bright's Injunction.
How the Mitchel Rifles did Police Duty.

Sunday, two weeks ago, the Mitchel Rifles, Irish-American citizen soldiers, gave a complimentary picnic at Oakland Park, but the bars did not make much money, and in order to give them a chance to make up their losses, the Mitchel Rifles consented to become the sponsors of a second picnic at the Park yesterday.

At the first picnic police officers were in attendance, and though present, could not prevent a few pugilistic encounters. Some things passed shortly after this picnic which caused Mr. George L. Bright, the proprietor of this resort, to go into court and sue out an injunction prohibiting the police from entering his grounds. The injunction had a beneficial effect—that is to the hoodlums who visited the park last Sunday and broke up the festival given by the German order of Huragari.

The Mitchel Rifles, after the scene enacted at the Huragari festival had been ventilated by the press, made application for police to Chief Boylan, who very properly refused unless the injunction was set aside. Therefore the Mitchel Rifles proceeded to the picnic grounds with the determined purpose of doing police duty, and to bounce out the first spalpeen who would create a disturbance.

Sentries were placed at the door, as a warning to the hoodlums and women who entered the park that they must behave themselves. The sentries were not there to order anybody away. Oh, no. Everybody who desired walked in unmolested, just to help the bar along. The bar thrived; cheap whisky was peddled out at a lively rate, and by eight o'clock there were many and many suffering from whisky indigestion.

As the music gave the signal for each dance, tussles were seen here and there on the platform with the remarks, "Say, drap that girl, this is my dance"; "I'll clout you in the ear if you dance with that fellar," and many other pet sentences of like strain were heard, but the time had not yet arrived for action.

At half-past ten o'clock, when one drunken woman was seen staggering around, a young girl scarcely sixteen years old was trying to hold her up, while their two escorts were just able to stand. "That woman must go out," ordered a soldier. "Now don't, please don't put her out," pleaded the young girl. This seemed to take effect, but it was soon dispelled by their fellows holding, "They can't put her out."

The captain of the Rifles seeing the crowd congregate, and as he had just taken off his heavy coat for a bit of fresh air, rushed coatless in the crowd and drawing his sword called out, "Mitchel Rifles, respect your colors, will ye see your picnic disgraced? Fall in, file."

The captain's orders were obeyed and the two women and their escorts bounced.

While the Rifles were attending to this little party, a crowd of hoodlums jumped upon one Frank Angelo, the keeper of the peanut stand. One blow felled Angelo, and when he came to, he found his stand demolished and his peanuts strewn around. Frank, considering discretion the better part of valor, left the grounds and made a report of the occurrence at the suburban station.

It appears that the two women and the two chaps who were bounced from the picnic boarded the train for the city, and finding that all the seats were occupied, one of the chaps began creating a disturbance. The train was soon stopped and the quartette landed in jail, and booked as follows: John Cunningham, John Maher, and May Heller were charged with being drunk and disturbing the peace. Mary Hamann, the only one sober in the crowd, was charged with disturbing the peace.

Things got so lively about this time, and as one of the Milesians expressed, "there was forty fights to a dance," that the Rifles concluded to break it up.

Two of the Rifles, jaded at their day's work, left a little before the command, and chanced to get in the same car with *The Item* man, who heard the following conversation:

"That's the last picnic of this kind they get me at."

"You bet," answered the other, "they won't see me there, aythur."

"Amen," whispered *The Item* man to himself.

Saturday, July 10, 1880
CITIZEN-EXECUTIONER SHERMAN+

À la Guillotine!

The whirligig of time is bringing in his revenges.

Defeated in his great ambition,—overthrown with great slaughter in the political battle at Chicago, Sherman still possesses the authority and the determination to punish the faithless or unfortunate generals entrusted with his campaign.

The Carthaginians crucified unlucky generals. The crime of defeat was punished by many nations of antiquity with the extreme penalty of the law. Oriental races pursue the same policy to-day. Precedent is not wanting.

But the naval dignitary whose head appears under the guillotine at the head of the page was not merely an unfortunate general of the Sherman armies.

He went over, bag and baggage, to the enemy.

He waited until he saw how the fight was going, and then deserted to what he believed to be the stronger side.

It profited him nothing; and his execution will not provoke a solitary sigh.

The General of the Cigar whom he aided can serve him in nothing, being buried beyond resurrection,—politically embalmed and mummified,—leaving the traitor to the mercy of the great Resumptionist who can not be expected to have any mercy.

Why, indeed, should he have any?

The look of vindictive determination with which he pulls the string of the guillotine, assures us that he does not intend to have any.

The checquered pavements of the Customhouse will run red with slaughter.

So much the better. But this shameless system of utilizing the offices of government for political campaign organization is destined to end before long. Wait until Hancock is elected, and the granite building will be disinfected. It smells of camphor at present. Its odors are pestiferous.

Those who can hold the fort of office until that time will make all the money they can. They have no time to lose either.

And don't you forget it.

Sunday, July 11, 1880
IN THE VISE

Lithographed copy of a letter to all the small office holders in the government employ throughout the country.

"*Dear Sir*—You are holding an office from the government. That office was bestowed upon you less because of the small political service already rendered by you, than because of your ability to serve that government in the coming campaign. You are sensible enough, I trust, to comprehend that you are not employed in the ———— Department because of ability to perform the routine duties assigned to you. Had we listened to the complaints of your incompetency received by us you would have been long since removed. A thousand infinitely more capable men are ready to step into your place at the word. You must understand thoroughly that you are employed really as a *political* servant of the government, although nominally as a department clerk. One condition of your retention is that you aid that government with money as well as with all the political influence you may possess. It is to your interest as well as ours to contribute at once what is demanded of you. We must buy votes by thousands in the coming campaign, and if the Democratic party obtain a victory you may rest assured that your tenure of office will be exceedingly brief. In order to buy votes it is necessary for us to draw upon you and all in our employ. Money must be had and plenty of it; and the Republican party must take advantage of all the means within its command to obtain it. You will therefore be prompt in your payment and place not less than FIVE DOLLARS in the proper hands. The amount of salaries has always been regulated with a view to this end, so that clerks may pay without being seriously embarrassed by their contributions. In case of a refusal, your place will be speedily filled by some more intelligent and efficient servant of the Republican party. If called upon again to contribute, it will be your duty to do so promptly and cheerfully. This circular is strictly private, and must be destroyed at once. To show it to any person will be sufficient cause for your dismissal."

"John Sherman."

The authenticity of the above seems to be further confirmed by the following dispatch, which appears in the columns of a contemporary this morning:

> Subscriptions are going on actively in the executive departments, and nobody dares to refuse paying for fear of removal. The Republicans seem to be decidedly ahead of the Democrats in raising money for campaign purposes; but the current seems to be running for Hancock, and it would not surprise me to see him elected by a great majority like that of Harrison and Tyler in 1840. There are signs strongly indicating that the people want a change in the government.

Monday, July 12, 1880
ILLUSTRATED LETTERS FROM THE PEOPLE+

Editor City Item—As your paper has been paying graphic attention to public nuisances, let me say a few words about the loafers at the street-corners, and especially on our block.

About five o'clock in the evening they congregate about the steps of vacant houses, at the corners of beer saloons and groceries, about lamp-posts and upon empty barrels.

Then they commence to curse and to swear and to laugh and to spit tobacco juice over everything and everybody.

In front of my place the pavement is often covered with tobacco juice. It is enough to make anybody sick to look at it.

They are a drawback to trade, and it is no use to order them away. In fact it is dangerous to order them away; and the police seem to be afraid of them.

When a policeman comes along it is always, "Hello, Pete," or "Hello, Jim," and then the policeman joins the crowd and squirts around like the rest of them.

Moreover, these fellows don't spend any money; they will drink one glass of beer, and loaf around the grocery all day after.

Is there no ordinance to prevent this kind of nuisance?

Tuesday, July 13, 1880
THE LAST SHAKE OF THE BLOODY SHIRT

Come, fire up the Northern heart,
    O Ruler of the Night!
And Hate's dark venom now distill
    With all your hellish might;
For if you don't, Peace will descend
    With healing on its wings,
And Brotherhood, with kind accord,
    Will break the rascal Rings.

Come, fire up the Northern heart!
    Shall hands, to plunder given,
Exchange the rule of hate and hell
    For that of peace and heaven?
No, by the Fiends! The bloody shirt
    We must wave once again,
Thus proving, though we win by fraud,
    That we are loyal men!

Come, fire up the Northern heart!
    The Solid South must know,
That, whilst pretending love and peace,

It's still the Nation's foe.
It must be crushed; so, worthy Fiend,
In malice steeped and sin,
Aid us to crush Democracy
And with our Garfield win.

Wednesday, July 14, 1880
HOW THEY DO IT

It is a well known fact that when a ward bummer or rowdy is under arrest for cutting or shooting somebody, heaven and earth is moved by his fellows to intimidate or spirit refractory witnesses who consider it their duty to obey a subpoena, and to tell the truth, the whole truth, and nothing but the truth.

Any man who "cuts and shoots" is a valuable man in a ward. The oftener he has cut and shot the more valuable he is. If he has killed somebody he is still more valuable. He has a name and a reputation which inspires fear to timid people; and fear is the belt which runs the ward political machine.

Violent means to intimidate witnesses, however, are resorted to only in extreme cases.

It is generally managed in a better or safer way. Sometimes the small ward politicians will club together and pay the doctor bills and expenses of the injured party in order to get him to "let up." It often happens that he refuses to "let up" under any circumstances. Then the witnesses must be taken in hand.

Sometimes the witness meets a ward acquaintance who calls him into a barroom and treats him. After a short conversation the acquaintance observes:

"That's a terrible looking hat you've got on, Jim. I'd be ashamed to be seen with it on. I tell you what I'll do with you. Just come along with me and I'll get you a decent roofing." And he treats him to a five dollar hat.

A few weeks after, the recipient of the new hat meets his friend again, as if by accident; and the latter says:—

"Why, Jim, I hear you're a witness against poor Mike. Are you going to swear against him?"

"Well, I'm subpoenaed."

"Now, you know Mike's a friend of mine. It would be a personal favor to me if you'd let up on him."

"But I've got to go to court."

"No, you haven't. We'll fix that all right. You need only keep out of the way until after the 18th, when the case comes up. If you ain't got money to go over the lake, I'll settle all that."

And the witness, remembering the new hat, bound by ties of gratitude, mysteriously disappears when most wanted. He never gets into trouble about it, either. The affair has been "fixed up."

An obdurate and determined and fearless witness is simply told to "look out." The boys will "fix" him.

"Are ye goin' to swear against Pat?"

"Shure, I will. There ain't no love lost betune me and that same."

"Whin Pat gets out again, he'll kick the livers out iv you."

"An what ud I be doin while he was kickin the livers out iv me?"

"If he can't do himself, there's others as can; and ye'll sup sorrow the day ye swear agin him."

"Divil the sup!"

"It's for your own good I'm telling yez. I know Pat and his crowd, and they'll lather the lights out iv ye. Now you take me advice, and lave that business alone. Mind what I'm tellin yez!—mind what I'm tellin yez."

Thursday, July 15, 1880
THE WOLFISH DOG+

The dog days approach and the dogs continue to abandon themselves to midnight orgies with a sense of perfect security.

The dog ordinance is not put into execution except in the case of fine aristocratic dogs belonging to rich people.

Those fine dogs are all well brought up and know how to mind their own business. It is the nasty, snarling, mongrel, vulgar dog which ought to be looked after, the dog which never minds his own business and is always poking his nose into other people's affairs.

The currish and vulgar dog shows his wolfish instincts at night, when he and his brethren render certain streets like unto the streets of Constantinople. Woe be to the wayfarer who walks without a big stick in such neighborhoods after dark. The dogs circle about him in packs and threaten to tear him limb from limb.

Friday, July 16, 1880
ILLUSTRATED LETTERS FROM THE PEOPLE[+]

Street Car Nuisances.

Editor City Item—Your article about Men and Mules seemed to me eminently just. Not only are street-car drivers obliged to do the work of two men, but their other duties render it impossible for them to protect passengers against nuisances and against roughs in the cars. They have their mules to look after; they have to keep a sharp lookout for passengers; they have to make change; they have to see that everybody puts his or her nickel in the box—a difficult thing to do when a car is crammed full; and it is no wonder that passengers are sometimes subjected to annoyances which in other cities are prevented by the employment of conductors.

Is it any wonder that horses are sometimes driven into street cars, as in the sketch which I venture to offer you for publication. The driver has so much to do that he can not look after other vehicles, as a conductor might do.

When roughs get into a street car, the driver must leave his mule, and go to fight the crowd single-handed. In other cities he would have a conductor to help him; and between the two of them the roughs would be piloted out.

And, Mr. Editor, while on this subject I would like to ask why those people who sell flowers are permitted to board street-cars and annoy people. They never address any except those who are accompanied by ladies, and one is obliged sometimes to buy these things just because the seller is able to take advantage of him. It is well enough to allow newsboys to sell their papers and their fans on the cars;—these are really conveniences. But if people want flowers they know where to buy them at reasonable rates, and ought not to be bullied into paying these prices for ugly little bunches of sickly blossoms.

A Victim.

Saturday, July 17, 1880
ULTRA-CANAL[+]

"Is the old man in?"

"Ah! De ole man! He not been live here since more as tree year. He have lef all his furnizer here; but I not know vat him become. I tink vat he lose himself."

"Lose himself?"

"Yes, I tink he lose to himself. Monsieur not speak Français? No? *Eh bien* I make try you explain, zough I not good English speak."

"You see, he have to him ze brain attach, I zink, of recent. We lost vat to him belong. Some time he lose coat, some time pant, some time shirt,— all time night-key. I vas oblige for him order more as tirteen night-key, for vat I make him to pay. He live in one kind of dream—*il s'embêtait*—he embeast himself much—he seem all day like vat you call *sonambule*."

"Yes, yes! Well?"

"*Eh bien!*—some time he put on tree pair pant. Some time on hot day he put him on ze overcoat. One day I see him try to put on to him ze pant for ze shirt. He have put to him ze arm in ze leg of ze pant; an' he swear *sacre roucht* for dat he not could put on—"

"Yes, I understand. But what has become of him?"

"*Attendez un peu.* I tell one. One oder day he not have any clothes on, an' he try to find his key, an' he swear at tailor for *sacre charogne* for dat he not have made him pocket vat he can easy find. He forget vat he not be dress. Den he lose to him money all time vat make him angry much. One time he take by mistake coat vat not to him belong, and take it to tailor for dat he put tail to it; an' he has to pay to de oder man, of which he spoil de coat."

"Yes. But where is—?"

"Vait—I explain you. He lose everyting—handchef, towl, pockbook, monee, key—all time. One domestique he employ only for find vat he los'; and domestique run himself away, for dat he not more can so hard work endure."

"But, for God's sake, what has become of him?"

"Monsieur, I not can you tell. He go out one morning, and I not have hear or see of him after. His furniser an' all be in my house. He have pay of advance. He owe me notings. He have not ever come back. No one have see or hear. I be satisfy vat himself he lose—like as he lose every oder tin—vat he lose never more find. Vell, he lose to himself. He never more himself find. *Que voulez-vous?*"

Sunday, July 18, 1880
DR. TANNER[+]

A New York correspondent sends us a photograph of Dr. Tanner as he appeared upon the seventeenth day of his fast. We reproduce the Doctor's portrait in wood-engraving, and will continue to publish portraits of him at intervals of two or three days, until the fast is over.

Each portrait will show a remarkable decline and fall in the Doctor's physical condition.

It is possible we may have to terminate the series by the picture of the Doctor's coffin. In that case special pains will be taken to do justice to the subject.

We trust that the public will exhibit their appreciation of our journalistic enterprise.

Monday, July 19, 1880
"SHINE?"

The bootblacks, notably those posted on our big thoroughfares, always address passers-by according to a graduated scale of estimation of rank and wealth, made up from exterior observation. It runs up *crescendo* in about this fashion:

To a seedy-looking man—"Shine?"

To an energetic, simply-dressed man—"Shine 'em up, Captain?"

To a well-dressed man—"Shine this morning, Colonel?"

To a very well-dressed man—"Will you give me a chance this morning, General?"

Tuesday, July 20, 1880
DR. TANNER[+]

The above sketch of Dr. Tanner was made by our correspondent on his shirtcuff, as the Doctor has got recently very nervous and refuses to be photographed. Our readers may already perceive a marked falling off in the appearance of the Doctor, and a marked increase in the size of the jug. This sketch was made at the moment when Dr. Tanner's watchers were sitting down to dinner in the next room. The smell of the viands seriously affected the Doctor's nerves, and he insisted that thenceforward the dinner should be served in some other part of the house.

If the Doctor does not die in fourteen days more, he will certainly live for two weeks.

The chief value of his experiment, according to our correspondence, is its solution of an economical question. Families in reduced circumstances may be able to do with one meal a month, if they can not procure nourishment oftener.

The Doctor, claiming his right to drink water, recently expressed a desire to have Mississippi water shipped to him regularly. To this his friends object on the ground that Mississippi river water is thicker than soup and that to drink it would be a violation of the Doctor's solemn contract with his stomach.

If Dr. Tanner can live on clear spring water for forty days, how long could he live on our Mississippi water, so thick, so rich, so nourishing?

Anybody that could not live for one year on Mississippi water alone ought never to hold up his head in society. We do it very easily; but we do not hanker after it. We are not in want of money, and we believe in eating all the roast beef and drinking all the good wine our stomach will bear. We are energetic,—and believe in making our stomachs work as well as the rest of our body. An idle stomach is an abomination. Dr. Tanner is simply proving that he has the laziest stomach in the Western Hemisphere. We do not care to compete with any one else in a contest for superiority in laziness.

We rush things; we hump ourselves; we move around on wheels—and don't you forget it. No Dr. Tanner in ours.

Wednesday, July 21, 1880
ILLUSTRATED LETTERS FROM THE PEOPLE+

Mischievous Boys.

Editor City Item—One of the vilest nuisances in the way of toys invented to amuse the mischievous boys of this country at the expense of quiet people is the thing commonly termed a "nigger-shooter." Why it should be called nigger-shooter I do not know, for it is not exclusively used to shoot at Ethiopians with.

I was sitting in my room the other day, when a small round stone came through the window, and passing directly over my head, shattered the glass covering a fine engraving in my room and spoiled the engraving itself. It was a very pretty engraving after Greuze, and is entirely ruined. The stone came through the window with such force that it only left a clear round hole in the glass, from which small zig-zag cracks radiated in all directions. Had it struck me in the head I might have been seriously injured. It was thrown from a catapult, or "nigger-shooter," if you please.

This is only one instance. Children have had their eyes put out with these infernal machines; and out of a little flock of pigeons I used to have more than half were killed by the use of these things.

They are positively dangerous; and I think their sale ought to be prohibited just as much as that of pistols to minors.

It is curious how some boys delight in torturing and annoying birds or animals or quiet people. Nothing seems to give them such pleasure as to injure some weak little creature or destroy the comfort of inoffensive people.

Parents are greatly to blame for this. They allow their children to run idle about the streets, and

> *Satan still some mischief finds,*
> *For little hands to do.*

The police ought certainly to prevent such nuisances from continuing. In other cities where I have lived such things are not allowed; and I cannot see why they should be allowed here.

A Subscriber.

Thursday, July 22, 1880

ILLUSTRATED LETTERS FROM THE PEOPLE+

Editor City Item—It seems to me that this is the only city in the world where the sidewalks are turned into lounging places. After a certain hour every evening during the summer, the sidewalks of the city are covered with chairs, and the whole population gets out upon the sidewalk. While the old folks chat and the young folks make love, the children play leapfrog and all other kinds of games upon the little clear space left on the sidewalk. Then the dogs all come out and stretch themselves at right angles across the sidewalk,—made insolent by the presence and example of their masters. It is no easy matter at such times to walk along a street without tripping up over a chair, or standing on a baby or a dog. Nobody pays any attention to you if you fall over a chair; but if you tread on a dog's tail you may have reason to regret it; and if you tread on a baby the whole family give you to understand how great is the length and breadth and depth of the human tongue. Naturally this does not take place on the chief thoroughfares; but on the quiet back streets. Yet it seems to me that these people ought either to confine themselves to their doorsteps or their front rooms or their backyards. Would this be allowed in any other city? Are not the sidewalks intended for people to walk upon, and not for sitting upon?

A Bewildered Pedestrian.

It hath been so from time immemorial, and will doubtless be so for all time to come. The why and the wherefore we can not explain. Our correspondent must resign himself. Instead of walking along the back streets let him seek the great thoroughfares.

Friday, July 23, 1880

ILLUSTRATED LETTERS FROM THE PEOPLE+

The Banana Curse.

Editor City Item—How can I do justice to the subject which haunts my mind, even though like one of Mahomet's angels I had seventy thousand heads, and in each head seventy thousand tongues!

How treacherous and deadly a foe to human happiness is the abominable banana peel!—how many human beings have been killed by them!—how many arms and legs broken!—how many suits of elegant clothes destroyed!—how many frightful and diabolical oaths have been extorted from the lips of suffering humanity by the vile skins, which like fiends, lie in waiting to tempt men to do what Job obstinately refused to do! And how many of us have the patience of Job!

In some Northern cities to throw a banana peel on the sidewalk is to incur a severe fine. Why should it not be so here? No fine could be severe enough. All the worldly goods and possessions of a man who throws a banana peel on the sidewalk should be confiscated. Had I the power I should fine every man who throws a banana peel on the sidewalk not less than a million of dollars; and keep him in prison at hard labor until paid. So much the worse for him, should he have to remain all his life in jail. I think a man who throws banana peels on the sidewalk ought to be caged for the term of his natural life in any case. He is a dangerous animal in the community, as dangerous as a sea serpent or a wild-cat. He risks the lives of the passers-by.

If he does not remember, he ought to be made to remember it. If an Awful Example were made of some one of these wretches, the morals of the community might be improved.

If a boy is the offender he ought to be whipped within an inch of his life—whipped until he faints, and then revived with ice water and whipped again until he faints again. And then brought to again with ice water and whipped much worse than before; and even kept up with brandy in order that he might be able to endure still more whipping. After this he ought to be kept in prison for twenty-five years and whipped twice a month with piano wire.

No: I can not find words to paint the iniquity of this practice. If a woman throws banana peels on the sidewalk, she ought to be sent to a House of Correction for five years; and all her family ought to be tarred and feathered for not having taught her better when she was a child.

An Enraged Citizen.

It seems to us that our correspondent is a little too severe. Perhaps he is at present taking his meals off the mantel-piece.

Saturday, July 24, 1880
DR. TANNER+

from a photograph

We present our readers to-day with an authentic portrait of Dr. Tanner as he appeared before his fast. The Doctor was a fine-looking man, it will be perceived, before he commenced to starve himself. The difference between his present aspect and that of his normal condition, as shown by the above portrait, reminds one of those advertising cuts respectively labeled "Before Taking" and "After Taking."

The Doctor is still keeping himself alive on ice water, and hopes to do so until August 7; when his fast will be broken by the deglutition of a gigantic watermelon, if everything turns out as expected.

Sunday, July 25, 1880
THE KNIFE-GRINDER+

Ding-ding, dingy-ding, ding, dingy-ding; ding, ding, dingy-ding!

A sleepy sound, which one hears through all the drowsy hours of a summer's day,—at first afar off, dreamily, like goblin bells; then nearer and clearer, then dying away like the music of the Turkish Sentry. A sound as of cymbals in the distance.

And hearing that sound, we begin to think straightway about naughty boys whittling the backs of chairs and the legs of tables and the Russia-leather binding of valuable books, and the molding of window sashes, and the frames of doors, and the edges of signs, and the tops and sides of desks, and various parts of benches, and the ends of map-rollers, and the pillars of old-fashioned bed-posts, and the ends of wooden chimney-pieces, and the corners of picture frames, and every article of value which yields to the edge of the knife.

With what delight does a boy rip up the entrails of a well padded sofa or easy chair; with what martial fury does he drive the keen blade into the heart of valuable mattresses!

And this is partly the fault of the knife-grinder.

But the knife-grinder is a necessary evil; partly because the character of modern education is not sufficiently practical, and boys are not taught to sharpen their own knives, and they are bound to get them sharpened somewhere.

Without a sharp knife how can chair-backs and desk-tops be whittled and padded chairs ripped up and family heir-looms destroyed?

And if these things were not destroyed, how could chair menders and upholsterers and cabinet makers and furniture dealers earn a living?

Therefore, let us bless the good knife-grinder.

Monday, July 26, 1880
DR. TANNER'S PRESENT ASPECT+

from a sketch

Dr. Tanner's present aspect may be fairly imagined from the fact that the above sketch was made nearly a week ago, since which time he has lost considerable flesh, and even stature. The wasting of cartilaginous substance has caused a curvation of the body and a shortening of the spinal column.

Dr. Tanner once before fasted for forty days, successfully, at Minneapolis. It is possible that he will accomplish the feat again.

Tuesday, July 27, 1880
"THE DIREFUL BOOST"

Deep in the mud sat the candidate—
    Mud he had gathered in by-gone years—
And the more he tried to cover it up
    The more it aroused his fears.

For the past misdeeds of a candidate
    Come back, as chickens come home to roost;
And though he cries, "they're nothing but lies,"
    They give him a direful boost.

Thus Garfield sits in the gathered mud,
    And Nemesis goads him with vengeful aim;
While the Fates are whispering in his ears:
    "You've only yourself to blame."

Beside him stands, in his manhood's pride,
    With a record fair as the flow'rs of May,
Another chieftain who wore the Blue
    And is honored by the Gray.

'Tis Hancock! Thus did de Garfield speak:
    "O honored rival, you see me down;
Please keep your fellows from throwing mud
    And soften your stately frown."

The answer came: "I throw no mud;
    And besides, I have seen none thrown;
If you've been spattered, it's surely by
    The petard you call your own."

Thus foul deeds rise to the sad surprise
    Of the parents that give them birth,
And like an accusing angel comes
    A frown from the brow of Worth!

Wednesday, July 28, 1880
——!——!! MOSQUITOES!!!

The mosquito is the most cunning of all living things which fly. She sees by night even better than by day. She knows by heart all the holes in every mosquito curtain in the largest hotels. She is a first class judge of dry goods, and distinguishes afar off the quality and thickness of socks and stockings. She poketh her little bill through the finest material that modern machinery can spin.

We say "she" because our tormentors are females; the male mosquitoes are respectable, well behaved boys who remain where they are born. Only feminine malice can explain the ingenious capacity for torment possessed by the mosquito which plays vampire both by night and by day.

When a mosquito lights softly with a subdued scream of triumph on the end of your nose, or any other end, she always keeps one leg hoisted high in air, so as to be ready to flee at a moment's notice. It is only when she puts that leg down that you have any chance of ending her pernicious existence.

Another matter in which biting mosquitoes show their feminine characteristics is their dislike of tobacco.

But they also possess feminine patience, and will wait hours for a smoker to finish his pipe. Then they will take ample revenge.

Nevertheless mosquitoes have their uses.

If it were not for mosquitoes we should all become terribly lazy in this climate. We should waste our time snoring upon sofas or lolling in easy chairs, or gossiping about trivial things, or dreaming vain dreams, or longing after things which belong to our neighbours, or feeling dissatisfied with our lot, instead of humping ourselves and scooting around and making money. Idleness is the mother of all vices; and mosquitoes know this as well as anybody, and not being lazy themselves they will not suffer us to be lazy.

It is for this reason that they hum around only in summer when everything is lazy and drowsy,—especially on one of those quiet summer days when everything is so silent that one can hear the cocks crowing to each other at long distances, and answering each other like sentries in the old cities of Spanish-America. For in winter time the cold forces us to make ourselves useful as well as ornamental.

And so, even while we curse, let us also bless the mosquitoes, for making us move about and root around, instead of dreaming our lives away.

House Hunting Nuisance.

Thursday, July 29, 1880
ILLUSTRATED LETTERS FROM THE PEOPLE

Editor City Item—As you are engaged in the philanthropic purpose of abating nuisances that afflict humanity, I implore your good-will to alleviate the unmitigated nuisance attached to house hunting. A family council is called, and in executive session, after an exciting debate of three days, pro and con, the better-half has carried the day and a change of residence must take place. Move is the word.

1. There must be a cheaper rent; buckle and tongue won't meet, because that heartless old pirate, "debt," has kept us in a fatiguing stern chase for three years.

2. We must have better appointments about the new residence—I can't say new house—for most of them are buggy, roachy, ratty, and catty, especially catty.

3. We must have some yard for the children, to keep them off the street, beside a long codicil of wants.

The word of command from headquarters rings out clear, "Be quick about it!"

Out we go house-hunting. Find one up town, on Constantinople, or down town, on Esplanade street, and a red-lettered card says: "For rent. Apply to S., on Carondelet, or B., on Poydras." Good Gracious! After all our tramp, tramp, tramping—let's see; one, two, three, four, fifteen squares to S. or B.—suffering flesh and tired legs, must I navigate a continent just to find out the price of the house?

If that card had only stated the price per month, I could settle the matter at once. Where are the keys? I will look through the house. No information on the card.

Now if I go by car I am out a dime; if by foot I am disgustingly worried with heat, and this unfeeling landlord—what does he care how I suffer? But I like the house; wife said be quick about it; I pluck up courage, and away I go fifteen squares; find the number on Carondelet, climb up the pair of stairs and inquire of a grim looking man, "Is Mr. G. in?"

"He's out," and goes on writing.

A day is lost—hot, tired, disgusted, mad, out four dimes and no house; and perhaps the same thing over again tomorrow, because those dumb, provoking red-lettered cards give me no information.

The City Council orders the price of bread; orders me to keep my back yard in a sanitary condition; orders the bucket of garbage to the sidewalk; orders me around as if I cared nothing for my own health or comfort, rating me as a blockhead in general and a fool in particular. But sir! I've stood this matter of house-hunting just as long as I can. And now, Mr. Editor, lecture these City Fathers, lash the landlords without mercy, and have an ordinance compelling these heartless men to always put the price on their cards, where the keys can be found, and at what time or hour they can be seen.

The nuisance is insufferable and unpardonable, especially where a delicate lady is concerned.

Friday, July 30, 1880
ATTENTION, ROWDIES![+]

Do you know who Judge Lynch is?

Judge Lynch is the magistrate who gives a short shrift and a short rope, and saves the expense of erecting a gallows.

Judge Lynch makes his appearance when matters become desperate in a community.

When lawyers openly boast their ability to get anybody off who pays the price;—when police are untrustworthy and even criminal;—when judges are unfaithful to the duties of their office;—when political influence constitutes immunity from crime;—when officers of the law descend to blackmailing;—when the lives and property of respectable people are jeopardized by the general demoralization.

There are a good many who think that the time is not far off when Judge Lynch will be needed in these parts.

There is a general feeling that conditions brought about by corruption and rowdyism are reaching a climax.

Judge Lynch's decisions are final. There is no appeal to a higher court, no *nolle prosequies,* no writs of *habeas corpus,* no postponement of trials in his court.

He wastes no time, permits no trifling, and his judgments are executed in Turkish fashion immediately they are pronounced.

Better not force him to pay us a visit.

If he comes it will be to some purpose. Some lamp-posts will be ornamented.

"Surely the churning of milk bringeth forth butter; and the wringing of the nose bringeth forth blood; so the forcing of wrath bringeth forth strife."

Saturday, July 31, 1880
TAXPAYERS' CATECHISM+

Question—Why do you pay taxes?

Answer—The theory is that we pay them for the maintenance of civil government.

Q.—Is this theory vindicated by the facts?

A.—A good deal of what is collected finds its way into unauthorized pockets.

Q.—Is it supposed that the Civil Sheriff whose term expires to-day has made any unauthorized profits out of the office?

A.—Rumor has it that he has been exceedingly exacting in his demands and correspondingly slow in his settlements with both State and city, so far as taxes are concerned, and that he has profited to an immense amount by special act 93, which is a disgrace to the Legislature that enacted it.

Q.—Is there no law regarding the settlement of city taxes collected by the sheriff?

A.—The law says he shall make weekly returns.

Q.—Is there no remedy?

A.—We shall see.

Monday, August 2, 1880
AH SIN ON THE SITUATION+

Dlam rascle! Dlam rascle! that black Melican!
Heim say, "I no votee: I dlam Chinaman,"
Heim "thlink Chinaman flool: h'm litlee, h'm lean;
(Uf savee h'm money): h'm Chinaman, mean."

Heim all time schreechee; heim allee time yell:
"Ballee-head Chinaman; h'm glot h'm longh tail;
No speakee Ginglish; Chinee no 'ndlerstent;
Sicky Chinamen washee ole shirts, tlen cent."

Hligh! Melican man, allee fooloolee manz,
Dlemoclats foolool. Foolool Plublicanz.
Allee time talkee, Johnie Chinaman GO;
Hli! ho so; plobboblee, yes:—plobboblee NO.

Melican man, loonee manz; walkee dark nights,
Dlink whisklee; screechee tchcop-la; wavee
    big lightz.
Shoutee "Thlantchok!" "Ginglish!": "Thlantchok!"
    ah whoop-law!
Whoopl! whoopl! "Glah-flee" ah-whoopl "Ah-Tah!"

Good Chinaman I: eatee rlice: keepee tclean.
I smartee "tlike tlitenin'"; I sharpee; no gleen.
I no stealee nice thling. I allee time work.
I no dlinkee whisklee; no eatee stlink pork.

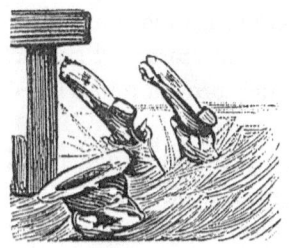

Tuesday, August 3, 1880
THE FATAL PLUNGE

How calmly Big Muddy continues to flow!
    How fierce are the tortures I feel!
Will a plunge in its depths release me from woe,
    And the book of my misery seal?

Whatever betides, the plunge I must take;
    The fiends and my woes urge me on:
My hunger still gnaws, and my thirst I can't slake,
    And no one will weep when I'm gone.

My body is racked with the pangs of disease,
    And my soul I have soiled by neglect;
Opportunities wasted now urge me to steal
    From the life I have made such a wreck.

O dark river's depth! if surcease I could find
    In the pulse of the infinite flow,
How gladly the torture of body and mind
    In thy Lethean flood I'd forego.

> But with terrible doubt and with terrible dread,
> And a body with rottenness rife,
> I plunge in alarm to the dark river bed
> To be free from the anguish of life.

Wednesday, August 4, 1880

ILLUSTRATED LETTERS FROM THE PEOPLE

Editor City Item—The dog-days are coming; but the poisoned sausage cometh not. Why?

I am tormented by a new idea. I should like to know whether a city can exist without cats and dogs. Why is it that in all parts of the world cats and dogs abound? Philosophers say that whenever a practice is generally adopted by mankind there is a necessity for it. But what is the necessity for cats and dogs?

It is no use telling me that cats are good to catch rats and mice; for I used to have five cats, and the rats were not less numerous. I got rid of the cats and bought me traps of all kinds, which proved much more valuable.

It is all very well to say that dogs keep away burglars. When I had dogs thieves used to steal my chickens every night. A good dog would be useful, but not always reliable; and the evil he does when he goes mad more than counterbalances all the good he can do.

I think keeping dogs is a relic of barbarous and patriarchal days. In primitive times men living in districts where lions and tigers abounded were obliged to keep enormous dogs to protect themselves. So in the days when wolves devastated Europe there were wolf-dogs, one of whom was a match for a dozen wolves. But all these dogs have disappeared probably because there is no more use for them.

A dog that could take a lion by the back of the neck and shake him like a bull dog in our day might shake a rat, must have been useful in ancient times; but of what earthly use are all these snarling curs of today? I think, Mr. Editor, that the practice of keeping dogs is a vice,—a widespread and universal practice, but a vicious one all the same. All these stories about dogs saving people from drowning and from robbers are very pretty; but for one person saved by dogs there are a hundred who die of hydrophobia. I really think that a price ought to be set on dogs' heads just as there used to be in England upon wolves' heads.

In my neighborhood several children have been seriously bitten by dogs; and you have already published cases of hydrophobia in your paper. Do you think that all the good done by all the dogs who ever lived in New Orleans since the time of Bienville can compensate for one death by hydrophobia?

For goodness sake, let there be something done to lessen the number of dogs and cats. I recommend the immediate application of strychnine and the subsequent establishment of a glove factory.

Anti-Carculum.

Thursday, August 5, 1880
INS AND OUTS+

Now do the ravening office-seekers prepare for the onslaught.

Wolf and buzzard; tooth and claw!

There is no idea on either side of striving to be useful to the community. It is a mere fight for the quarry of office, for the carrion of political spoils.

It would be a pretty safe maxim to hold that office-seekers should never be permitted to hold office.

The man who lives by politics alone is usually in these days a very poor specimen of humanity.

He is only a veneered specimen of a loafer, too lazy or too proud to work, but not too lazy to concoct schemes of plunder or too proud to accept money which does not legally belong to him. He is a species of parasite which clings to the body-politic.

When men are too lazy to wash themselves they are apt to be troubled by vermin. When communities are too apathetic to purify themselves they will be devoured by political vermin.

A professional forager for office, incapable of pursuing any other occupation, ought to be regarded as a suspicious and dangerous character, and be given twenty-four hours to get out of town.

To be fit for office a man should be industrious, intelligent, honorable and patriotic, conscious of his ability to serve his country to some purpose, and determined to consecrate his talents to that end.

All this, then, the professional office-seeker is not. He neither works nor knows how to work. He is neither energetic nor intelligent—except as a beast of prey is intelligent. He produces nothing and consumes a great deal. What he can not consume he beslimes and spoils like certain reptiles.

There was a time when men considered political office a high honor. Now it is being made a dishonor to run for it. This is the truth and nothing but the truth and will continue to be the truth until the respectable part of the community undertake to purify matters and run all municipal branches of government themselves. If our citizens can purify the city in the material sense, they can purify it in a moral sense. We need a Moral Sanitary Association.

Friday, August 6, 1880
UNDER THE ELECTRIC LIGHT+

A sound as of the boiling of a prodigious pot, the bubbling of a witches' cauldron, under the electric light. Such was the music of the insect orchestra at the West End last evening.

It was worth the price of the trip alone to behold the spectacle,—a veritable realization of the swarm of flies that afflicted the land of Egypt.

The insects hung about the lights like thin clouds about the face of the moon. The sky was actually obscured at intervals. But the little creatures did not bite. They only uttered their wailing music, and formed a living canopy above the heads of the people, like the canopy formed by the enchanted birds above the head of Solomon in Arabic tradition.

They entered Micholet's restaurant uninvited, and pounced like Harpies upon the viands, spoiling what they could not carry away.

Whether the wind brought them or the lights or the music, we can not positively say; but at ten o'clock they disappeared as if by magic.

It seems not improbable that the electric lights exercise a certain fascination upon them, and perhaps also the sound of music; for mosquitoes have a fine ear for harmony.

At all events they came to the fort together with the crowd of human visitors, and thinned away as the people began to withdraw, after having enjoyed the evening as much as anybody, and secured all the privileges and pleasures and luxuries of the resort without paying therefore. The phenomenon was certainly a most curious one.

Saturday, August 7, 1880
DR. TANNER[+]

Special Telegram to THE CITY ITEM.
New York, 12:01 P.M.

Slams the Door on the Undertaker's Nose.
End of the Forty Days' Fast.

11:50 A.M.—Dr. Tanner is about to break his fast. It is doubtful, however, whether his friends will permit him to begin with the watermelon, as he wished to do. His condition is ghastly; but he does not complain. His face looks like a skull with a thin skin drawn over it, and his eyes have a spectral brilliancy. He maintains his good humor, stimulated by the triumph of having completed his great feat. Letters and congratulations have been pouring in upon him. He will not be permitted to receive visits for some little time, probably, as his condition is really dangerous.

Dr. Tanner is a fanatic in his way, and believes in bringing children up without eating. This is said to have been the cause of his divorce from his first wife. He has received many offers of marriage since he began his fast; but treats them with philosophical indifference.

The dispute has been settled. The Doctor will begin with the watermelon.
NOLEM RETAW.

Sunday, August 8, 1880
SCAT!

As hearty as Tanner's wife was he.
    And midnight suppers were his delight,
But his after slumbers were never free
    From the direst nightmare fiend's affright.

The burglars gather to seize his stores,
    And wolves glare at him with horrid eyes,
While into his ears a lion roars,
    As if just ready to grasp a prize.

And then assassins, with bloody knives,
    All ready to plunge into heart and brain,
Stand over him, while their heartless wives
    Mock at his fears and deride his pain.

He rolls in torture! He thought the damned,
    From infernal regions, upon him sat,
And into his stomach vile poisons crammed;
    He awoke, and saw but the household cat.

"Scat! scat!" quoth he, and the cat withdrew;
    But his stomach refused to be comforted;
He tried to sleep but the furies flew
    With taunts and curses around his bed.

Monday, August 9, 1880
SEEKING A SENSATION

A Day Among a Pile of Bones Found on the Lake Coast.

His story was plainly told, but the interest of his listeners was intense. He had just returned from an alligator hunt, and while up one of the many small bayous on the lake coast had discovered the skeleton of a man, the bones of which formed part of a turtle's nest, in which was deposited thirty eggs. Some of his listeners doubted the truth of the story, while others, with a romantic turn of mind, in the skeleton saw a terrible tragedy; some rich planter waylaid, murdered, and buried in the swamp, or perhaps a fugitive fleeing from the majesty of the law, seeking shelter among the rushes and weeds, loses his path and is overcome by starvation and death.

But the bayou was not far, so bright and early yesterday morning the train to West End carried an *Item* reporter, bent on solving the mystery.

Canal street was crowded with happy looking people, all bent on a day's enjoyment in the suburbs, and countless covered baskets on the train mutely testified that the inner man would be properly cared for.

The bridge at the lake end is reached at last, and finally seated at a table in Joe Astredo's, the story-teller, who was to act as guide, is impatiently waited for. An hour passed, and still he came not, and in the absence of better amusement, he is denounced in unmeasured terms.

Breakfast is served and for a time the story-teller and skeleton sinks into insignificance, but only for a time, for as the *Camelia*, laden with excursionists, steamed out into the lake the story-teller appears. His apologies are profuse, and while explaining his detention with ready hands bails out the cat-rigged yawl, provided by the host, who also takes a rifle from the shelf and places it securely in the craft. From Astredo's to the bridge, and thence into the Basin the craft quietly glides and all hands make ready to set sail.

A strong pull on the throat halyard, and another on the peak, and then something breaks and down comes the sail with a run. A stiff wind from the northeast, accompanied by a heavy rain, drives the yawl hard against the piling on the west side of the basin, where she remains until the halyards are repaired and the sail set. The squall becomes more violent, and after splitting the sail, going over on beam ends and filling up with water the mouth of Bayou Tchoupitoulas is at last reached.

Taking a pirogue and paddling about two miles, a turn in the bayou disclosed three large mounds of shell, circular in form, which tradition says were built for burial purposes many years ago by an extinct race. Large trees, bearing the imprint of age on their rough bark, surmount the mounds, while a luxuriant undergrowth almost prevents access to the high land on the top. The mounds are surrounded by an almost impenetrable swamp, and save the occasional visit of a moss gatherer or alligator hunter, this evil but romantic spot is never disturbed by the presence of man.

In a secluded spot, in this secluded region, and in a hollow formed by the wash of incessant rains, reposes the bones and skull just as described, eggs and all. But then, what of it? These mounds, which were formerly burial grounds, are filled with human skeletons which may be unearthed, or rather unshelled, with but very little trouble.

Over-heated, mosquito-bitten, wet, down-hearted, disgusted, and muddy, the sail was again set and the yawl headed for West End. The wind had died out in the meantime, and the oars were brought into use; at a snail's pace the voyage homeward was made, and it was with a feeling of joy that the delightful odor of fried fish and turtle soup was wafted to the "dampened" mariners as the now almost wrecked yawl was made fast alongside of Astredo's house.

Tuesday, August 10, 1880
LAKE-SIDE LICKINGS

Sabbath Amusements of the Covington and Madisonville Boys.

The numerous excursionists on the steamer *Camelia* were highly entertained on their arrival at the Old Landing by several fights between the boys of Madisonville and Covington. There is an animosity peculiar to boys existing between the two places, and as the good steamer reached Madisonville some twenty of the belligerents boarded her, and at a glance the most casual observer could see mischief in all their actions. On reaching the Old Landing about a dozen "pine tops" were seen leaning on the wood piles and apparently not expecting the enemy. In a few minutes both parties divided and taking their stand on either side of the road, prepared for action.

The Covington side concluded that they were too weak to tackle the boys from below, and sent a messenger to their stronghold for reinforcements. In about half an hour they commenced to arrive, and after both sides were considered equal a parley was held, and it was agreed to select three champions from each side and settle the question by a square rough-and-tumble fight, the victor to be open to a challenge from either side.

Three boys were then selected and placed in the road, and the other side matched them in age, weight, and height as nearly as possible. The first fight was for strictly light weights and two tough little rascals pranced and fluttered around like Bantam cocks. Covington got in the first lick and the boys clutched, with the throw down in favor of Madisonville. Then came the tug of war, and after ten minutes fighting with varying results the fight was given to Madisonville.

The second fight was for medium weights, and the two boys stepped to the front and faced one another. The Madisonville boy was jubilant over the former victory and threw himself off his guard, while the Covington lad was determined to make up for his side's loss, and settled down to business with a will and soon had his opponent on the ground doing him up as handsomely as possible.

In about five minutes the Madisonville boy was declared whipped, and the second event recorded for Covington. Excitement was now at its highest pitch when the two heavy weights approached each other. Covington opened hostilities by a well directed blow on the left eye of his opponent, and with a rush doubled him up in a knot and raising him about three feet in the air, threw him to the ground with sufficient force to almost dislocate every bone in his body. After the first round, Madisonville concluding that their man was no match for the Covington champion, threw up the sponge, and gracefully yielded the fight to the Covington boys.

Wednesday, August 11, 1880
SARAH BERNHARDT+

We present our readers to-day with a portrait of the great and gifted woman,—greater, it is true, in mind than body, but by no means insignificant even as to body. The stories about Sarah's leanness are, of course absurd exaggerations. She is very slender, like the great Rachel; but replete with elegance and grace. She has been spoken of as possessing the grace of the serpent, a compliment which any woman might be proud of in its true poetic sense, as applied to physical attraction. Some people would perhaps prefer to look at a very plump figurante with colossal understandings; but Sarah comes only to give us a feast of reason and a flow of soul—not to amuse the baldheaded people who monopolize the front seats at ballets and Black Crook performances.

Thursday, August 12, 1880
ILLUSTRATED LETTERS FROM THE PEOPLE

Editor City Item—I think there are no greater public nuisances than the men who force people to buy things they don't want.

There are different ways of making people buy what they don't want. Sometimes it is done by mere force of jaw and muscle. Men talk and talk and talk until you have to buy something just to get rid of them.

Again, people are made to buy what they do not want by having their feelings titillated, their sympathies cunningly worked upon, their vanity flattered, etc.

But the meanest way of making people buy what they do not want is the fashion now in vogue among flower-sellers to take advantage of a man's situation when he is out with his girl.

They poke their nasty little bouquets under the young lady's nose, and then under your nose; and they know that you don't just exactly know sometimes whether it is your duty to buy or not.

They never ask anybody who is not out with a young lady to buy flowers. They have sharp overseers who tell them how to "work the game."

Did you ever see them offer flowers to the father of a family or any staid and elderly person? I never did. It is only to young folks, sweethearts, you know.

This is what makes one mad. You know that they offer you flowers just because they think they have got the advantage of you, and I don't like to be taken advantage of. I think the habit of peddling flowers in street cars is a nuisance and ought to be stopped.

A Hater of Flowers.

Friday, August 13, 1880
VOLUNTARY CONTRIBUTIONS

I Sherman am, big Ingen heap—
    Chief of the Treasury;
And with my little hatchet, I
    Cut down the barren tree.

Your voluntary offerings,
    Subalterns, I invoke,
And if you do not freely give,
    You'll feel my hatchet stroke.

I force no man; but great results
    On our success depend;
He who refuses is a foe,
    And he who gives, a friend.

Garfield my ALTER EGO is;
    Both are from O-high-owe;
And he who fails us in our need
    Shall feel my secret blow.

Your money, or your head, my friend;
    I give you your free choice;
He who says "No," shall feel the blow
    Responsive to his voice.

But he his answer: "Yea, amen!
   I give with pious trust;
The ticket must be well sustained—
   The just must serve the just."

Then all for him right well will be;
   His head erect shall stand;
And he shall eat no Tanner's meat,
   But fatness shall command.

Yes, fatness, and the best of spoils,
   Brought from my Treasurie;
But if my tomahawk descends,
   Down falls an enemie.

Saturday, August 14, 1880
JEWELL'S DEFENCE OF GARFIELD[+]

There was once a man who offered to carry his friend over a muddy place, because the latter had a new suit of clothes on; but when the wader got to the middle he fell over and the friend was covered with slush and slime from head to foot and the new suit of clothes was irretrievably ruined. Then the owner of the new suit got mad, and thought to himself, "If that fellow had minded his own business this would not have happened."

Sunday, August 15, 1880
BY THE MURMURING WAVES

Those quiet little resting-places beside the lake could tell such tales had they only tongues. Perhaps it is as well that they have none.

How many little romances have taken place there!

It is so shadowy and quiet. Only the stars are looking; the frogs pay no attention to what does not concern them; the sobbing of the wavelets never interrupts a love; and the distant music of the land, the cries of waiters, the clinking of glasses, and the murmurs of the crowd are too far distant to destroy the delightful sensation of being all alone together by the lake shore.

But they talk in whispers nevertheless.

Doubtless there are many lives of which the fate has been decided by these quiet rendezvous by the lake shore.

Doubtless there are many who will remember to their dying day the story of these evening chats, the whispering of the waves, the chant of frogs and crickets, the winking of the silent stars above, and the distant murmur of the joyous crowd.

Monday, August 16, 1880
HUNTING FOR THE HONEST EIGHT+

When old Diogenes of the Prose
    Walks forth with his glowing lamp,
He searcheth early and searcheth late,
In the narrow paths, at the palace gate—
    What cometh of his tramp?

Of Eight that are honest he is in quest;
    And with his electric light,
He peereth East, and he peereth West,
And hopeth among our oldest and best,
    To find Eight men of might.

He findeth one, and he findeth two,
    He findeth three and four;
And his heart elate with the smiles of fate,
Doth palpitate at a gladsome rate:
    He hopeth to find four more.

Thus far, however, the other four
    Have failed to come to time;
So he peereth still through the open door
Of the City Hall, with its marble floor.
    And tries the effect of rhyme.

Tuesday, August 17, 1880
NAUGHTY BOYS

Among the various woes of street car conductors, not the least is caused by the pranks of mischievous boys who climb on the tall-end of the vehicles, and disappear only when the conductor, finding that patience ceases to be a virtue, seizes his blacksnake whip and rushes to the attack. But the moment he returns to his seat, they also return like a swarm of flies to pester him. Not long ago, one of these mischievous imps fell off and was severely hurt.

This sort of sport is highly dangerous, nor is it wholly confined to street cars. We have seen boys leap upon and off of trains in motion—a piece of folly which often costs a life. If boys will jump upon street cars they are also likely to jump upon trains, and this mischievous practice deserves the attention of the police. We do not refer to newsboys, who seldom give trouble or commit such folly, but to the idle urchins who spend their days in playing pranks and practical jokes instead of going to school or learning a trade, and who bid fair to grow up loafers and rowdies.

Wednesday, August 18, 1880
GHOSTESES

Midnight in an Ultra-Canal Pension.

You not know vat be dat noise of foots up de stair. Dat be de ole man vat die in my house ago ten year.

I see him now in my t'ought, 'sleep in ze *berceuse;* afraid to go to his room for cause of vat you call *farfadet*—goblin and ghosteses.

He was very, very old, and he see always of tins vat not exist. He be much torment by goblin and ghosteses vat valk all roun' de house in de night; an' he say it vas one curssed house and one curssed city. He tell me dat people dressed like vas dress since one hoondred year come in his room in de middle of de night; dat he lock de door but not could dem keep out; dat dey sit silent and make at him face horrible and not speak and not make shadow on de door.

Den he commence to us avake. In de middle of de night he knock at mine door and say,—"Monsieur, mount to my room for dat dere be one man dead in my chamber." So I mount and look and not see no man dead. "He go himself away," say de old man, "for dat he hear you on stair. But have made stop my clock and vatch." And I see dat de clock and de vatch not more march,—I not know how.

After dat he often tell me vat dere be in his bed dead vomans; and dat dead beoples him look at trough de vindow. So he become afraid more to bed go, and ven he mount he not himself sleep, but valk all night on de gallery, one lantern in his hand, and shoes all vat be of mos' heavy for drive away ghosteses-ta-ta-tatatatata—all de long of de night. Much also he sing in de night and swear for dat dis be one curssed country of ghosteses. Also he swear at proprietor of house; for dat he not chase ghosteses.

So it arrive at las' dat not person in de house could himself to sleep go, and dat all de vorld begin to demselves much fatigue. Den dey construct one goblin of vatermelon and inside one candle light; and dey it put on stick and one sheet of bed to make look like fantome. So it come to arrive dat ven de ole man march himself he see one goblin march more horrible dan he have before eve see. So he let fall his lantern—vat cost tirteen dollar,—and try to descend stair for me avake for dat I chase him de goblin. But he fall de top to bottom of stair, and make himself much of hurt. Never again he not speak and soon he be dead, and no person much sorry himself. But it vas much vicked!

It ten year since he be dead; but all de night he march like he march oder time. No one afraid; de ghost of de ole man not make much hurt to personne!

Thursday, August 19, 1880
COMING EVENTS CAST THEIR SHADOWS BEFORE[+]

It will come sooner or later; but the parties who should be most interested in such matters do not pay any attention to the shadows of coming events. The Widow with Wooden Legs, as the Spaniards call the Gibbet, is waiting to celebrate her nuptials with some of our hoodlums; and yet the latter do not seem to know it. A long time has elapsed since the Widow was last married here, although the number of fellows who ought to have been married to her by force is legion. She is becoming tired of widowhood; and this is leap year. She is going to propose pretty soon; and when she proposes it will be no use to try backing out.

Friday, August 20, 1880
QUACK! QUACK![+]

Quack! Quack! I am on the rack,
    You promised to end my pain;
For a little wealth you'd restore my health,
    You said; yet here I've lain
For weary weeks and for mournful months,
    With pangs that are only known

To the tortured victim of the Quack,
    When his faith to the winds has flown.

Death's shadow falls on my barren walls;
    It sleeps on my chamber floor,
Its marrowless bones mock at my groans,
    And point to the shining shore,
While a jeering, mocking, ugly grin
    Spreads over its fleshless face
At a double triumph—the Quack's success,
    And the Quack's supreme disgrace.

Saturday, August 21, 1880
THE CHINESE VICE+

The Board of Health, adopting the suggestion of the energetic Dr. Beard, has requested the City Council to pass an ordinance for the suppression of opium dens and the punishment of those who keep them.

It is doubtful in our opinion, however, whether the penalty proposed by Dr. Beard is sufficiently heavy or sufficiently extensive; consisting only of a fine of from $25 to $100, or a term of imprisonment in default.

This punishment is to apply only to persons who keep the opium dens. Why not increase the severity of the penalty and make it apply also to those who enter the dens as patrons of the vice?

In San Francisco it was found necessary to enact severe penalties against the practice of entering Chinese opium dens or Chinese houses of prostitution. The result, we believe, has been very satisfactory.

The great point in the suppression of these nuisances is to prevent Chinese vices—which are many and revolting—from contaminating even the lowest class of our community. To keep Chinamen from privately indulging their Mongolian habits and proclivities will be impossible; but to prevent white persons from imitating them will not be difficult.

We would respectfully suggest, therefore, to Dr. Beard and the Health Board,—while thanking them sincerely for their action in this regard—that they also request the City Council to enact that any citizen who shall enter an opium den, for the purpose of smoking the drug, shall be severely punished by fine and imprisonment. Short as the time has been, comparatively speaking, since the growth of this vice began to attract public attention, it has already spread to a shocking extent among certain classes, and unless promptly and severely checked, may do incalculable mischief to public morals.

Sunday, August 22, 1880
CAT-ANKAROUS[+]

Hear the yelling of the cats! Horrid cats!
How vain are bottles, boots, brickbats!
In the silence of the night, how we shiver with affright,
At the melancholy menace of their tones,
And each note, from each infernal feline throat
Goes right to the marrow of one's bones.
Yet catskins may be used for a variety of stuffs,
    for robes and rugs and muffs,
And for the rubbers of electrical machines,
And we have repeatedly suggested the means
Of preventing the night from being made hideous, and enjoying that sleep that knits up the raveled sleeve of care.
    Scat!—scat!
They are only too well aware
That they can safely yowl beyond the range of human wrath, and howl,
Instead of attending to their legitimate business and trying to catch a rat.
    Darn a cat!

Monday, August 23, 1880
GO-IT

There's nothing either ashore or afloat
That the small boy loves like a prim toy-boat.
He wades and paddles to see it go
As a living thing o'er the water's flow,
And when he returns, from heel to hat
He's just as wet as a drowned rat.

But amid brick walls where there are no pools,
Save those at which big boys bet like fools,
The small boy that can not sail his boat

Is bound to harness a dog or goat.
A cart or wagon he'll improvise,
Though the box and wheels may not suit in size,
And a fall in the gutter is just as certain
As a Candle lecture behind the curtain.

Comment, avant: let the picture tell
Of the sad disaster which befell
The youthful hoodlum that early went
Abroad on a mission of merriment,
And found himself in a stifling splatter
Amid the filth of a dirty gutter.

Tuesday, August 24, 1880
MURDER AND VIOLENCE+

The papers are still obliged to record daily a variety of bloody crimes and casualties. It is true that this is a month in which crimes of violence are especially apt to occur. But we doubt if the present condition of affairs simply indicates that we are passing through a season of epidemic sin. We fear that the present state of affairs is likely to assume a permanent form. It is the result of a steadily increasing demoralization of the police force and an increased difficulty in securing a proper administration of justice. The prospect is really serious; and it is time that every honest citizen should consider it in a serious light. Men hold mass meetings upon matters of far less importance. Public opinion should express itself on the subject strongly and promptly. We have stated on another page our opinions in regard to the chief source of many of the present evils. We need a dozen hangings or so in order to restore order and security.

Wednesday, August 25, 1880
CHAR-COAL

Black-Coalee-Coaly!
   Coaly-coaly; coaly-coaly; coal-coal-coal.
   Coaly-coaly!
   Coal-ee! Nice!
   Cha'coal!
   Twenty-five! Whew!

O charco-oh-oh-oh-oh-oh-lee!
Oh-lee!
Oh-lee-e!
[You get some coal in your mouth, young fellow, if you don't keep it shut.]
Pretty coalee-oh-ee!
Char-coal!
Cha-ah-ah-ahr-coal!
Coaly-coaly!
Charbon! Dû charbon, Madame! Bon charbon? Point! Ai-ai! Tonnerre de Dieu!
Char-r-r-r-r-r-rbon!
A-a-a-a-w! High ya-a-ah! High-yah!
Vingt-cinq! Nice coalee! Coalee!
Coaly-coal-coal!
Pretty coaly!
Charbon de Paris!
De Paris, Madame; de Paris!

Thursday, August 26, 1880
ROWDYISM SUPPRESSED+

Something that has not yet occurred and which not even the most fervid imagination dare hope for; but which should nevertheless take place here at short intervals is represented in the above cut. We dreamed of the scene therein depicted; for in our wakeful and rational moments such an idea could never enter our head. And if anybody should tell us that we had seen such a thing in reality we should either denounce him as a prevaricator or condemn him as a fit subject for the dungeon room of a lunatic asylum. Anybody who thinks that the above cut represents anything possible or earthly, should have ice applied to his feverish brow, and leeches to his extremities, and be subjected to douches and electricity and all sorts of violent remedies until cured of his hallucinations.

Friday, August 27, 1880
NOT A DREAM AT ALL⁺

Yesterday we ventured to chronicle and illustrate a mad and fantastic Dream which haunted us in the dead waste and middle of the night. Today we chronicle the Reality which haunts us in our waking moments. Anybody that says it is not true ought to have his head put under the pump in order to wake him up to the actualities of life.

Saturday, August 28, 1880
OUR GHOULS⁺

In the first sweet dawn of dawn the garbage boxes are placed upon the sidewalk; and the sluggish morning air becomes thick with the smell thereof.

We do not believe that there is another city in the United States where garbage boxes smell so insufferably.

It is a stink which makes the bravest hold his nose,—a stink far beyond the horror of dead cats or the abomination of rotten eggs,—a most vile stink which turns the stomach.

Judging by its vileness it must also be a very unhealthy and poisonous stink.

Then the Ghouls come.

They ferret about in the garbage boxes, stirring up the smell, and causing it to expand and lift itself.

The Ghouls are always followed by lean and wolfish dogs, which would fight for the horribly booty were they not afraid of the Ghouls.

Phew! phew!

The Ghoul has a stick or a wire lash with which she lacerates the noses of the dogs who try to fight for their share of the rottenness.

Poor Ghouls! We should not wish to deprive them of the right to make a living; but it is not necessary that they should make it at the public expense. We think the garbage box nuisance ought to be modified for sanitary reasons, and the Ghouls only permitted to haunt the dumping grounds in quest of what they seek.

Sunday, August 29, 1880
THE WITCH

The Witch wanders about throughout the city seeking whom she may devour; but unlike other witches she practises her art by day.

She knocks at a hundred doors and rings about a hundred bells diurnally, and asks to see the "lady of the house." She is too sharp to tell the servant what her business is.

Then she proposes to the lady to tell her fortune—to "draw the cards" for her. In nine cases out of ten she is successful, because she knows exactly what kind of people will be her best customers.

These belong to all classes—the rich and the poor; the wicked and the just; the wise and the foolish.

The best paying class are the *demi monde,* who are superstitious to a superlative degree. Here the fortune teller reaps a rich harvest.

Then there are the intelligent people who never saw a fortune teller before; and who "would like to see how it is done," although they do not believe in it.

Lastly there is a large class of respectable women who are just superstitious enough to pay for a prediction which they secretly believe will be fulfilled.

The fortune-teller is an English Gipsy. Her hair is black with tints of blue,—coarse and thick like a horse's mane,—a mass of elf-locks. In the hottest period of summer she wears heavy woolen wrappings. Her skin is like bronze, her strength like that of a man.

While she relates the future of her patrons, she abandons herself to extravagant gestures. She leaps in the air; wildly brandishes her arms; and mutters words of Romany. She speaks a little of many languages,—French, Spanish, and German.

She told us our fortune the other day for the insignificant sum of twenty-five cents.

—"Jealousy and misfortune—Red and black—a light-haired man will make you much trouble—He is stronger and richer than you—You will be badly treated—He will try to kill you—But a friend comes to save you—He will lend you money—But he will also come to misfortune—You will marry a woman who will murder her child—Your business will be ruined—Your health will be destroyed—Your life will become a burthen to you."

Then we gave her twenty-five cents more to take back all she said. And she lifted up her voice and spake:

"You will be married three times. The first time to a rich young lady. The second time to a widow who keeps a coffee-house and a corner grocery. The third time to a German girl whose father is worth a million. You will go to Europe. There you will live to be 175 years old. Another twenty-five cents, and I will tell you how you will die."

But we lifted up our feet and departed with exceeding good speed, putting our fingers in our ears as we vanished in the distance.

Monday, August 30, 1880
DES PERCHES

Daily he goeth out beyond the limits of the city into lonesome and swampy places where copperheads and rattlesnakes abound.

And there he cutteth him clothes-poles, wherewith he marcheth through the city in the burning glare of the sun; singing a refrain simple in words but weird in music.

A long and lamentable sobbing cry, as of one in exceeding great pain and anguish.

So sorrowful in sooth that the sorrow of the city drowneth the sound and sense of the words,—the words chanted in ancient Creole patois—

And we, listening to the cry, gave ourselves up to solemn meditation;

Dreaming of the cries of anguish that arise when a clothes-line, heavily burdened with its snowy freight, falleth upon the mud;

And the poor little woman sitteth down and crieth till her eyes are red, ere she findeth courage to commence all over again, and mend the clothes-line.

It is to avoid these things that men should buy clothes-poles.

Des perches!

And hearing the ancient negro once more lifting up his voice, we also remembered.

That often in the dead waste and middle of the night, while meandering about the black backyard,

We were suddenly and violently smitten on the nostrils by the treacherous clothes-pole, hidden between lines of white sheets and shirts that waved their empty arms like spectres.

Also, we remembered how the wet linen fell upon our sacred person; and how we tried to lift up the clothes-pole again but could not;—

For the cunning of the washerwoman was not given to us.

But notwithstanding these things we do bless the clothes-poles, and him that sells them, remembering the service they do to the indispensable washerwoman.

Des perches—des perches!

Tuesday, August 31, 1880
WASHERWOMEN+

The washerwoman is a creature of which there are various species.

There is the washerwoman who works very cheap; but who never gives you back your own socks or undershirts; and the exchange is invariably to your disadvantage.

There is the washerwoman who makes it a rule of life to wash off all the buttons of your shirts and pull all the strings off your drawers and never dreams of putting them on again. This washerwoman charges like sixty.

There is the washerwoman who puts the thinnest kind of starch in your shirts, so that they become limp rags after being worn an hour. This kind of washerwoman gets rich fast. She has an eye to business.

Then there is the washerwoman who promises to bring your clothes at a certain hour, and never does so under any possible circumstance.

But there is also the good, honest, industrious, prompt, and motherly or sisterly washerwoman who puts buttons on your shirts and darns up your socks and does not charge extra therefor.

We looked for such a washerwoman for two years before we found her. Now we wouldn't give her up for a small fortune.

If washerwomen have their faults, it must be remembered they have their trials and afflictions. Many of them have been spoiled by bad treatment.

There is no sort of thieving so contemptible as to beat one's washerwoman; but we doubt if any other class of working-people are so much victimized.

It is pretty rough to labor hard all the week, working until one is ready to drop down with fatigue; obligated to watch changes of weather; obliged sometimes when a clothes-line breaks to do all the work over again; obliged to furnish one's own soap and starch and blueing;—

And then to carry the work to those who ordered it,—all nice and clean and pretty,—expecting to receive the just reward of one's labor;—

But, on the contrary, to receive nothing but lying promises and sometimes even hard words;—

And then to go home hungry; and to sit down and cry because there is not a cent in the house!

No wonder the poor women often say it is better to be a sieve than a washerwoman.

No wonder that washerwomen should sometimes feel disgusted with their work, and cease all effort to try and please, and tear off buttons and pull off drawer strings with rage and fury.

It isn't their fault if they are not always angels.

Wednesday, September 1, 1880
SONS OF THE SEA

They come to us from the uttermost parts of the earth, with the winds that swell the white sails of their vessels. There is a sparkle in their eyes like the sparkle of a distant sea; and a faraway look acquired by the habit of gazing over the infinite expanse of rolling water. They walk with a swaying motion learned from the gait of their own ships, and there is a tone in their voices like the tone of sea-winds roaring through the rigging.

They have passed over all seas, and heard a hundred tongues spoken.

And coming into a city; leaving the rocking deck for the motionless search, they still wear a quiet dreamy look, as of men accustomed to the sight of Nature in her most infinite aspect, and not liable therefore to be impressed greatly by the sight of the handiwork of Man.

But at times human frailty asserts itself;—the stern discipline of the sea has made the sailors long for some wild frolic on land;—strong drink and women hold out siren-temptations.

What wonder is it? Was not even Ulysses, that wisest of sailors, once obliged to bind himself to the mast lest the song of an enchantress might lure him to destruction?

The old sea-dogs are usually wise, like Ulysses; but the young ones will have their day.

Then again we have swarthy sailors from sunny West Indian ports, who wander about seeking for those who speak their own tongue, in order to sell odorous packages of cigars concealed in their pockets—cigars in which all the soporific fragrance of the tropics seem concentrated.

And having performed their little work of *contrabandistas,* they depart to enjoy a little fun with the profits thereof.

So do they sail from port to port;—more wearied by their stay on shore than by mighty wrestling with the Giant of Storms; for the whisky is not good, and there are other things which are worse.

But the sea who loves her children braces their strength up once more with the elixir of her bright winds; and drives away the fumes of a night of orgy, as evil dreams are scattered by daylight.

And as the sailors call east and west and north and south; buffeted by wild winds; struggling with raging waves; making brief visits to strange ports; collecting dreamy memories of foreign lands;—until the time comes for them to sail into that weird sea which is waveless and shoreless and shadowless and forever silent, and from which no mariner ever returns.

Thursday, September 2, 1880
A SMALL NUISANCE

Just for the same reason that selfish people stand exactly in the middle of a street-crossing to talk, and oblige passers-by to bestraddle the gutter;

And for the same reason that folks block up a doorway to gossip instead of going to one side and letting people pass;

And for the same reason that people sit on the bottom steps of a staircase, so as to prevent folks from going up and down;

And for the same reason that some folks walk four abreast with disgusting slowness so that busy and energetic people must go into the middle of the street to pass;—

So do wagon drivers persist in slowly driving beside street cars on narrow streets instead of driving before or behind, and leaving the thoroughfares clear to others.

Friday, September 3, 1880
THE MILKMAN+

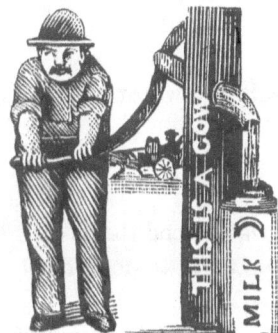

The milkman ariseth exceedingly early in the morning to milk his cows.

More especially the Cow with the Iron Tail, which can furnish more milk in one hour than the thousand she-asses of Job could have done within the space of seven moons.

Inasmuch as all mankind are aware of this fact, it might seem needless to mention it.

We only mention it as we make allusion to universally known facts,—as we make allusion to the late war, or the siege of Jerusalem by Titus.

Just in order to preface a few remarks.

The milkman doeth good when he doeth anything, just like certain doctors without diplomas—

Who give us bread pills and flour powders and weak tea tonics, and who cure people notwithstanding;

Because as Napoleon observed, Imagination ruleth the world;

And when people imagine that something does them good, it is almighty apt to do it.

So also is it with the contents of the milkman's can;—at least it is so when the Cow with the Iron Tail is not in a feverish and unhealthy condition.

But this so often happens, that we deemed it best to purchase a lactometer.

And having even done so, we discovered that the proportion of water was prodigiously great and that of milk most ridiculously small.

And having accused the milkman he swore a great oath, and hoped that jackasses might defile his grandmother's grave if the milk was not pure even as Nature could make it.

And we in silence exhibited the testimony of the lactometer; and lo! the milkman's face became even as the color of the setting sun.

And he swore that no living man could give pure milk at the price which he had been accustomed to ask;—

But he said that should we pay him "so much," the quality of the milk would be improved.

And, we having paid it, received that which we desired; and the milkman also pretended to be satisfied.

Saturday, September 4, 1880
PRICKLY HEAT

One man told us that borax would cure it.
It didn't.
Another party said salt and water.
No good.
A third said carbolized soap.
Ain't worth a darn.
A fourth said starch was a good thing.
A fifth said that all you had to do is not to scratch yourself and then the prickly heat would go away.
He also said that any person could keep from scratching himself if he only made up his mind to do it.
He was a liar and a horse thief.

O prickly heat! it is hard to beat;
   Though people say, 'tis "a healthy ill":
With the sun-dog's rage it begins its wage,
   And it spreads o'er all its fiery will.

The little prattler, the half-grown tattler,
   The lover, blest with extatic dreams,
And the blooming maiden that roams through
   Aiden,
   Show their annoyance by pretty screams.

But sterner manhood, in deeper banhood,
   With curses fret at the fiery pain;
Through puff and powder they shriek the louder,
   And of their arms and their sides complain.

Still medication and meditation
   To their affliction bring no relief.
Their nails are harrows, which sting like arrows
   Their epidermis is filled with grief.

Come, cooling breezes, cure the diseases,
   Which make us healthy by giving vent
To rash and humors, and unripe tumors,
   That spread abroad o'er this continent.

Sunday, September 5, 1880
THE HAND-MAIDEN

She poketh one's shoes so far under the bed that it is necessary to crawl under it on hands and knees in order to fish them out again.

If there be any water, however little, left in the bottom of the water jug, she troubleth not herself to fetch more;

And leaveth the stale water there even until it becometh a museum of natural history.

Never thinketh she to clean out the bottom of a jug or of other utensils which we need not name.

Also she forgetteth often to put a certain indispensable article in its accustomed place;—

So that in the middle of the night one hath even to dress himself and go out to look for it in vain.

Also she sticketh one's comb in the blacking brush;

And she bangeth the blacking brush and the hair brush together.

Never doth she dust the chimney-piece or disturb the repose of the ancient spiders that spin in the four corners of the room.

Never doth she overturn and arrange the mattress; but only flingeth back the covers to their former place, and all is over.

Never doth she remember to pull the mosquito curtain;—

Or, if otherwise, she pulleth it in such a way that it were much better she had not pulled it at all.

Perpetually she forgetteth to bring up clean towels,

Or to take the soap out of the basin instead of throwing it away,

Or to leave things alone which she hath been bidden not to meddle with;—

Such as precious papers and books arranged in a certain cunning fashion, in order to aid the possessor in his literary researches;—

And which she musseth up and disarrangeth so as to make one even wish that he were dead; seeing that it must take weeks to arrange it all over again.

When a stranger cometh he always findeth his room swept and garnished, but not because of the good will of the hand-maiden;—

But, forsooth, because she knoweth that the landlady visiteth the chamber of a stranger to see if all be well.

After a week everything is all that it ought not to be; and the traveler being often a shrewd man, knowing that "a new broom sweepeth clean,"—

Getteth his traps together and lighteth out to other quarters without a word,—

Knowing also that words are vanity and complaints vexation of the spirit in such cases—

For no man by word of mouth alone hath ever been able to prevail against a maid-servant.

If the maid-servant be pretty, and that one doth not tickle her under the chin, and much admire her,—

She will despise him for a man of bad taste; and will take little heed to his comfort. Whereas, if he flirt with her, she will say,—

"Lo! now we are friends; what profiteth it that I should labor for him."

And if the servant girl be ugly, she only asketh for money secretly, as a condition of doing the work her employer hath already vainly paid her to do;

And if one giveth her money he findeth his room in no better condition than before.

And asketh himself why he is the most doggoned infernal —— —— fool that ever lived.

Seeing that he hath been sold out and bamboozled by a lazy woman.

In a few words, let it be understood that a maid-servant liveth by pretending to do what she is paid for doing; and we much marvel that men still allow themselves to be so greatly humbugged; and we also admire the author of *The Coming Race,* who saith that in a perfect society there will be no servants—only mechanical automatons.

We say:—

"Give us the mechanical automaton in ours."

Monday, September 6, 1880
DANDY-TRAPS

The rain being over, the well-dressed young man blacketh his boots and walketh out to see his sweetheart;—

When unawares he steppeth upon a stone that looketh dry; but it is really a trap for the unwary;

And resenting the pressure like a reptile, it squirteth a geyser of brown slime over the beautiful pantaloons of the enamored, so that he uttereth language it would not be pleasant for his sweetheart to hear.

Nor does he feel as though balm had been poured upon his wounded feelings, when she exclaims:—

"Oh, my goodness, George, where *have* you been? You look as if you had been rolling in the gutter,"—

Not *knowing* that he had only stepped upon a *valscuse*.

Tuesday, September 7, 1880
CONTRABAND+

Stolen waters are sweet and bread eaten in secret is pleasant.

Therefore is it that the seller of contraband cigars makes great profit. People have to buy what they are prohibited by law from buying; and it is human nature to do as speedily as possible that which it is forbidden to do.

Consequently numbers buy cigars under surreptitious conditions—not so much because they are cheaper, but because it is so delightful to do something wrong.

Moreover, few think it a very great sin to rob the government of the United States out of a little revenue.

But these are often punished just wherein they offend; for there are numbers of people going about who pretend to be smugglers and sailors, and who are nothing of the kind. They simply buy a few thousand cigars from some factory at the rate of $1.75 or $1.50.

Wednesday, September 8, 1880
THE INDIGNANT DEAD+

If they are not indignant as a certain worthy Administrator declared they were, they ought to be.

During the last ten years three hundred and three persons have been murdered in New Orleans or vicinity.

And yet only FIVE of the murderers have been hung.

Only five—although eleven were actually sentenced to death.

Consequently the chance of being hung for committing a murder in this community is as five to three hundred and three.

Almost as little danger of being hung for having committed murder as of being run over by a railroad train or cut in two by a buzz saw or brained by a brick falling from a chimney.

It is really horrible to read the report made to Governor Wiltz.

Of perhaps more than three hundred murderers—for many of these murders were committed by several persons—only three escaped from justice. What became of the rest? Where are the three hundred?

One hundred and sixteen were declared NOT GUILTY.

A *nolle prosequi* was entered in fifty-nine cases.

In nine cases it was "not a true bill."

There were three mistrials.

Twelve cases were transferred to the dead docket.

Without going much further into particulars we need only remark that the rest mostly escaped with light sentences, or were pardoned out of the Penitentiary.

Only five murderers were punished by death.

And that was only because they were strangers,—

Because they had no money to pay lawyers,—

Because they had no political influence.

Two Italians, two negroes, and a Malay—probably less guilty than some who are now walking the streets!

There are nearly three hundred unavenged dead,—the blood of nearly three hundred victims crying vainly to heaven for vengeance!

If the dead are not indignant, in the immortal words of our Administrator, they ought to be.

Thursday, September 9, 1880
WHITED SEPULCHRES

It is rather ghastly to have death in the midst of life as we have it in New Orleans; but ghastlier when it is presented without even the ordinary masks. The skeleton of our public closet is exposed to broad day-light. Are we becoming like the Orientals who never repair?—do we accept all things with the fatalistic *Kismet?* Our bat-haunted prisons and our ruined cemeteries seem to answer in the affirmative.

They are hideous Golgothas, these old intramural cemeteries of ours. In other cities the cemeteries are beautiful with all that the art of the gardener and the sculptor can give. They are often beautiful parks, in which shafts of rosy granite or pale marble rise in pleasant relief against a background of ornamental shrubbery;—birds are singing in the trees;—flowers are growing upon the gently swelling eminences which mark the sleep of the dead. There horror is masked and hidden. Here it glares at us with empty sockets.

The tombs are fissured, or have caved in, or have crumbled down into shapeless masses of brick and mortar;—the plaster, falling away, betrays the hollow mockery of the frail monuments;—the vases are full of green water and foulness;—the flowers are dying in their coffins of glass;—the crawfish undermine the walls to fatten upon what is hidden within;—and instead of birds, the tombs are haunted by lizards.

If we must have intramural cemeteries, at least let them be worthy of a civilized people. As they are, they are nightmares.

Friday, September 10, 1880
DEAD SEA FRUIT[+]

The small fruit vendor usually buys only damaged fruit at a nominal price, and sells it for good fruit at an imperial price.

He turns all the apples with the holey side down and the sound side up, so that nobody can see that the worms have a prior lien thereon, until the abomination is paid for.

And once paid for, you needn't imagine the Italian will ever give you back your money or change the fruit for sound fruit.

In fact, he couldn't if he tried; because he never has any sound fruit!

Sometimes he moistens the corner of a cloth in his mouth, and therewith washes the rosy side of the apples.

Oranges and bananas are always cunningly arranged so as to make them look what they are not.

Of course these small dealers can not do business in our big thoroughfares;—no! They establish themselves in obscure side streets, like spiders waiting to catch flies.

They catch so many that after a few years they can open a corner grocery; and after a few years more they become wholesale merchants.

The profit, you see, on selling spoiled fruit at the price of good fruit is several thousand per cent.

And if a man can make five thousand per cent by selling rotten apples and only a hundred per cent by selling good ones, would he not be an infernal fool to sell anything else but rotten apples? There may have been a time when little corner-stand fruit sellers preferred to sell good fruit at a small profit to selling rotten fruit at a prodigious and incredible profit,—but it was so long ago

> *—That mountains have arisen since*
> *With cities on their flanks.*

We did know a nice little Italian boy with a Corresgiesque face who never sold anything but perfectly sound and healthy fruit; but he disappeared years ago.

Mysteriously and suddenly.

We suspect that he was too good to live in this world and that the angels must have flown down and taken him right up to heaven.

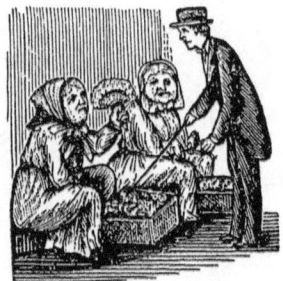

Dedicated to "The Little Maids."

Saturday, September 11, 1880
THE FLOWER-SELLERS

They sit forever under the shadows—silver-tressed and ancient—calmly weaving their flowers into rainbow-tinted gifts for youth and beauty.

And I, gazing upon them impassibly weaving the bright blossoms together, dream of the ancient Norns of Scandinavian legends—

Weaving the warp and woof of human destinies;—measuring terms of life as the stems of flowers are measured;—

Mystically mingling Evil with Good; Joy with Sorrow; Love with Grief;—tints of Passion with tints of Melancholy,—even as in a bouquet the hues of a hundred flowers are blended into one rich design.

Evanescent as the beauty of Woman are the colors of the flowers;—volatile their drowsy-sweet odors as the perfume of youth.

And thou, O reader, when thou receivest, from the wrinkled hands of the Norns, who measure the lives of summer blossoms, an odorous gift for the ivory hand of thy living idol,—

Knowest thou that the gift is in itself a voiceless symbol of the fragility of all which thou worshippest?

Fair girl, a mightier Norn than that grey woman who silently weaves her flowers in the sun, has measured the golden thread of thy life:—

Though sweeter than the presence of Esther, bathed six months in palm-oil and rich odors before entering the chamber of the King—thy youth will pass like the breath of a flower;—

Though thy lips be as those of the Shulamitess, they will wither and crisp and wrinkle like the petals of a scarlet blossom;—

And as a flower between the leaves of a book, thou shalt be pressed between the marble covers of that ponderous volume in which Death, who is, alas! strong as Love, keeps the weird record of his deeds.

Sunday, September 12, 1880
THE MAN WITH THE SMALL ELECTRIC MACHINE

Br-r-r-r-r-r-r-r-r-r-r-r-r-r-r-r-r-r-r-r!!

—"Want to try it, sir. Take hold of these two handles. Lower down, please! Now! Tell me when to stop."

Br-r-r-r-r-r-r-r-r-r-r-r-r-r-r-r-r-r-r-r!

—"One hundred and eighty-six,—seventy-five above the average!"

Then the man goes away, thinking he has done very fine, and looking proud of himself.

The machine sometimes runs only to a certain figure, say 150. Almost anybody can hold on till the needle goes clear round. Then the man shuts off the current, pretending he is going to put on more force.

The visitor holds on again, and is told that he has stood an electric pressure of three hundred.

Then the same thing is done again until he believes that he has stood nine hundred!

Everybody is told that he goes above the average.

No average people ever visit the Man with the Single Electric Machine. They are all giants and giantesses,—all people of mark.

Everybody is flattered and pleased until they pay a visit to the man who has a Big Electric Machine, which one must be a hippopotamus to vanquish, and then they find that they are not so far above average as they supposed.

Monday, September 13, 1880
THE ALLIGATORS+

None discover aught of beauty in them; yet they were once worshiped as gods.

They were not of this world, in truth, but of another—the Antediluvian world of monsters and dragons and vast swamps broader than continents—where there were frogs larger than oxen, and alligators longer than the serpent slain by the army of Regulus.

The Ichthyosaurus, the Pterodactyl, the Megatherium, the Plesiosaurus—have passed away with the Antediluvian world.

This strange being, with its dull cuirass marked like the trunks of the primeval tree-ferns, still endures—although new strata have been formed since the birth of his species—although the monstrous vegetation of the swamps in which his ancestors crawled has been transformed to beds of coal!

Alligator, crocodile, or cayman—it matters little—they alike belong to the age before which history began.

And looking upon them, must not one dream of the sacred Ganges and the most ancient Nile—of South American rivers that flow by dead palaces buried in the vegetation of virgin forests—of dead civilizations—of Karnac and Tebes and Crocodilopolis—of catacombs and broken-limbed colossi—of empires and of races that have been swallowed up by Time? The world has changed, but the Giant Lizard changes not.

Tuesday, September 14, 1880
THE POLICE BOARD

The Victims of Last Night's Session.

The Board of Police Commissioners met last night. Present—Mayor Patton, Administrator Meallie and Messrs. Hagan and Byrne. Commissioner Phillips was not expected to attend, as his resignation is in the Mayor's hands, but Commissioner Lanaux was again absent. The proceedings, as usual, were characterized by the peculiar decisions that have brought the board into so much unenviable notoriety.

The much continued cases against Patrolmen James Farrell and Mike McDermott were called. McDermott appeared, but Farrell, who was at the Charity Hospital, suffering from a bullet wound received from Mr. Lauer's pistol, when he attempted to shut that gentleman's eye for a round of drinks, did not show up.

Mr. Byrne claimed that as Ferrell was not present the cases should be continued. Mr. Meallie remarked that the cases had been continued too many times already, and Mayor Patton came to the rescue by announcing that the board had full power to proceed with the matter. Mr. Byrne withdrew his objections.

A number of witnesses were examined, one of them, Peter Sims, stated that he had attended the meeting that was to have been held August 16, but as the board did not meet, and not having received any other notice, he failed to appear. Subsequently another of the witnesses, R. Walsh, from whose grocery Farrell and McDermott threw eggs at an old Italian fruit vendor, testified he knew nothing of their capers.

Mr. Hagan moved that the accused be dismissed from the force.

The charge of sitting down, while on duty, against Patrolman P. Devine, A. Martin, and M. A. H. Porter, first precinct, was discharged.

Patrolman H. Gainer, third precinct, pleaded not guilty to the charge of refusing to arrest the party who had assaulted Mr. M. Quintero, at the corner of Canal and Royal streets on the night of July 18. Mr. Quintero wrote to the board that he could not appear. The board continued the case, but issued an attachment for that gentleman's presence at the next meeting.

Supernumerary V. Cuital, fifth precinct, was not ready to be tried, as some witnesses who could prove his innocence were not present. The case was continued.

Patrolman T. Burnett, fifth precinct, changed with drunkenness and disturbing the peace of his board-house on the 11th and 12th of July pleaded not guilty.

Patrolman M. A. H. Porter, eighth precinct (Algiers), pleaded guilty to a number of charges, such as sleeping on his beat, holding unnecessary conversation, etc., and was fined ten days' pay.

Patrolman W. A. Boynes, eighth precinct (Algiers), pleaded guilty to the charge of drunkenness. Mr. Hagan moved to dismiss him from the force, but was outvoted by Commissioners Byrne and Meallie, who had him fined ten days' pay. Boynes, when informed by the Mayor of the Board's decision, said he would quit, whereupon Mr. Meallie had his motion reconsidered, and then Mr. Hagan's proposition was carried, and Boynes given the bounce.

Chief Boylan's report showing the condition of the force was read. There is a total of 247 men on the force, 91 doing day duty and 156 night duty. Of these, 48 are doing detailed duty, leaving only 199 men doing actual police duty.

Wednesday, September 15, 1880
THE VENDOR OF WISDOM[+]

The Vendor of Wisdom selleth and also buyeth at a moderate price all the wisdom that hath been crystallized into the shape of books.

In his antiquated and darksome little shop, the thoughts of thirty centuries reside.

Every wave of civilization that has ebbed over the face of the earth, has drifted something into that little dusty bookstore.

Every great event in the history of the earth has contributed something to those dusty shelves.

All nations and tongues are represented there; all the philosophers have riches there; and there all the poets have preserved their word-music.

As for the antiquarian, he thinketh much of these things; for he knoweth by heart the story of each book, and now rarely openeth any save new ones,—works of this age of ours.

Then he saith,—

"Pshaw! They call that new, and I have beheld the same in books that were written lo! three thousand years ago!

"The founders of the Semitic and Aryan religions knew these things; and forsooth these modern fools offer them to us as something novel!

"The Egyptians were versed in the very profoundest philosophy of all these questions;—they were taught also in Rome and Greece.

"Nevertheless, there are people in these days who imagine they can write something new upon the subject."

And saying these things he putteth the new book aside, and he taketh a duster and dusteth tenderly the thoughts of Plato and Aristotle and Socrates, and patteth the good old books on the back.

Never doth he lose patience,—not even when bibliophilists steal his books,—

Nor when cockroaches devour the backs of Aristophanes and Pliny, and of Diodorus Siculus, of Athenæus and Sophocles and Petronius,—

Nor when book-worms bore holes through the Elzevir text of the Fathers of the Church,—

Nor, when, having bought a book for a good price, he afterward discovereth that the person who sold it to him had previously torn out the engravings,—

Nor even when having been told to "lay books aside," the person for whom they are laid aside never cometh back,—so that they lay there until all hope of selling them has departed.

He putteth works of godly piety in the waste-basket.

And books in the French language, robed in yellow like Roman courtesans,—these he selleth for a good price.

"For such," he saith, "is the depravity of human nature."

Never have I been able to learn whether he saith this seriously or not,—so much doth his eye twinkle when he saith it.

He is never absent from his post;—for twenty-five years he hath lived every day with his books from 7.30 A.M. to 7.30 P.M.

And there will he remain, let us hope, for many years more.

Until they take him from his books and file him away, even as a roll of manuscripts in the marble pigeon holes which are never dusted and whose contents are never looked at.

Thursday, September 16, 1880
THE CURSE OF THE NEWSPAPER VENDOR+

What do people buy newspapers usually for?

(We say usually, because some buy them at so much a pound for wrapping paper and other purposes which it is needless to mention.)

People buy newspapers generally in order to see what is in them.

But if they see what is in a paper without buying it, they do not care to buy it afterward.

What do people buy illustrated periodicals for?

Why to look at the pictures and inspect the contents.

But when they can do that without buying it they are not apt to buy it.

Therefore it is that our news vendors are seriously annoyed by people who want to read papers free of charge.

For one man who buys a newspaper to read, there are at least fifty who read a newspaper in order not to buy it.

The man who enters a news-store to buy a paper, buys the paper generally without looking at anything except the date.

The man who goes to a news-stand in order to save himself the expense of five cents, usually spends half an hour at the table.

Frequently he monopolizes the last copy of some paper which others want to buy, and destroys the news vendor's chance of selling it.

He is greedily hurried, like all who obtain pleasure by doing wrong, and he seldom turns a paper inside out.

No: he simply sticks his greasy head inside the pages, which he sometimes tears. When he tears a paper he sticks it under the pile to prevent the news-dealer from seeing it.

He looks at all the magazines,—at the engravings in *Scribner's* and *Harper's;* and dirties the pages, and never thinks of buying a periodical.

He thinks that if he buys a five-cent newspaper once a month, he is justified in spending an hour a day in clawing newspapers and reading magazines for nothing.

When he does buy a five-cent newspaper, he does so reluctantly and under compulsion;—

Because he knows that the news-dealer will not let him loaf around unless he buys something once in a while;

And he hates the news-dealer because he is obliged to spend five cents. Such is human nature.

Friday, September 17, 1880
AT THE PHOTOGRAPHER'S

When the half-grown youth gets photographed, he wishes in the most unmistakable manner to show that he is a terrible person.

Therefore he cocks his hat on the side of his head, and sticks a cigar in his mouth, and has an empty beer-glass or whisky-glass stuck on the table beside him, or a mint julep with a straw in it.

He always takes a companion with him; for in spite of his cheek he would not like to go through this farce all by himself.

The two sit together, looking as rowdyish as they can, and grieving at heart that they are not yet even more like hoodlums than they are.

They want to "be taken" so as to look like drunkards and corner-grocery loafers.

Sometimes they want to be represented at a card table,—sometimes in a barroom; and they grin at each other approvingly.

If the photographer wants to "arrange" them in a decent attitude they say,—

"Guess we're paying for this, Mister,—

Or: "Now you just mind your own business, will you?"

Or: "We're running this biz, old man; and if you don't like it, by G—— we can go somewhere else."

So the photographer does just as they want him to do.

And then he places their beautiful portrait in his window,—especially if his establishment happens to be in a back street.

Thus he revenges himself.

For every person who comes by thinks that these young men are about the "rattiest" and meanest that the city can turn out,—judging them even worse than they are. For they are often not really half so much addicted to whisky and cards as they pretend to be.

They only want to be thought men; and they think it is very manly to get drunk and to swear and to sling slang and to gamble.

Some of them find out the contrary sooner or later. Others don't.

But there is not one of them, perhaps, who will not feel small some day when he remembers how he tried to stick on style in the photographer's gallery.

As for the photographer, he cares nothing; for he has seen all kinds of stupid vanity, all kinds of ridiculous eccentricity, and all varieties of absurd people on his little gallery.

Saturday, September 18, 1880
CAKES AND CANDY[+]

She buyeth little cakes and selleth them to little children.

Sometimes, especially if she be Creole, she maketh them herself, and great be the cunning skill wherewith she prepareth the little dainties.

Then, whenever little boys and girls get five cents to spare, they go to spend it at the cake-stand.

Children are the only customers;—it is childhood supporting age.

Some of these ancient women have been selling dainties to little ones through two generations.

Many of the infants who trotted to them with five cents in their dimpled fingers are now grown-up men and women.

Others have now children of their own, and these too toddle to the good old woman with their nickels.

So that the old woman knoweth much of the history of families and the vicissitudes thereof.

During the epidemic of 1878, the business was not good. Little ones who used to buy suddenly ceased to come. And many came no more.

And the aged woman, sitting in the sun, smiled not as was her wont, and spake less than usual,

Wondering what had become of her little darlings.

Of many of them she never heard again;—and never will hear, and she wonders still.

So that, asking her one day where was little fair hair baby, whom we had not seen since last summer, she answered only—

Bon Dieu, li connais!

Sunday, September 19, 1880
THE PULLER OF NOSES+

Thou, O barber, pullest the noses of the oldest and best.

Also dost thou tickle the most dignified under the chin.

Thou tellest the vainest that their heads need washing badly.

Thou stickest the teeth of the comb in the rims of the ears of judges.

Also thy patience is great and thy good nature large.

Otherwise thou couldst not be a barber at all.

Nevertheless thou hast thy faults.

After having smoked cigarettes thou shouldst carefully wash thy fingers, and yet thou dost not.

And the odor of burnt paper and tobacco is not soothing to the olfactory nerves.

Wherefore, one wisheth that women were barbers,—nice young women who do not smoke.

Old women smoke sometimes, you know.

This is why we should like young girls to shave us.

Don't you believe that is the only reason?

Then you mean to say we are not telling the truth;

That we are prevaricators and equivocators!

Then we have nothing more to say upon the subject.

Monday, September 20, 1880
YE PILOT+

Bravely the Pilot at his post
   Stands, and the guiding wheel
Resolves, responsive to the touch
   Of his strong arms of steel.

Fierce winds may blow, fierce storms assail,
   Fierce fires may rage around,
But fires, nor lightnings, nor the gale
   Can this brave heart confound.

A thousand lives on him depend,
   And, careless of his own,
He firmly tries; he does or dies;
   And, with his latest moan,

He thinks of those he could not save—
   Should fate against him rise—
And sinking in a watery grave,
   Still holds the Pilot's prize!

Tuesday, September 21, 1880
AWFUL CONSEQUENCES OF POOR SHOOTING+

Nightly visions of the inhabitants of Jersey Farm! Dedicated to the Louisiana Field Artillery!

Wednesday, September 22, 1880
A WARNING TO ADVERTISERS

Advertisers sometimes think it is cheaper to get circulars printed by the thousand and pay naughty little boys two bits to distribute them to the public than to advertise in the daily papers. Now we have seen the boys distribute them.

The way they distribute them would not probably suit employers, but it suits the boys first-rate.

Do you really think boys are such fools as to slide one circular off the pile with his fore-finger and thumb,—one after the other,—and give each circular to a different person?

For two bits!

No danger.

Don't worry yourself.

The boy distributes the circulars all at one time as above described in our engraving.

He just slamms up against a wall;

Or lamms against a post;

Or slathers them against the pavement with such violence that not one remains upon another.

It is like the rains of Jerusalem after the Romans got through there, and left not a stone upon a stone.

What is the remedy?

It is very simple.

Also, it is very efficacious.

Don't print circulars to be so distributed;

But advertise in The City Item.

Thursday, September 23, 1880
FRANTIC APPEALS FOR HELP

We reprint the following from the *Democrat* of this morning. It was received by a leading firm of New Orleans, and met with no response. The fact is encouraging, however; for it shows that the Republicans are at the end of their pecuniary resources. They can no longer rely on these great corporations which formerly poured out money like a flood to keep the South down by keeping the old Republican war party in power.

Headquarters of the Republican Congressional Committee
Washington, D.C., Sept. 14, 1880

Dear Sir— To the business interests of this country the success of the Republican ticket is indispensable. The election of Garfield and Arthur means stability to legislation, continuance of existing business prosperity, and speedy development as the infallible result. This issue is higher than politics, and appeals to the business interest of every class.

The Republican Congressional Committee is actively engaged in connection with the national committee in the work of organizing and reaching the voters of the country. Both are crippled by want of means.

Relying upon your fidelity to the cause of the Republican party, which is eminently the cause of the country, I confidently appeal to you for help. All funds received by us are divided with the national committee, and are rigidly applied by both to the necessities of the campaign.

The occasion is urgent, and prompt action is requested.

Please send a liberal contribution to George F. Dawson, treasurer congressional committee, 1317 F. street, N.W., Washington D.C.

Respectfully yours,
Jay A. Hubbell, Chairman

Saturday, September 25, 1880
POLICE EFFICIENCY+

We think that the killing of Bares was in all respects a shameful affair. The man did not belong to the class of hoodlums and law-breakers;—he was violent only when upon periodical sprees and then his violence was not generally of a very terrible character. The lives of the police were not endangered. The man resisted and kicked and bit, according to statements made, and being a strong man no doubt gave trouble. But the legitimate weapons of policemen are not fists and feet. They are furnished with clubs to quell riotous characters; they have their pistols to use in cases when they are attacked with murderous weapons and their lives are really endangered. The city does not pay police to kick and gouge and bite prisoners. It pays them to quell them by more rational and less brutal measures. Had the officers contented themselves with using their clubs on Bares' legs and arms, the man would be alive today, and probably not much the worse. But he would, nevertheless, have been placed *hors de combat*. Even if he had been clubbed judicially on the head, nothing very serious would have come of it. However, it must be remembered that his offense was only a petty one, deserving a simple fine, and he had never been up for any grave breach of law. It is natural that policemen, especially when kicked, as they are said to have been, should lose patience; but if such loss of patience endangers the life of a prisoner who is not a recognized desperado, men of greater coolness and efficiency should be chosen to take their place. Gentle firmness goes a long way in making arrests,—except where professional ruffians are concerned; and many fights between police and their prisoners are caused by unnecessary and unjust roughness on the part of the former. Nine ordinary men out of ten will walk quietly to a stationhouse if treated like men, but none out of ten will resist if treated like brutes. This is human nature. If a policeman finds a drunkard too strong to manage, it is his duty to summon assistance. As we have said before, if a gang of regular hoodlums attack the police to the discharge of their duties, and a few of the rowdies get their skulls cracked, we should sustain the police under reasonable circumstances, but when there are three policemen and only one drunken man, and the former choose to stomp and kick the latter to death, we can not but consider it simply a case of murder.

Sunday, September 26, 1880
THE MASTER SPIRIT[+]

The Devil, unseen, sat on the box,
    Into which the ballots fell,
And he grinned a grin—the sly old fox—
    As he sent a dispatch to hell.

Oho! 'tis fun, when the game's begun,
    To see these mortal fools
On my darksome errand of mischief run,
    At work with my hellish tools.

And some with whisky, and some with tin,
    And some with the bludgeon, I
Lead hotly on from sin to sin,
    While their pauper souls I buy.

But they go too fast—these mortal fools—
    For they arouse the ire
Of the good, who disregard my rules,
    Of the true, who avoid my fire.

But my crop is certain to be large,
    And to deal with the rascal Ring
Is worthy the proudest demon's charge—
    The undying serpent's sting.

Monday, September 27, 1880

THE POLICE MUTUAL AID SOCIETY

Until there is a complete reorganization of that ridiculous and pernicious thing we call a police force, it will be in the last degree difficult to bring members of the force to account for any misdemeanor which they choose to commit.

If a policeman kills somebody or commits some grave abuse of authority, it is almost impossible to convict him.

Suppose there are five witnesses for the prosecution, who are not to be intimidated or coaxed, and all of whom tell one straightforward story, the police always seem to have the marvelous faculty of invoking a very cloud of witnesses, who give a directly opposite version of the affair, and who will swear that everything the uninterested witnesses swear to is untrue.

It is the same way when cases come up before the Police Board (which, by the way, has had unjudged cases pending before it for two months). A policeman accused of a certain misdemeanor in a certain place seems to find it wonderfully easy to summon a cloud of witnesses to prove he was not there at all.

If it is a case of assault and battery, witnesses seem to rise up from beneath the ground to testify that the policeman's life was in awful jeopardy, that the battered-up man had a knife or a pistol, and that the police showed great forbearance.

We have no doubt a policeman could, if he wanted to, find witnesses to swear that they had seen him in seven different parts of the city at the same time.

We like to call attention to this fact at the present time, as this case of the Bares' homicide will doubtless confirm the truth of what we have above observed.

Another Chance for Reform. What an Administrator Gets Paid for Not Doing.

Tuesday, September 28, 1880

ILLUSTRATED LETTERS FROM THE PEOPLE+

Editor City Item—Riding in a street car the other day I overheard the following conversation:

"I see that the Mayor and Administrators have paid themselves their August salaries. When were you paid last?"

"When were we last paid? Not for months. It is very discouraging. I spent all day yesterday trying to borrow on my October time from the broker, but could do little better than give my yet unearned claim away. I did get a bid of sixty-five per-cent for my next January certificate, but for the remainder of this year it seems we poor teachers must work for virtually nothing more substantial than—with a desperate necessity for retaining our situations—the hope of better times next year. Ah! me, how long deferred hopes of those better times makes sick the heart and desolates the homes of such as I."

Was this not sufficient to arouse your correspondent's ire? The chat was a sort of confidential one between two ladies, who, judging from their prayer-books, were returning from church. Looking as if intently absorbed in his newspaper, your correspondent sank back in the corner of the car and waited for further developments.

"Have you asked Administrator Isaacson what he can do toward relieving the distress of teachers?" soon spoke out the original querist.

With a little tinge of bitterness came back the words: "Mr. Isaacson gets a hundred dollars a month for paying off the teachers, and his interest apparently ceases when that item of school expense is liquidated."

This brought fairly before your correspondent a palpable question of public finances. In addition to six thousand dollars a year as Administrator, is a gratuity of one hundred dollars per month given to Mr. Isaacson in payment for his merely nominal duties as treasurer of the School Board? If so, it may be claimed that he gives an additional bond, but the fact fails as a defense for squandering an altogether insufficient fund, as he incurs no additional risk. It might further be alleged that the present incumbent is justified in thus depicting the school moneys by the example of his predecessors in office; but a similar justification might be set up for all the waste and thriftlessness which characterize other departments in our municipal system. Nor would such defence hold good in this case. The duties of the department have been so reduced by governmental changes that leisure seems to be the most abundant thing left in the offices, when compensation for paying off the school teachers was initiated, the salary, although nominally drawn by the Administrator was, I learn, given to the clerks, who, in extra hours, performed the work.

In view of these facts I feel impelled to call upon the Administrator to relinquish this gratuity to the underpaid, ill-treated school-teachers. He is rich and "rides in chaises"; they are poor—so wretchedly poor that their condition is a disgrace to this city, and should stir every impulse of manhood to assist in relieving them. Private individuals may be discouraged from giving further aid in the face of such official misapplication of what is collected for school purposes, whereupon, the condition of the teachers must become distressful indeed. With his quick sense of right your correspondent is certain that the Administrator will act promptly on the gentle hint herein given.

HAWKEYE.

Wednesday, September 29, 1880

YOU PAYS YOUR MONEY, AND YOU TAKES YOUR CHOICE+

Some of the testimony in the Bares case has been even more contradictory and extraordinary than we had anticipated.

P. Bares, S. Jacobs, and Alexander Armant swore they saw Driscoll kick Bares in the stomach and pull him up from the ground by the hair.

John H. Vigers and Officers Welsh and Martin swore on the other hand that nobody kicked Bares at all, but that Bares kicked Driscoll with such force that he knocked him thirty feet away!!

Louis de Lavas swore that Jacobs, the most important witness in the case, was not there at all! He did not see him, you know; and if he had been there he must have seen him.

Then other witnesses swore that Bares hurt himself by falling on his side on a barrel in the station house.

Yet another swore that it was by flinging himself down on the floor.

The physician stated that the accident might have been produced by falling on a barrel, or might have been produced by kicks in the stomach; but he does not appear to have expressed any opinion as to which caused his death.

In the face of this contradictory statement the jury failed to agree; and it looks doubtful whether any jury would ever agree under such circumstances.

After a while we may expect to hear witnesses swear that the ground jumped up and hit Bares in the stomach, or that Bares hit himself in his own stomach, or that his own stomach hit Bares, or that a brick fell off of the top of the house and fell on his abdomen while he was standing up, or that Corporal Driscoll was kicked so far away by Bares that he could not find his way back to the scene until the morning of the next day.

Thursday, September 30, 1880
THE *GREAT EASTERN*+

The *Great Eastern* was designed by I. K. Brunel.

Ten thousand tons of iron were used in her construction.

Her hull, masts, and all her framework are iron. She was registered for 18,915 tons.

Her deck is 695 feet long, or one-eighth of a mile; and more than eighty feet in width. A walk around her deck is equal to a quarter of a mile.

She draws twenty feet of water; and thirty feet when laden.

She has four decks. From the upper deck to her hold is a depth of sixty feet.

Her paddles are sixty feet in diameter.

The diameter of her screw is twenty-four feet.

She is five thousand tons heavier than Noah's ark.

She can spread 6500 square yards of canvas.

In addition to her boats, she formerly carried swung to her sides, four small tug-steamers. Whether she continues to do so now, we do not know.

She can carry 10,000 soldiers; or 800 first-class, 2000 second-class, and 12,000 third-class passengers; and a total of 22,500 tons.

Her engines have a power of 3000 horses.

If the people of New Orleans are not too crazy to act within judgment and decency, she will moor her vast bulk at our wharfs,—occupying a distance of two blocks along the river front.

Friday, October 1, 1880
THE WAGES OF SIN+

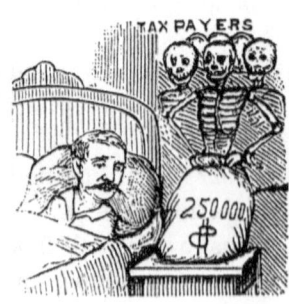

They are ready now to go through Gauthreaux.
   But Gauthreaux first did go through them
As with loaded dice, and when he did throw,
   He seemed quite certain of his game.

Two hundred and fifty thousand dollars!—
   'Tis a good round sum in these trying times
When a fellow has that amount it follows:—
   You can't convict him of fiscal crimes.

How careful have been both State and city
   Not to bring the offender under ban.

They waited and prated and—more's the pity—
    Adopted the mild, persuasive plan.

No small amount would do for Gauthreaux;
    He wanted the whole of the hog or none;
And e'en at the Ring he was not loth to
    Twirl his fingers, though just in fun.

But things have changed; and now he lieth
    With fraudful gleanings under his bed:
He can't enjoy them; mayhap he dieth
    While phantoms fill him with direful dread.

Saturday, October 2, 1880
THAT VERDICT[+]

We, the intelligent coroner's jury, do find that the deceased did come to his death through peritonitis.

There are not less than nine hundred and ninety-nine different causes which may produce peritonitis.

The deceased might have been kicked in such a manner as to produce peritonitis,
Or he might not.
He might have fallen down the stairs and hurt himself.
Or he might not.
He might have fallen upon his back so as to destroy his stomach,
Or he might not.
He might have kicked himself in his own abdomen by accident.
Some witnesses swear that they saw the deceased killed by the policeman,
Others swear the contrary.
We live in the immediate neighborhood and deem it judicious to give the policeman the benefit of the doubt.
We think it might not be healthy to do otherwise.
Therefore we simply find that the deceased died of peritonitis.
And that, according to the testimony of the police, he received falls enough to produce peritonitis.
And if the public are not satisfied with this verdict, they can just hold the inquest over again themselves.

Sunday, October 3, 1880
PONEY UP!+

The above scene is laid in one of those streets where respectable people object to live, and where the police are able to make up the deficiency in their salaries. The police are No. 1 collectors. They have their own private dodges for enforcing payment.

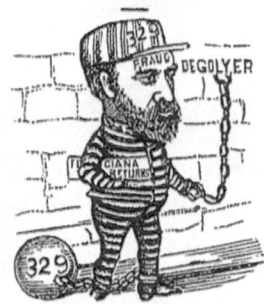

Monday, October 4, 1880
329+

Addition, Division, and Silence
   Are the Radical Rule of Three;
They were taught to James A.
While the boat-muse would bray:
   "That's the sure rule in Congress for me,"
   Quoth Garfield; "that plainly I see."

With perjury, fraud, and corruption
   He did up the business for Hayes:
"Some votes we must steal,
Or our doom we will seal,"
   Quoth Garfield; and ere many days
   The figures of fraud he displays.

With treachery, treason, and guile,
   He did up the business for Grant:
At Chicago's Convention
Was done what we mention.
   While the Sphinx that was silent did pant,
   He said unto Grant, "No you shan't!"

Tuesday, October 5, 1880
WANT TO INVESTIGATE

Like all rings, the Police Ring is indignant at hearing a little truth.
   It wants an investigation.
   It wants to investigate the *City Item*!!

It is so confident of its skill in manufacturing false witnesses and bullying honest ones that it cries out for a chance to whitewash itself.

If the *Item* has not noticed special cases of blackmailing or bribery by the police, it has been for the sake of saving the victims further persecution.

We have asked an investigation at least fifty times; but the proper authorities do not want to investigate.

They know these things as well as anybody else.

And now that the police are perfectly well convinced there will be no investigation by others in power, they propose to investigate themselves.

We accept the challenge.

We said many months ago, at the time of a cowardly assault upon one of our representatives, that we proposed to keep up the fight against the police ring till we should break it up or break up ourselves.

And we shall do it.

But do not let Chief Boylan suppose that we are going to turn our office into a detective agency to suit his momentary whims.

We shall make an investigation, but no such investigation as the police want.

Our investigation will be very broad and long, and will be carried on through months and months.

You won't get the *City Item* to whitewash you, gentlemen of the police.

Hitherto we have only spoken of scandals in a general way,—such scandals as are known to every intelligent resident of the city. Hereafter we shall give precise details and names and facts and dates without mercy,—except in such cases where we deem it probable that informants need the protection of secrecy. And we shall take our own time about it. Meanwhile, the Chief of Police can go through the process of self-analysis and investigate himself as much as he wants to.

We have no doubt there may be some good men on the police; but we have not yet had the inestimable pleasure of becoming acquainted with them.

Wednesday, October 6, 1880
STATEMENT OF A VICTIM[+]

The following is the substance of a statement made to a person connected with this paper, by a representative of that class of unfortunate creatures who although compelled to pay for the right to follow their calling, are refused the protection of law:

"I think such women as I ought to have some right to protection as long as we pay the police. We have none. If a man comes into my room and breaks up my furniture and abuses me, the police arrest me, and not him. Yet I have done nothing. I have often been starving because the last cent I received was taken from me by a policeman. They have no mercy. They come in and beat us and take what we have and oblige us to treat them as if they paid us. We have no redress.

"When we are brought up before the judge, he will not allow us to tell our story. No one will take our word. If we say that we have been robbed and beaten no one will believe us. Everything that the policeman says is believed. And they will all swear the same thing against us. If they have some spite against us they will do anything. And if they kill us, they have nothing to be afraid of. Two years up the road for killing a woman!

"I know it is against the law to live this way; but if we pay we ought to be left alone. Sometimes, when they have a spite against us, they allow nobody to come near us, and if we go out of the house they arrest us. They do not think anything of hitting a woman with a club or knocking her down and kicking her.

"Perhaps they are not all as bad as those here. I am told in some parts of the city, they leave the women alone. Perhaps they have rich friends, those women. We have none. And if we are sent up we lose all we have, and often have no place to go when we come back. Is it true that in other cities the police are not allowed to do these things?"

Thursday, October 7, 1880
THAT VILLAINOUS BROKER

Ha! Ha!! Ha!!!

Foul fiend, we have thee now.

Revenge is sweet, and a long enduring public shall wallow in the luxury.

The broker did it! Long as he evaded the Argus eye of the law, but the rigid investigation of the Gauthreaux defalcation by the City Council developed him in all his amazing turpitude.

Seizing an unsuspecting and unsophisticated sheriff, this vile broker compelled him to take money instead of scrip, as the law directs, for taxes.

Cunningly shutting the eyes of the Mayor and Administrators to the oft-repeated warnings of the *Item*, the broker bullied them into fancied security in which they neglected to exact prompt settlements.

The broker buys the claims of the police and school teachers and laborers—not the chief officials—at seventy or eighty cents, and they shrivel by consequence of official inaction, in his hands to a value of twenty or thirty cents on the dollar, but this is only a blind.

The broker makes the oppressed Mayor and Administrators feel their feebleness, while plunder-gorged as he is, he goes about with his coat binding frazzled out and exhibiting a general air of seediness. Yet this is only done to deceive.

Hang this villainous broker! Shoot him!—stab him!

Sit down on him! He has no friends.

Friday, October 8, 1880
IMPROVED POLICE IDEAS+

The happy idea of one of our patrolmen in turning in a fire alarm the other day, and thus dispersing a mob, ought to be universally adopted.

We should recommend that the present police be simply employed to stand at street corners and turn in fire alarms when arrests ought to be made.

We'll bet on the fire department every time.

We don't think the fire department would ever back down when there is good hard work to do.

In other cities firemen hold commissions as guardians of the peace; and if policemen are not around when there is trouble the firemen usually turn up. And when they lay their hands on a disturber of the peace he always goes where they want him to go.

Firemen never stand any nonsense. When they go in to work they mean business.

We recommend an occasional application of the cold-water cure to hoodlumism, as above represented.

Saturday, October 9, 1880
BLACKMAILING+

We are daily in receipt of reports regarding the manner in which the police collect money from the houses of ill-fame; and the brutal abuse which they make of their power. Our testimony is accumulating.

We would suggest to Judge Miltenberger,

for example, that certain women arrested and brought before him, be allowed to testify occasionally in their own behalf.

If the city authorities made a fair investigation of the existing evils, and would assure the witnesses protection, a mass of disgusting testimony could be obtained ample enough to fill a thousand newspaper columns.

The police know, however, that their victims are at their mercy; and under present circumstances dare not testify.

Names of officers have been given to us which we have filed away intending to use as soon as we receive such testimony as will not leave the witnesses without protection.

This sort of abuse of authority is something which did not exist as it does now even under the Radical regime.

It must not be supposed that in speaking of these things we do not desire that social evils be properly restrained by law.

On the contrary, we speak of them because we desire that they shall not increase; and also because it is a disgrace to any city that her police should draw money from the practice of crime.

It is said that if a humane policeman be assigned to certain patrols, where their practices are carried on, and that he is unwilling to disgrace his manhood, he is quietly shunted off to the outlying districts.

A good patrolman—we happen to have met one or two very recently—said to a person connected with this paper: "Why do you give it to us poor peelers; it is not we who make the money; it is the men with the double row of buttons."

Another said: "That article in *The Item* the other day, entitled the 'Statement of a Victim,' is true. I have been on the police twelve years; and I can tell you that these things happen almost every day."

And will the citizen-voters of New Orleans allow this state of things to continue forever?

Sunday, October 10, 1880
NOTHING LIKE SELF-ESTEEM

The theatre matinee assembles a queer lot of young men who arrange themselves on sidewalks at close of the performance. They have a blank expression of countenance, and all look alike, though none of them are pretty enough to warrant their being so posted for exhibition.
—*Picayune.*

Perhaps they are not pretty; but they think they are, and stand there in the fond hope that some woman will fall in love with them.

Monday, October 11, 1880
SCOURGED TO THE BALLOT[+]

See how the stalwarts use the lash!
    They scourge the negro up to the poll,
To blacken the ballot with perjury,
    Though, in doing so, they peril his soul.

The people's verdict they falsify
    With darkest fraud wherever they can,
And then they swear, with a curse for a prayer,
    It's all for the good of their fellow man.

The darkey squirms when he feels the scourge,
    Though on the wages of sin he smiles;
And the cheating stalwart who deals in fraud
    Cares little the way he the dupe beguiles.

Tuesday, October 12, 1880
THE SMOKERS OF PIPES

The sky being grey and sad, and the world looking dull, the editor taketh some yellow tobacco and having stuffed it into a pipe lighteth up, and dreameth of a subject to write about.

And straightway it seemeth to him right and proper to utter some observations upon the virtues of the pipe.

For the pipe is the most faithful friend of man,—simple, frank, and honest.

He that smoketh a pipe hath always energy; and he that smoketh a pipe in the street hath not a lazy bone in his body,—although it is not *à la mode* to smoke a pipe in the street.

He that smoketh cigars in the street may or may not be lazy; but is generally energetic when he wants to be.

But he that smoketh cigarettes is apt to be lazy. A friend of ours says that everybody who smokes cigarettes is lazy. But we know a few, a very, very few, who smoke cigarettes and are not lazy.

But he that smoketh cigarettes perpetually is always lazy; for no man can smoke cigarettes continually and attend to anything else.

And those who go to foreign lands where cigarettes be smoked all the time cometh back so lazy that his life thereafter becomes a burthen to him.

But he that smoketh a pipe may toil unceasingly and the pipe never interfereth with his work.

Wednesday, October 13, 1880
THE FESTIVE

He maketh ghostly noises in the dead waste and middle of the night.

He hath a passion for the green and crimson of beautifully bound books, and after he has passed over them they look as if they had been sprinkled with a shower of vitriol.

He loveth to commit suicide by drowning himself in bowls of cream or stifling himself in other eatables or drinkables.

When trod upon he explodeth with a great noise.

In this semi-tropical climate he sometimes attaineth to the dimensions of a No. 12 shoe.

He haunteth printing offices, and fatteneth upon the contents of the editor's paste-pot, and upon the bindings of newspaper files.

He haunteth kitchens and occasionally getteth himself baked and boiled.

Five hundred thousand means have been invented for his destruction; but none availeth.

If a house be burnt down to the ground he will momentarily disappear; but when the house is rebuilt, he cometh back again.

His virtues are these: He amuseth young kittens, who practice mouse-hunting with him. Also is the deadly enemy of the cimer lectaries. *He is used for medicinal purposes.*

But none care to recognize his good qualities, because of the mischievous and disgusting propensities, and all creatures wage unrelenting war against him, and nevertheless he continueth to propagate his species and to drown himself in cream.

Thursday, October 14, 1880
AÏDA+

We translate the following extract which the *Bee* republishes from the *Journal de Nice,* regarding the scenery which M. de Beauplan will import to this city for our opera season:—

Aïda at New Orleans.

The Americans of the United States are not contented with being the first people in the universe, and eclipsing us by the strength of their political institutions;—they also wish to rival us and even surpass us, if possible, in the interpretation of works of art. In point of splendor and magnificence, nothing will surpass the scenery of *Aïda* which will shortly appear upon the stages of the great theatres of New York and New Orleans.

We have had the pleasure of viewing and admiring several of these scenes, now being painted in the studio of the artist, Bertieri, whose talent, well appreciated by all the Italian *impresarii,* is commencing to obtain a reputation throughout Europe; and we must say that the paintings leave nothing to be desired in point of historical truth, perfect design, and strength of color.

The scenery for the second act, especially, representing as every one knows a vast public square at the entrance of a great Egyptian city, is a veritable marvel. Avenues of sphinxes, gigantic palms, majestic porticoes, and in the distance, under the luminous and glowing Oriental sky, a vast mass of cupolas, minarets, and terraces. The illusion is complete.

Decorative art, thus displayed, is true art of the highest class. Our sincere compliments to M. Bertieri and congratulations to the impresario of the great theatre of New Orleans.

Friday, October 15, 1880
HOW HISTORY IS WRITTEN

The *Two Republics of Mexico* publishes the following in a recent issue:—

Railroads—The Conquest Of Mexico.

The *Hispano-Americano,* a paper published at Panama, is becoming alarmed at the prospect of the railway rivalry of Mexico. When the Mexican interoceanic railroads are built, there will be no further use for the pathway over the sickly Isthmus of Panama. Knowing this, the people in that region are waking up to their miserable prospect, and they begin to cant the bugbear of annexation. The *Hispano* is sorely troubled in this respect, and affects to assume the situation as dangerous, and quotes from an obscure paper in New York—*The Daily City Item*—to sustain its illusions.

The *Item* is one of ten thousand papers published in the United States, and its editor is one man in a population of fifty millions. The opinion of that one man is as a grain of sand on the seashore. Public sentiment in the United States, expressed by its thousands of journals, is diametrically opposed to incorporating ten millions of people of another race and different in language and customs. Besides where there are a few men who entertain similar ideas to *The Item,* and who would unjustly despoil a neighboring republic, there are millions of just men who would revolt at such despoliation.

This is very amusing.

In the first place *The Daily City Item* is not "an obscure paper published in New York," but a very popular illustrated daily published in New Orleans. In the second place we are not annexationists, if by annexationist be understood one who clamors for the absorption of Mexico by the United States. In the third place the view expressed in this paper is not that of "one man in a population of fifty millions,"—"a grain of sand on the seashore," but on the contrary the opinion of thousands of intelligent and cultivated people who appreciate the lessons of history, and have therefore a right to theorize on future probabilities.

We have never clamored for the conquest of Mexico. But we have stated that in years to come it is highly probable that Mexico will be absorbed by the United States, just as the Spanish possessions in North America were swallowed up, just as Texas and New Mexico were amalgamated into the vast confederacy of States. But there is nothing for Mexico to be alarmed about. Unless the folly of one or other government should precipitate a war, the change will be gradual and peaceful. It will be for the benefit of Mexico and her people. It will develop all the riches of this marvellous country, and bring her such prosperity as was never known before. We have written several times at length upon this subject, and regret that our articles should be so misinterpreted. Reasoning upon the future from the lessons of the past, the latter all tend to confirm our views. The Latin race must yield sooner or later to the predominance of the Anglo Saxon throughout all those regions formerly known as the Spanish-Americas.

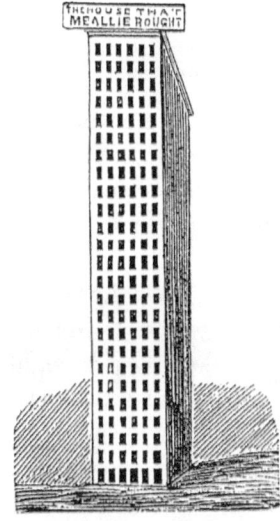

Friday, October 15, 1880
NOT 329 BUT 350+

Mr. Adams moved "that the committee be instructed to demand a settlement by candidates of previous assessments before making new arrangements. In other words," he said, "I mean that the committee be instructed to require Patrick Meallie to settle his indebtedness of $350 to the last Parish Committee. He has, I understand, bought a $5000 house out of the profits of his office, and should be able to pay the amount."
—*Democrat.*

Monday, October 18, 1880
AND HE SPAKE TO THEM ANOTHER PARABLE

The above will be comprehended by all intelligent, and even by a large number of non-intelligent, minds.

Wednesday, October 20, 1880
DREAMS OF THE ELECTOR—BEFORE AND AFTER

Something for our candidates to meditate upon. *Qui non exportant non disappointabuntur!*

Thursday, October 21, 1880
JOURNALISTIC DISSECTION+

The Professor of the *Democrat* goeth for the *Times,* scalpel in hand, making deep incisions into the abdominal and thoracic viscera, and exposing much true inwardness.

Saturday, October 23, 1880
YOUTHFUL SMOKERS

How horrified would the members of the British Anti-Tobacco Society become could they stroll through the streets of New Orleans, and behold the smoking infants that beg for a light in various languages.

Probably the effect of tobacco upon the human system has been greatly exaggerated by anti-tobacconists; but we must certainly believe that at so tender an age as eight or ten the adoption of the habit must have deteriorating physical effects.

It is detrimental, morally and physically, to smoke before seventeen or eighteen years of age; checks growth, saps vitality, injures energy, and lays the foundation of laziness. Then, as the little ones smoke usually only in order to imitate men, they are apt to imitate other habits of men which are worse.

With grown up men we have no doubt the moderate use of tobacco is beneficial. It quiets the nerves, aids concentration of thought on important subjects, and assists digestion after a good meal. But there are men who are confined by their occupation to desks and in warehouses; and tobacco is a great comfort to those deprived of natural exercise. It has healthy effect likewise, which every smoker knows.

But children have the tonic of bright air and liberty to run and enjoy themselves, and do not need the narcotic to comfort them. It is not here as in Panama, where it is even too hot sometimes for babies to toddle about, so that they are taught to smoke before they can walk.

Wednesday, October 27, 1880
COMMERCIAL STATUARY

American commercial statuary is not in the highest style of art; but there is a something artistic about it in the sense that it is a gross and stinging caricature.

On the art-taste of American commerce?

Well, we don't mean a caricature in that sense, although there is some reason to ask the question. What we mean is this:—

The average dummy which stands in front of a clothing store is certainly a type of something,—a type of something human. Not a type of the last generation, but a type of to-day. It is a caricature of the Young Man of the Period.

If it is not, what else is it, with hair plastered down in an inverted arch over an idiotic forehead, an air of superlative insolence, and a smile that is the "sickest smile" humanity ever smole?

No one can say that he has not seen in all great cities the living originals of these awful woodenheads,—at least no one who has observed human nature at all.

They were all supremely disagreeable persons, these originals: Some of them were knaves, some were fools, some were rowdies, some drunkards, some were criminals.

They represent the lowest types of well-dressed humanity to be found in civilized cities. They are horrible caricatures of living types; and yet standing before clothing stores with their insolent wooden grin, they seem to drawl out,—

"Come in here, and have some style about you and try to look like me!"

And is it wonderful that drunken men should occasionally become furious at the spectacle of the villainous smile worn by these snobby horrors, and should smite the dummies upon their wooden nostrils, and dash them down, and trample madly upon them until a policeman interferes?

Then our sympathies are certainly with the drunken men, not with the dummies.

Thursday, October 28, 1880
SPANISH MOSS+

In goblin looms,
Depending from the many-elbowed arms
of gnarled oaks, thou weavest Druid charms
    Under weird moons!

Thy night-mare hug
Stifles the moaning of the dying pine;
The cedars know that strangler's cord of thine,
    O vegetable Thug.

Thy robes of rags
The mightiest monarchs of the woods must wear,
And wreathe their crowns with locks of thy grey hair
    Like a Witch-hag's.

> What ghostly foods
> Sustain thy spectral sap, thy phantom breath?
> Thou Succubue, thou eldritch Life-in-Death,
> Thou Vampire of the Woods!
>
> L. HEARN.

Friday, October 29, 1880
FIRE!+

The time used to be in New Orleans when people dressed up to go to a fire. It was an occasion for toilettes. But that has passed away, just like the pretty custom prevalent formerly with young Creole ladies of taking an evening walk without any other head-dress than their own beautiful hair, decorated with flowers.

Still, if you want to see real excitement at a fire to-day, it is in the Second District where you can see it. There, where everybody knows everybody else, and a fire breaks out in one of those funny little stores which line the old fashioned street, the whole population of the quarter seems to turn out *en masse*. And there is none of the roughness which often characterizes an American crowd. Everybody is accommodating—a good-natured curiosity mingled with an audibly expressed sentiment of anxiety and regret animates the throng.

When the fire is out, it is pleasant to hear the voices of the firemen singing in the night, as they pass through the deserted streets in solid column.

It is the signal that the danger is over; the welcome news that all is well. "Sleep on, good folks!—pleasant dreams!—we are taking care of the good old city!"

Sometimes perhaps they do not sing. There is only a hurried trampling of feet. Their voices are lowered when they speak. And people feel anxious, and look out of the windows into the darkness. It is all well for the city. The fire is out. But the fire of a young life has gone out with it. Some brave boy has died at his post under the red rain of fire. And the singers can not sing, because their hearts are heavy.

Sunday, October 31, 1880
ALL SAINTS!+

As All Saints' Day approaches, a little village of peasant and lemonade stands grows up in the neighborhood of the cemeteries; and those who take charge of the tombs are busy laying in a great stock of shells and sand.

"Want any sand, sir?—any shells?"—a boy asks, as he passes by with his wheel-barrow.

And the stranger shakes his head, muttering,—"No: my dead are not here!"

The abrupt question makes him dream, perhaps, of a cemetery beyond the great waste of waters, where there are tombs inscribed with the same name as his own.

Or, perhaps, the query may seem like a reproach: "What!—hast thou no dead loves?—no tombs to decorate?—no graves to weep over?"

And dreamingly, he mutters to himself: "My dead ones are nameless;—my heart is their place of burial;—not with whispering shells and white sand can I make love-offerings, but only with those living thoughts and words which are as incense offered up to the memory of what has been loved and lost."

"Sand, sir? shells?" Life in the midst of death; activity in the shadow of the eternal rest; speculation upon human affection; profit upon grief;—is it not the great melodrama of all human life upon a small scale that we watch at the gates of the cemetery?

Tuesday, November 2, 1880
THE CHINESE POISON+

The Chinese opium-smokers have not departed from the city as we had fondly hoped. They have simply established themselves in other streets. An opium den has been opened in the vicinity of the old St. Louis Cemetery. What do your authorities propose to do?

[Wednesday, November 3, 1880]
DREAMS OF THE BALLET

Now the man whose pate is smoother than a billiard ball, dreameth of Terpsichore.

And straightway he secureth a front seat, and an opera glass with the power of a marine telescope.

Thursday, November 4, 1880
A DAY OF RECKONING

When wages are reduced to the lowest pitch possible in the great cities of the North and West;—

When, under the protection of the Republican party, the barbarians of Asia will take the places of the skilled mechanics who yet toil in the factories of the United States;—

When the condition of the working classes in the East shall have become worse, by unnatural competition with Asiatic labor, than in any of the great capitals of Europe;—

When the pride of free and capable artisans shall be broken down; and all the trade unions broken up;—

When riots provoked by the Chinese evil in the West and East shall have been bloodily suppressed by the military;—

When the monopolies and the ring-powers shall threaten the very foundations of American liberty, and the strangling coils of centralization shall begin to compress and shape American politics;—

Then the Democracy of the North will sit in sackcloth and ashes, and remember how they deserted to the enemy on November 2.

Friday, November 5, 1880
GLADNESS IN THE GRANITE BUILDING†

Great joy exists in the Granite Building.
    Great guns, three hundred and twenty-nine,
Roared out through their idiotic mouths
    The sulphurous and noisy sign.

Touched off they were by the brave Sambola.
    Their mystic number indorsed a fraud;
But they who expect the loaves and fishes
    Must always, right or wrong, applaud.

"So much per gun," quoth the brave Sambola.
    "We'll give it thee," quoth the grinning three,
"And if we'd music, we still would troll a
    High *tol de rol* for the victory."

Then off they went to the old San Carlos,
    And drank a basket of Roderer;
Though one or two of the colored brothers
    Said they would whisky straight prefer.

As they got tight their tongues were loosened,
    And each one told how he'd feather his nest,
And how he'd crush out the opposition,
    While he clasped Pitt Kellogg to his breast.

Oh! they had a jolly time—these fellows!—
    But they poured their ban on the Beattie crowd,
And again they hugged, and each to the other
    Said: "O, kind sir, you do me proud!"

Saturday, November 6, 1880
FRENCH OPERA+

Toilets, perfumes, opera-glasses, librettoes, oysters and wine, refreshments, and many other things.

Greatly rejoiced are those who deal in all those pretty things which add to the beauty of women under the gaslight.

Also those who fortify the stomach with good things late in the night and early in the morning.

Also the vendors of music.

Likewise the dealers in kid gloves.

Furthermore the owners of hacks and carriages.

Thus doth opera cause money to circulate and purses to grow fat.

Sunday, November 7, 1880
THE SHOOTING SEASON

Now there are Nimrods among us who go forth occasionally to shoot.

They are excellently provided with ammunition.

Ammunition for their own stomachs as well as for the stomachs of the wild beasts and birds.

So that sometimes they shoot themselves with their own ammunition instead of shooting the birds of the air and the beasts of the field with that ammunition which should be kept dry.

So that the birds of the air and the beasts of the field do mock them, even as above represented.

And they return home with much sorrow and empty game-bags and empty bottles.

Monday, November 8, 1880
THAT PIANO ORGAN

The Man with the Piano Organ is the new sensation.

In the French quarter the multitude of children, servants, and people of all descriptions who throng about the organ is astonishing to behold.

They are more attracted, perhaps, by the puppets who move inside a glass house to the sound of the music than by the music itself.

The man with the Piano Organ has a pretty little wife who travels about with him, and who speaks Italian, French, and German with equal facility.

And they seem to be more or less of philosophers, these strangers, possessing a serious aspect while all about them are laughing at the puppets,—unconscious that they themselves are after all but puppets on a larger scale, who dance to the music of all the passion and follies and hopes which agitate mankind.

Unconscious that the little puppets within the glass house are but silent mockeries of the large puppets outside.

Unconscious that the organ-player compels them to behold a satire upon themselves, and makes them also pay to see it.

And the lesson was well worth paying for, if it were properly appreciated.

Tuesday, November 9, 1880
UNE PREMIÈRE DANSEUSE

Signorina Augusta La Belle, whose portrait we offer to our readers, a *première danseuse* of the French Opera, is a native of Rome, and was educated in the great school of Milan, La Scala. She made her first debut in the ballet at fifteen years of age, and although still very young has made a brilliant reputation in many European capitals. In Italy, Austria, Germany, Poland, Russia, and Mexico she created enthusiasm by her grace and skill.

She is, moreover, remarkably versatile in her art; being familiar with the national dances of many of the countries she has visited. At the Teatro Nacional in Mexico she created a furore when she executed some of those Spanish dances which will always be popular wherever beauty charms or grace fascinates. Mexican poets wrote verses in her honor; and romantic editors spoke of her, to use their own terms, "*como los mahometanos de las huries de Paraise.*"

No doubt she will soon be as great a favorite in New Orleans,—which she now visits for the first time,—as she has been at Warsaw, Kief, Dresden, and elsewhere.

La Bella is worthy of her name;—she is slender, *svelte,* graceful, and possesses a very characteristic face, with a remarkable pair of Italian eyes.

Madame Emilie Ambre.

Wednesday, November 10, 1880
THE FRENCH OPERA

Madame Ambre made her first appearance last evening as Violetta; and at once captivated the public. She has a rich and powerful voice, admirably trained, and of remarkable compass. Her Violetta was a superb lyrical effort and a perfect piece of passionate acting. The cast being almost entirely different enabled the audience to judge of the admirable resources of this splendid company.

The audience appeared to be at once surprised and delighted with Madame Ambre. The applause frequently broke out, as if involuntarily, even in the midst of musical passages of striking beauty,—but was almost as suddenly checked. Such interruptions are by no means to the credit of those who make them, generally speaking; but last evening they were evidently due to the unexpected delight caused by Madame Ambre's remarkable vocalization. At the close of the performance the gifted soprano was repeatedly called before the curtain. Madame Ambre has a comely face and a beautiful figure, and a more attractive Violetta than there has perhaps ever been seen in New Orleans.

Madame Ambre is an Algerian; having been born at Oran in 1854. Perhaps some may find in this fact the explanation of that tropical grace which characterizes her. At Paris, London, and Brussels her successes were splendid; and it was in *Violetta* that she won her great triumph in the French capital. Her repertoire includes fifteen of the greatest operas.

Mdlle. La Bella and the ballet-corps charmed the audience with a novel and supremely graceful Spanish dance,—*La Danse des Matadores*. This charming exhibition must, however, be seen to be appreciated. A mere description would not enable our readers to realize what the dance is.

The preliminary performance, a pretty little comedy entitled *Les Sonnettes*, was rendered with capital spirit, and kept the audience merry throughout. To-night the dramatic artists of the company will perform Dumas' famous *L'Etrangère*.

Thursday, November 11, 1880
RECOLLECTIONS OF THE THEATRICAL SEASON⁺

This shows why some people can not get a good view of the stage.

When one wants to look at a pretty dancer for example, and the intervening headdress persistently bobs backward and forward and shuts off the whole charming spectacle, one can not help wishing that it were required that women, as well as men, should doff their hats in presence of the stage.

Friday, November 12, 1880
DISSATISFIED

One of that Type of people who are not at all pleased to learn that Judge Miltenberger will continue to be Recorder of the Lower Districts.

Jourdan

Saturday, November 13, 1880
THE FRENCH OPERA HOUSE

M. Jourdan, the basso of the French Opera Company, who figured as "Bertram" in *Robert le diable,* is a native of Marseilles. He is an accomplished gentleman and a fine lyric artist. Jourdan has not only a rich and admirably trained voice, but great power as an actor. To-night he will appear as "Balthazar" in *La Favorite.*

Sunday, November 14, 1880
THOSE FURNITURE MEN

Now is the winter of our discontent,—
    When people move in order to be more comfortable during the winter,
    And are obliged to call upon the furniture men,
    Who smash and crash and sliver things around,
So that a set of furniture worth $500 before being moved is worth about $200 on arriving at its destination;—
So that a bedroom set which might have been before insured for $250 would afterward only be insured for $100.
So that one must deliver up half his earthly goods and possessions for the privilege of moving them.
And three moves are worse than a fire.

Mauge

Monday, November 15, 1880
THE FRENCH OPERA HOUSE

There was a good attendance at the Opera House last evening in spite of the weather. It looks as though the public were waking up to an appreciation of the treat which Mr. De Beauplan has brought us.

    The performance of *Les Deux Orphelinée* was in every respect a master-piece of acting throughout;—so much so that the best renditions of the translated drama as given by English companies, seemed colorless and lifeless by comparison. It is to be hoped that the play will be repeated; for those who were prevented by the weather from witnessing it last evening missed a remarkably fine spectacle. The audience was fully alive to the merit of the performance; and the company could not complain that the applause was not warm or frequent.

We present readers with a portrait of M. Frederic Mauge, baritone of comic opera, who has already appeared in *La Traviata*. He is a native of Liege, and a pupil of the great Solomon. In Europe he has had much success.

Tuesday, November 16, 1880
THE BONE OF CONTENTION[+]

N.B.—The poor bone does not contain much nutritive substance; but it will contain less after the battle.

Wednesday, November 17, 1880
THE FRENCH OPERA HOUSE

Enrico Utto, the splendid baritone of the French Opera Company, is a Parisian by birth, but received his musical training, we believe, in Italy. He is well known in Europe, and has won brilliant triumphs with the fastidious public of Toulouse,—the city which has produced so many famous singers.

Utto has a fine massive head, and makes a splendid appearance on the stage. He is one of the handsomest European baritones who ever visited the United States. Last evening his impersonation of the Count de Luna in *La Trouvère* was something superb. He is an actor of uncommon power as well as a singer of rare merit.

The *première danseuses* treated the public to something very novel and pretty. Mdlles. La Bella and Gossi—the latter dressed as a boy—danced the Sevillana with a grace which brought down the house. The Spanish music was very pleasing; and the rhythm of the dancers' movements faultless. Mdlle. Hennecart's Gipsy dance was also a surprising display of grace, agility, and the poetry of motion.

There will be no performance to-night; but one of the most coquettish and amusing of comic operas,—*Les Dragons de Villars,*—will be given at the matinee with Madame Ambre in the leading role.

To-morrow evening, *Robert Le Diable*.

Gossi.

Thursday, November 18, 1880
THE FRENCH OPERA

We present our readers to-day with a portrait of one of the graceful *danseuses* whose performers have been so well received by the public. Mdlle. Gossi is an Italian, and educated for the profession at Termin, where she also made her debut. At Milan and other Italian cities she won triumphs. She had also much success in South America, and especially at Buenos Ayres.

Friday, November 19, 1880
THE PELICAN'S GHOST[+]

There used to be a Pelican in the neighborhood of Jackson Square.

We used to attach considerable interest to that bird. It seemed to us like one of the sacred geese at the Capitol must have seemed to the old Romans. The destiny of the city seemed somehow connected with it. It enjoyed universal respect. Even the wicked little Creole boys refrained from tormenting it. Yet one day it mysteriously disappeared.

We never knew whom it belonged to, and never discovered exactly what had become of it. A friend hinted that it was really a sort of guardian genius, and had left the State in disgust, owing to the corruption of politics.

But it would seem that it simply went the way of all flesh; for an aged man who haunts the Passage de Saint-Antoine declares that he sees its ghost sometimes of clear nights, perched upon the head of Gen. Jackson. He knows it is a ghost, because the stars shine through it.

And the bird says—according to the ancient—something to the following effect, shortly before the midnight hour:—

"I was a Symbol. I am still a Symbol in my ghostliness. I betoken the old-fashioned life of the Pelican State that is passing away. I represent the quaintness that is dying out, and the antiquated thing that shall soon become as ghostly as myself. The old city is becoming Americanized; and I am glad that I am dead."

Saturday, November 20, 1880
SOMETHING TO BE PROUD OF[+]

The New Orleans "banquettes" are famous. We therefore give a view of some of the beauties they exhibit at the present time.

Sunday, November 21, 1880
THANKSGIVING

The austere and philosophic *pater familias* goeth early in the morning to the market and buyeth a turkey at a just price, and returneth therewith to the bosom of his family.

But the roystering man goeth early to the grocery where a turkey is to be raffled,—at ten cents per chance.

He buyeth his chance and winneth the turkey, which having cost only $1 hath already brought the landlord $10,—the which is a profit of 1000 per cent, without counting the expenditure for alcoholic liquors involved thereby.

Then the winner treats the crowd. One dollar and sixty cents!
Then the landlord treats.
Then the "right bower" of the man that won the turkey treats.
Then the "left bower" also treats.
Then the landlord proposes to throw for the drinks. He loses.
Then the man who won the turkey treats again—$3.20.
Then everybody gets happy. From happy they become outrageously merry. And it is after midday.
They play cards and sing and drink a great deal; and the heart of the landlord is rejoiced.
Evening cometh; but the wife of the man who won the turkey vainly waiteth at the door,—

Until the midnight hour has arrived, and Thanksgiving Day has passed away.

And early in the morning—the man who won the turkey comes home.

And for three days after he lieth in bed, cursing himself and the turkey and the landlord and the whole world, and wondering if his stomach will ever get well again.

Monday, November 22, 1880
BRITISH RECOLLECTIONS OF NEW ORLEANS

The crew of the British bark *Modern* will probably retain *tenderer* recollections than of any other port at which they ever laid up,—or at which they were ever laid up.

Tuesday, November 23, 1880
THE MAN SOCIALLY LOVED+

The latest plan for collecting internal revenue at Lake Providence.

Wednesday, November 24, 1880
CURIOUS!

He does not know what it is. And he wonders exceedingly.

It is much better that he should not know what it is.

Were he to understand the real gravity of his situation he would not become fat.

The fear of coming events would harrow up his feelings and destroy his appetite; and the toughness of his being would seriously trouble our digestion.

There is a little moral in this Thanksgiving picture; but our intelligent readers can find it for themselves.

Thursday, November 25, 1880
AN ARTFUL DODGER

Old Man—"How are you, sir (to perfect stranger who has never seen him before)? I am getting old. Eighty-nine years of age! I want to see my brother, who lives in the Third District. It is too long a walk for my poor old bones. Can you let me have five cents?"

Stranger, who has heard of that dodge before, through reading the *City Item*—"Awfully sorry, but I have not really got any change."

Old Man—"There's a grocery at the corner; could you not get change there?"

Stranger—"Unfortunately, I have not got anything to change; but if I had I would be only too happy to—"

Old man turns his back in disgust, and refuses to hear explanations.

This dodge is getting to be quite common in the Second District. There are several who practice it quite successfully. As they are well dressed they often impose on people; and sometimes make two or three dollars a day. This they spend largely at the groceries. They speak several languages; but generally address their victims in French. Sometimes they forget themselves and address the same person twice. When taxed with this they straighten up, and declare themselves grossly insulted.

Friday, November 26, 1880
AFTER THANKSGIVING

How the turkey revengeth himself upon his murderers on Thanksgiving Night.

Saturday, November 27, 1880
OUR MODEL POLICE FORCE

"I was nearly shot in the back last night," remarked Aid David Hennessey yesterday evening in the detectives' room, at the central station, in the presence of Capt. Malone and the *Item* reporter.

A New Method of Keeping the Peace.

The scribe at once importuned the aid to relate the particulars of the occurrence.

"Well, you see, one fellow had his gun out and ran behind me before I knew it, but Gaster dropped on him."

"Where was it and who were they, Dave?"

"It was down the street some way," evasively answered the aid.

The *Item* reporter was not satisfied with the aid's answers and proceeded to investigate the case, and very soon dropped upon the cause of the evasive replies. It had been a policemen's row, and if there is one thing that a policeman religiously knows how to do, it is not to "give away" a brother officer to a reporter.

This little disturbance, which will not serve to elevate the moral character of the force, was about the most disgraceful that has ever occurred, and what is more, was enacted in that *crème de la crème* of precincts (the third), and opposite one of those Dauphine street saloons principally patronized by prostitutes.

The two model peelers are named Ducoing and Pellissier. They used their clubs, and Pellissier had his pistol drawn and would have fired but for Aid Gaster. The appearance of the aids put a stop to the row, to the disgust of many who had assembled to witness a duel to the death.

Charges have been preferred against these officers; but how much better it would have been had they both been arrested and charged with fighting and disturbing the peace, which they certainly were doing.

Sunday, November 28, 1880
"OFT IN THE STILLY NIGHT," ETC.+

These black and dismal nights recall the Plague of Egyptian darkness.

How many catastrophes have not occurred during the past week in unilluminated backyards.

Where those vile enemies of mankind, the wheelbarrow, the step-ladder, and the water-bucket lie in wait for the unwary,—

And where half-open doors and windows prepare to bump his nose and to blacken his eyes,—

So that he uttered words which are not in accordance with Christian teachings.

N.B.—*The flashes of lightning in the cut indicate the bursts of profanity in which the victim finds himself compelled to indulge. Also the "stars" which he sees while the step-ladder and wheelbarrow are getting their work in.*

Monday, November 29, 1880
UGH!!+

It is no use denying it. Whether owing partly to the rain or partly to negligence on the part of the city authorities, or partly to both, the streets of New Orleans are disgustingly dirty and horribly dilapidated. There are mudholes in nearly every thoroughfare, pitfalls in nearly every sidewalk, broken places over drains where there is danger of breaking one's leg, loosened bricks, and dandy-traps innumerable. The nuisance of garbage and rubbish is horribly accumulating. The street cleaners seldom make their appearance. Everything is soggy, slimy, slippery, filthy, and foul. The public are disgusted. We are disgusted. But until the weather changes, little can be done.

The public must now see that the only pavement capable of remaining solid and clean in such swampy weather is the square block pavement for the thoroughfares, and flagged pavements for the sidewalks. There is not a brick or boulder pavement in the city but has suffered from the rain.

Tuesday, November 30, 1880
THE FRENCH OPERA

Mr. Momas, Leader of the Orchestra.

The delightful little opera of *Rigoletto* was given last evening with Madame Ambre as "Gilda."

Tuesday, November 30, 1880
MORAL EDIFICATION+

How some of our guardians of the public peace and property do guard the city. Being a chapter from the records of the Police Board.

Wednesday, December 1, 1880
"WET ENOUGH FOR YOU?"+

The sun showed his face yesterday; and the people of New Orleans began to think that the world was coming to an end.

But even as they were trying to accustom their eyes to the light, it became dark again, and the floodgates of heaven were reopened.

So that people talked about rain-areas and barometers and colds and rheumatisms even worse than before.

Thursday, December 2, 1880
WEB-FOOTED

The above represents the physiological changes which will probably make themselves manifest in the pedal extremities of our people, if this weather continues. Nature adapts animals to their surroundings. Animals that inhabit swamps are web-footed. Let us prepare ourselves to become web-footed.

Friday, December 3, 1880
TAXES

Since brains are taxed, we respectfully submit to our legislators the above pictorial catalogue of objects that might be taxed also when "occasion requires."

Saturday, December 4, 1880
TANTALIZING+

The sun has made his appearance; but he couldn't fool us. We know perfectly well that he is going to hide himself again for an amazing length of time.

Sunday, December 5, 1880
OFFICERS OF THE LAW

How some of our constables serve writs of ejectment.

Monday, December 6, 1880
SIGNIFICANT PARAGRAPHS FROM THE PRESIDENT'S MESSAGE

Why the Country Needs a Captain-General?

Continued opposition to the full and free enjoyment of the rights of citizenship conferred upon the colored people by the recent amendments to the constitution still prevails in several of the late slave-holding States. . . .

Resistance to and nullification of the results of the war, will unite together in resolute purpose for their support all who maintain the authority of the government and the perpetuity of the Union, and who adequately appreciate the value of the victory achieved. . . .

I commend to the attention of Congress the great services of the Commander-in-Chief of our armies during the war for the Union, whose wise, firm, and patriotic conduct did so much to bring that momentous conflict to a close. The legislation of the United States contains many precedents for the recognition of distinguished military merit, authorizing rank and emoluments to be conferred for eminent services to the country. An act of Congress authorizing the appointment of a Captain General of the Army, with suitable provisions relating to compensation, retirement, and other details, would, in my judgment, be altogether fitting and proper, and would be warmly approved by the country.

Tuesday, December 7, 1880
WON'T WAIT TILL THE HOLIDAYS

The fire-cracker nuisance is becoming very annoying, and boys ought certainly to be prevented from indulging in it on the streets. There is plenty of room in backyards and other places to fire off crackers, without running the risk of frightening horses, and perhaps causing a death by a runaway.

Wednesday, December 8, 1880
A MILLER WHO COULDN'T MILL+

How a Sanitarian made it unhealthy for a bunkoman, and handled him without Kid gloves.

Thursday, December 9, 1880
THE SANITARY CONFERENCE

It is to be hoped that the fitful and fateful germ which plays will-o'-the-wisp to scientific pursuit may be finally seized and dissected and analyzed, so that we may be made somewhat wiser as to the origin of yellow fever than we were before.

Thursday, February 10, 1881
THE INUNDATIONS+

Mayor Shakspeare and His Relief Committee Doing Noble Work.

No Prospects of the Water Going Down for Some Days.

It is an ill wind that blows nobody good. The negroes that play the part of St. Christopher, and the boatmen that charge two dollars to ferry people a square or two, and the urchins who catch the fish that come up in shoals with the flood, do not complain. They will be sorry when the flood subsides.

It would be well, however, that the city itself provide against extortion in such matters for the future. If there be a law regulating hack-rates, there ought to be some regulation also regarding boat fares. People on the verge of starvation have been made victims of shameful extortion.

The relief committee, after having been out all day, assembled at the Mayor's parlor last night. The reports from all the districts showed that the suffering was terrible. It was decided that the provisions be brought to the needy.

The Sanitary Association have tendered their services, and will act in concert with the relief committee. Dr. J. F. Payne, of the association, has tendered his services. Generals Glynn and Reichard have tendered the use of the men of their brigades, which was accepted.

After the meeting, the Mayor issued the following proclamation:

PROCLAMATION TO THE PEOPLE OF THE CITY OF NEW ORLEANS.
The pecuniary necessities of a large number of the people of our city are such as call for prompt and liberal response from our fellow-citizens. The worst effects of the inundation are yet to come, and it is now an urgent matter requiring that the public should render all possible relief as early as practicable. Starvation stares many of our citizens in the face, and all are called upon to contribute to a cause so deserving.

JOSEPH A. SHAKSPEARE, Mayor.

NOTES ON COLUMNS

THE HAUNTED AND THE HAUNTERS

The titular source of "The Haunted and The Haunters" is a story by Edward Bulwer-Lytton. Hearn also borrowed from his own exposé "Balm of Gilead," which he wrote years earlier for the *Cincinnati Commercial*. However, the purpose of this piece and Hearn's other editorials on correctional institutions was to advocate prison reform. The campaign was partially successful: Hearn's editorials precipitated a Grand Jury investigation of conditions in Orleans Parish Prison and the founding in 1881 of the Board of Prisons and Asylums, whose members included George Washington Cable.

The Grand Jury reported the prison was indeed infested with bats, causing the air to be "vitiated, pregnant with noxious gases and, of course highly prejudicial to health" and recommended daily removal of the guano. The *City Item*'s continuous drumming on the issue also persuaded health inspector Dr. Mandeville to bring up the bat nuisance during August's meeting of the Board of Health, which decided against eradication, due to a belief the bats protected against yellow fever. The board's prescience was remarkable, as it was more than a decade later that scientists concluded that the disease is caused by a virus spread by the bite of the *Aëdes aegypti* mosquito. The Parish Prison was located in a poorly drained area of the city, which bred mosquitoes—a steady food source for the bats. After a new prison was built in 1892, the prison compound was abandoned and in 1895 was demolished.

Sources: "Balm of Gilead," *Cincinnati Commercial,* October 3, 1875; Hearn, "Penitentiaries and Punishments," *City Item,* February 17, 1880 (collected in *Editorials*); "The Prison and Asylum Commission," *City Item,* November 6, 1881; *City Item,* August 1 and 27, 1880; Jackson, *New Orleans in the Gilded Age,* 242.

FREE BOARD AND LODGING FOR THIEVES

Hearn used the same woodcut for this column, which was published on June 3 and a counterpoint to "The Haunted and The Haunters" above. (He also repeated several other woodcuts; the image always appeared on an inside page the second time it was used.)

Prison labor in Louisiana has a long history of controversy. In 1880 the *City Item* insisted prisoners would work on projects otherwise neglected by a city virtually bankrupt, unable to pay its teachers and police. "In a moral point of view the enforcement of hard labor as a penalty for those offenses which are usually punished by incarceration in this hideous building, would have an excellent effect. Loafers dread hard labor for a week more than they dread imprisonment for a month. A committal to the Parish Prison has been regarded by many of them as a sort of vacation—a term of free board and lodging." Later Orleans Parish Prison inmates were used as a labor force by the city, but the legality of the practice was challenged in court, resulting in a policy change: only volunteers among the prison population could be assigned work duty.

Sources: Hearn, "The Parish Prison and Dr. Jones," *City Item,* September 5, 1880; Jackson, *New Orleans in the Gilded Age,* 243. For a history of prison labor in Louisiana, see Mark T. Carleton, *Politics and Punishment: The History of the Louisiana State Penal System* (Baton Rouge, 1971).

THE DELIVERING ANGEL

Depicted here is Lt. Gov. Samuel D. McEnery, at the time acting governor due to the serious illness (tuberculosis) of Gov. Louis A. Wiltz. Wiltz had been criticized for pardoning several convicts serving time in the state penitentiary, but McEnery nonetheless pardoned more, for which he was ridiculed. An editorial of a *City Item* contemporary stated that "at this time the voice of mercy for criminals should not be raised or heeded in this city. With a disorganized police and a town full of lawless and daring characters, the law should deal with the utmost vigor with the criminals who are in its grasp."

The ten whose sentences were pardoned or commuted by Wiltz and McEnery included a murderer, a rapist, a grand-larcenist, and a forger. In "Condoning Crime," Hearn highlighted the serial forger who, having also been pardoned by a previous governor, had obvious political influence. "In some respects the Lieutenant Governor's mental vision may have been blinded—political dust thrown into it; but on the whole we believe that in making himself the friend of convicts he has made himself the enemy of the decent portion of the community. Pardons should only be granted in cases where the full severity of the law has really not been deserved by the condemned, or when some unfortunate error in a trial has resulted in the conviction of an innocent man." McEnery, an attorney, defended his pardons and commutations, claiming he was obligated by Article 66 of the state constitution to issue pardons when recommended by at least two of the attorney general, lieutenant governor, and presiding judge. It was widely believed that such actions undermined the criminal justice system, emboldened criminals, and contributed to a trend of vigilantism.

Public criticism of McEnery for being soft on crime was not enough to damage him politically in the long run. He succeeded Wiltz after his death in October 1881 and ran as the incumbent in the subsequent gubernatorial race. He was, however, replaced in 1887 by Francis R. T. Nicholls, who appointed McEnery judge on the state Supreme Court, where he served twelve years.

Sources: "Pardoning Board," *Daily States,* May 29, 1880; *City Item,* August 4, 1880; Hearn, "Condoning Crime," *City Item,* May 24, 1880; *City Item,* May 19, 1880; Dawson, *The Louisiana Governors,* 182–86.

THE IDEAL COMMISSIONER

Making up the Board of Commissioners of the Crescent City police were the mayor and administrator of police, both of whom served as ex-officio members, and four mayor-appointed members who served staggered one-year terms. In response to the *City Item*'s criticisms, Commissioner Byrne claimed that "the innate defects of the system . . . [were] responsible for all the wrongs done." The paper was unconvinced, for Hearn targeted Byrne in this satire that ran alongside the latter's defense.

This burlesque is the first of many satires on the Crescent City police. In April 1880, a police officer attacked *City Item* police reporter Harry Michel when he was investigating a story on police brutality. The paper responded by declaring war on the police department.

Sources: "Wayside Notes," *City Item,* May 26, 1880; "Police Ruffianism," *City Item,* April 25, 1880.

THE OPIUM VICE

A contemporary newspaper reported that between 1879 and 1880 the volume of illegal opium and opium extracts imported into the United States had more than doubled—

from 147,489 pounds (valued at $554,834) to 296,617 pounds ($1,485,141)—and that the opium habit was "100 times more demoralizing and enervating than the alcoholic habit."

The previous day, the *City Item* described an opium den on Dauphine near Customhouse Street. While acknowledging the argument that "both gambling and prostitution are necessary evils," the editorial stated that "opium smoking is not a necessary evil for this community and can be prevented." California legislation prohibited Caucasians from entering Chinese opium dens, and New Orleans' city council should follow suit, the paper argued. If it was impossible to prevent citizens from smoking opium, Chinese residents of New Orleans should be prohibited from opening their dens to white visitors, and no Chinese keeping a laundry or restaurant should be allowed to use rooms for opium smoking.

The sanitary organization alluded to in Hearn's illustrated column is the Auxiliary Sanitary Association (A.S.A.), a private-citizens group founded in 1879 primarily to address drainage, whose neglect by the Department of Improvements was believed to be a cause of the city's yellow fever epidemics. The A.S.A. also funded "nuisance boats," which carried the city's garbage downriver and dumped it midstream. The State Board of Health had jurisdiction over health matters in New Orleans and conducted inspections of dwellings within the city.

Sources: New Orleans Times, November 21, 1880; "Wayside Notes," *City Item,* May 27, 1880; Waring and Cable, *History and Present Condition of New Orleans,* 289, 283.

FRANK J. MUMFORD

Mumford was celebrated as the rowing champion of the South in the 1870s and 1880s, and a national sports magazine also called him "the finest oarsman who has ever pulled" in the competitions of the National Association of Amateur Oarsmen. He won the single-scull championship of the Mississippi Valley Rowing Association twice, and in 1880 he not only successfully defended his 1879 title as Champion Amateur Sculler of America but finished the course in record time.

Initially, New Orleans rowing was, like yachting, a sport of the upper class, but laborers found they could make the sport more accessible by pooling funds to purchase boats and equipment. Numerous organizations were founded during the 1870s, including the Orleans Rowing Club, by cotton press workers; the Riverside Club, by metal foundry workers; and the Hope and Perseverance Clubs, by firemen. The motto of the Perseverance No. 13 fire station, established in 1837, was "Rough and Ready." Mumford was a fireman and cotton weigher.

Source: Dale Somers, *The Rise of Sports in New Orleans,* 151–57, 219, 225, 230–31.

MUMFORD OF OURS

This column, headed by the same woodcut printed with "Frank J. Mumford," was published on July 10, 1880. On a Friday evening less than two weeks later, a large group of New Orleanians, including a military band, greeted Mumford's arrival by train. The procession meandered from the station through the main streets, stopping to serenade the newspaper offices and the households of the hero and Captain Fitzpatrick, of the Perseverance fire station. It ended at the Perseverance boathouse, located on the Old Basin Canal, where the Magnolia Bridge was decorated with flowers, bunting, Chinese lanterns, and a transparent banner welcoming home "Our Champion."

In the weeks following, the celebratory atmosphere was clouded by questions raised by the National Association of Amateur Oarsmen over Mumford's amateur status, and he was suspended from competitions until his exoneration the following year. Several years later he was again suspended for four years. Sadly, while training for the national competition of 1900, the robust athlete and fireman contracted a fatal case of pneumonia; he died at the age of forty-three. His legacy, however, continued for years: in three of the next six races, his protégé C. S. Titus won the national single-scull championship, thereby inheriting the title Champion Amateur Sculler of America.

Frank Mumford may have been a close relation of William B. Mumford, who was hanged in 1862, during the Civil War, on the order of Benjamin Butler (for which he earned the name "Beast Butler") for tearing the U.S. flag from the top of the U.S. Mint and ripping it to pieces following New Orleans' capture by the Union.

Sources: States, July 24, 1880; Somers, The Rise of Sports in New Orleans, 153, 156; Dawson, Army Generals, 149–52.

THIS WAY? OR THIS?

In New Orleans in 1880, adversaries of all classes occasionally still resorted to the illegal *duello*, which by that year was more akin to wild frontier anarchy than to the earlier custom that had observed gentlemanly protocol.

The duel alluded to here was between William Rafferty and James Eagan, rivals for the affections of a fickle young resident of Tchoupitoulas Street who refused to choose between her two suitors. The delay in choosing weapons—pistols or knives?—added to public suspense as rumor raced through the city about a duel to take place at Tiger's Park (at the corner of Thalia and New Levee Streets) at nine o'clock on Sunday morning. The duelists had chosen their seconds (John Daly for Rafferty and Dave Shannon for Eagan), who sent out an agent to reconnoiter the dueling place. However, the Crescent City police department, not excluded from the rumor mill, had a squad waiting to arrest the entire crowd. When the principals and their friends learned that the police had already arrived, they decided instead on Orange Grove of Upper City Park. Due to effective police intelligence, a telegram was sent on the police wire about the change of venue so another squad could be dispatched in time to intervene.

Meanwhile, the dueling party decided on a third site and stopped on the way to City Park at Delachaise Green (near the Louisiana ice works). "There a crowd soon formed a ring, and James Moore, the referee, called 'time.' Rafferty and Eagan came smilingly up to the scratch and took up their respective positions." The weapons decided on were neither guns nor knives but (wisely) bare fists. After two rounds, Rafferty conceded the fight to Eagan, whom he told to "take the girl." A policeman arrived after the battle, but since no one was willing to provide any information, no arrests were made.

Source: Account from the *Daily Picayune*, May 31, 1880. Edward Larocque Tinker in *Lafcadio Hearn's American Days*, 89, attributed the inspiration for Hearn's cartoon "This Way? Or This?" to a duel between the *City Item*'s editor-in-chief Mark Bigney and Henry J. Hearsey, then editor of the *Democrat*. However, the altercation between these two had occurred two years earlier; see Wilds, *Afternoon Story*, 8–9.

DOG DAYS

A city ordinance of 1856 empowered police to distribute poisoned sausage to dogs running at large within the city limits. A local law providing for the licensing of dogs and impounding strays—none addressed feral cats—did not go into effect until September 1879. Even then it was not enforced; nor were there city funds to maintain pounds effectively. Therefore, strychnine was still used for animal control, especially for rabid dogs. During 1880, hydrophobia was the cause of several human deaths.

Source: Ord. 6140, in Jewell, *Jewell's Digest*, rev. ed., 531–32.

POLICE BOARD

According to a literary sketch by Hearn, police were hard to find after dark.

> It was midnight—not the dark, damp, rainy night when the wind howls and flashes of lightning make the gas lamps look sick; but a clear, cool night with a brilliant moon and a soft wind from the south fanning the tired denizen of the pleasant city to sleep.
>
> "What is up?" asks a white robed figure.
>
> "The whole neighborhood," comes back from one of the tall white houses.
>
> "Are you a policeman?" from a female voice; "for if you are, that man over there is killing that woman."
>
> "No, I am not a policeman, but what woman is getting killed?"
>
> No answer came back, but the sound of many windows, as they descended with a crash, could be heard, and it was evident that in the absence of the police the white figures would not get outside of their castles to prevent "that man," as the white figure called him, from killing the woman.
>
> But where was the policeman? Patrolling his seven thousand square miles down by the Barracks.

In 1880 the patrolman of the Crescent City police was responsible for the purchase of his uniform and whistle; the city furnished only his club. He was paid only fifty dollars a month (compared to the chief of police at $290, the chief of aids $150, and aids $100), and he, as well as public school teachers and other city employees, had been receiving, in the place of paychecks, certificates of indebtedness, which often had to be cashed by a broker, who kept a sizeable percentage. This state of affairs contributed to low morale and discouraged the recruitment of more conscientious men to the force. But these adverse conditions did not quiet cries from the press for reform. "If we cannot have a thoroughly good police," said the *Picayune*, "at least we should be saved from a thoroughly bad one; and we can be saved from a thoroughly bad one only by a process of purification."

Source: Hearn, "Midnight in New Orleans," *City Item*, August 1, 1880.

THE DEVIL ON CARONDELET STREET

Because of city officials' mismanagement of finances, funds were unavailable to run the city and pay bondholders, who were in favor of raising the necessary funds to pay bond indebtedness with new taxes. But opponents claimed the law did not allow taxation over ten mills. Ultimately, the matter had to be settled by the State Supreme Court, who announced on this day a decision that was to the advantage of bondholders and brokers.

THE OARSMEN

The St. John Rowing Club was one of the most prominent and long-lived rowing organizations of New Orleans. Rowing had been a popular competitive sport in eastern cities since the late eighteenth century, but the first rowing team was not formed in New Orleans until about 1838. One of the eight boat clubs in existence several years later hosted the city's first regatta. The popularity of rowing among New Orleanians doubtless would have increased over the next decades, but a flood in 1844 destroyed the boathouses and racing boats, discouraging organized rowing for the next fifteen years, and the Civil War preempted further activity until after 1865. The St. John Rowing Club led a revival of the sport in 1872, when it and the Pelican Club built boathouses on Bayou St. John and began hosting regattas. Within two years a dozen clubs had sprung up, and by the end of the century thirty had been organized (although not all survived).

Races attracted large crowds of spectators, especially to watch state championship races. In 1885, the St. John Rowing Club built an elaborate grandstand that seated five thousand spectators and featured a bar and poolroom. But the public preferred local and state championship races to intersectional competitions, and when an ambitious regatta of the latter sort ended in financial loss, the grandstand deteriorated as public interest turned to baseball and other attractions. By the turn of the century, rowing had again become, much like yachting, a leisure sport exclusively for the well-to-do New Orleanian.

Source: Somers, *The Rise of Sports in New Orleans,* 46–47.

EXTHRACT FROM THE SPACH OV PADDY WHACK

An Irish reader wrote to the *City Item* to complain about this sketch, which the editor defended while praising the many Irish contributions to the city.

THE TROPICAL PALM

Hearn had also written about Thomas Bailey Aldrich's story "Père Antoine's Date-Palm" in a *Cincinnati Enquirer* article of 1873 and an 1877 dispatch to the *Cincinnati Commercial.* The Creole historian Charles Gayarré recorded a legend, handed down to him from previous generations, about a mysterious Turk who had arrived in New Orleans. Said to have fled the Ottoman empire to escape justice for an offense against the emperor, who was his kin, he was found by compatriots, executed, and buried in a garden on Orleans Street. A marble tablet left at the grave was said to have been inscribed: "The justice of heaven is satisfied, and the date-tree shall grow on the traitor's tomb. The sublime Emperor of the faithful, the supporter of the faith, the omnipotent master and Sultan of the world, has redeemed his vow. God is great, and Mohammed is his prophet. Allah!"

Sources: See Hearn, "Marjorie Daw and Other People," in *Literary Essays;* "At the Gate of the Tropics," in Hearn, *Inventing New Orleans;* Gayarré, *History of Louisiana,* 1:386–89.

(AWAY, AWAY)

Light-draft passenger steamboats regularly plied Lake Pontchartrain to Mandeville on the north shore. Throughout the summer, daily newspaper advertisements gave the excursion schedule of the *New Camelia* (a U.S. mail steamer), which cruised between West End (in 1880 still often called "New Lake End") on the south shore and Mandeville, Old Landing, and Madisonville on the north, and on Wednesdays to Bay St. Louis.

Streetcars to West End left at regular intervals from the corner of Canal and Carondelet Streets. The last return left Old Landing at 8:00 P.M. Other steamboats running during the summer were the *Sunbeam,* the *Heroine,* and the *Ariel,* the latter of which ran between the south-shore lake resorts.

Source: Waring and Cable, *History and Present Condition of New Orleans,* 269. For a photograph of this popular side-wheel steamer, see Huber, *New Orleans,* 235.

THE SMILE THAT JOHNSON SMOLE

Since January 1880, New Orleans had been plagued by a series of mysterious ship fires. A sluggish police investigation prompted the Cotton Exchange to form an investigative committee. In April, the arrest of a tugboat worker in connection to a fire on the *Iron Cross* led to the unraveling of an insurance scam involving the notorious junk dealer Charles Johnson, who was confident he could bargain for a light sentence by naming other conspirators.

Commenting on Johnson's cavalier attitude, the *City Item* (probably Hearn) wrote, "If he smiled and smiled, it was not because he is a villain and utterly reckless, but because of the involvements of the case, and a refrain of the old Tyburn song that came into his head: 'Since laws were made for every degree, / To curb vice in others as well as in me, / 'Tis a wonder we hadn't better company / Upon Tyburn tree.'"

Source: "Wayside Notes," *City Item,* June 7, 1880.

CRUSHING OUT THE VIPERS

Roscoe Conkling led the Republican Party's "Old Guard," which favored giving the presidential nomination to Ulysses S. Grant, who had already served two consecutive terms (1869–77). James Abram Garfield was formerly an antislavery Ohio state senator, a major general in the Civil War, and a U.S. congressman. After the war, he supported a Radical Republican program for Reconstruction and played a role in the compromise agreement in the disputed election of 1876, in which Louisiana surrendered its pivotal electoral votes to grant Rutherford B. Hayes victory in exchange for concessions that included ending Reconstruction in Louisiana. "Satan Sherman" refers to the Union general William Tecumseh Sherman, whose brother was Treasury Secretary John Sherman, also a candidate for the Republican Party's presidential nomination. James Garfield was John Sherman's campaign manager but became the compromise candidate and won the nomination.

BOOM-BOOM

This woodcut appeared under two different headings, the second on August 29, after the christening in Luling of the notorious cannon of the Orleans Artillery, an event which Hearn covered in an article subtitled "Sambola's Little Gun Created Mischief but Gains Popularity." The party—including Capt. Anthony Sambola, the Fifth Regiment of the Orleans Artillery, the cannon, and Hearn—boarded a steamer at the foot of Canal Street.

> The christening ceremonies took place upon the plantation at two o'clock Sunday morning, and were opened by Capt. Sambola (after having nearly shattered every glass upon the *City of Augusta*).

Suffice it to say, that at thirty-five minutes past ten last night the good *City of Augusta* left Donaldsonville and at seven o'clock this morning arrived in the Crescent City; in the interim, men evidently dead although not wounded, covered the cabin floor; valor was pillowed upon the shoulder of beauty, and Sambola's mischievous gun broke one head light and knocked off a plank from the stern wheel. Selah!

Source: Hearn, *City Item,* August 28, 1880.

ILLUSTRATED LETTERS FROM THE PEOPLE (JUNE 24)

This is the first extant "Letters from the People," which may have been based on actual letters but appear to have been written by Hearn. A city ordinance of 1878 made it unlawful "to encumber or obstruct any of the streets, gutters, public roads, public grounds, pubic squares, public places or promenades, banquettes or sidewalks of the city by depositing . . . any box, bale, hogshead, barrel or any goods, wares or merchandise, or any article whatsoever, except for the necessary time of loading or unloading the same." Enforcement of existing city ordinances has remained a problem into the twenty-first century.

Source: Ord. 4797, in Jewell, *Jewell's Digest,* rev. ed., 339.

ILLUSTRATED LETTERS FROM THE PEOPLE: "BOOTS!"

The cry of an inn guest to summon the resident bootblack was "Boots!"

THE LAST OF TILDEN AND THE LAST OF GRANT

Samuel Jones Tilden, elected governor of New York in 1874, was in 1876 the Democratic presidential candidate running against Republican Rutherford B. Hayes. The race ended in a dispute similar to that between Al Gore and George W. Bush in 2000. Hayes was ultimately awarded the victory, and Tilden chose not to contest the outcome. Tilden was considered miserly by Southerners after contributing only five hundred dollars to a Memphis relief fund during a yellow fever epidemic.

Source: City Item, September 21, 1879.

THE UNSPEAKABLE VELOCIPEDE

The 1850s French invention of the velocipede, the high-wheeled bicycle said to be "every man's horse and every man's gymnasium," went relatively unnoticed in the United States until the 1860s, when the purchase of twenty-five velocipedes was considered for the New Orleans' fire companies. Several young men who invested in them gave indoor exhibitions and instruction sessions, making these occasions social events, complete with dances, in order to attract young women. Firemen, among the greatest enthusiasts, featured velocipede races at Sunday outings. But the metal wheels grinding over irregular surfaces like New Orleans' shell roads jarred the body and riders soon dubbed the machine the "boneshaker." Two decades later the British improved the design, using an enormous front wheel and a small rear one, and interest in cycling was renewed. When this "ordinary" was exhibited at the 1876 Centennial Exposition in Pennsylvania, it created a sensation that spread to New Orleans within four years.

In May 1880, the *Picayune* briefly mentioned in its sports column the popularity of bicycling in Britain and New England, where a National Bicycle League was to be organized.

Source: Somers, *The Rise of Sports in New Orleans,* 219–331.

THE BICYCLE FIEND'S DEFENSE

Published on July 21, this column is a counterpoint to the above piece and was illustrated by the same woodcut. The two-wheel contraptions appeared to quickly gain popularity in the city. In December 1880 issues of the *Democrat,* Fred N. Tayer (a store on Gravier Street, across from the St. Charles Hotel) advertised bicycles and velocipedes— "an elegant assortment especially adapted for Christmas Presents." In 1886, an ordinance was passed requiring bicycles ridden in city streets be equipped during the day with an alarm bell and at night with a light; another prohibited the riding of bicycles over (but not across) the banquette (sidewalk) of any street.

After his illustrated series ended, Hearn published an epilogue to these two pieces in which a boy on a velocipede collides with a "gigantic man" rolling a barrel: "'So you wouldn't get out of the way of it?' grimly observed the gigantic man. 'Ah, ha!—so you wouldn't get out of the way of it!' And the boy wept. And each of his tears was to us more precious than the balm of Gilead or the roses of Gulistan."

Sources: Ords. 1641, 1750, in Jewell, *Jewell's Digest,* rev. ed., 325–26, 329; *City Item,* January 18, 1881.

THE ORGAN GRINDER

Organ grinders of other cities were usually identified as Italian and associated with Italian fruit dealers and vendors. They were scorned and often satirized in journals as belonging to the same tribe of nuisances as beggars. Hearn's juxtaposition of "The Organ Grinder" with the professional beggar of the following day suggests a similar bias. But if he represented him as a species of beggar, Hearn's earlier tribute suggests the organ grinder deserved respect.

> And already is the music of *Carmen* flying abroad through the medium of the ubiquitous barrel-organ. Surely there is even room for philosophic meditation in the career of the organ-grinder. Viewed as an integer the organ-grinder may not seem important; but how vast a mission is that of the world-wandering and multitudinous guild of organ-grinders. To the millions of the poor who have never heard and never will hear the human music of an opera in their lives—to millions who know nothing of Verdi or Lecocq—to gamins playing in the fetid backalleys and courts of a thousand overpopulated cities—to myriads of weary laborers plodding homeward from the work that is begun with each succeeding morning—to the children of the poor in all parts of the civilized world—the barrel-organ teaches the melodies inspired by tragedies unheard of by the unlettered, and charms with French gaiety or mystic Italian melancholy souls that know nothing of France or Italy.

Hearn also mentions organ grinders in a literary sketch describing a charivari inflicted on a newlywed couple at their home near the Ninth Street Market, in which "all the available hand organs in the neighborhood were hired at an immense expense."

In other cities laws were passed to limit organ grinders' numbers through licensing and outright banning. Since 1867, it had been illegal to "make charivari" in New Orleans and to "beat a drum, or blow a horn, or sound a trumpet in any street or public place within the limits of the city," unless those instruments were part of a military band or other procession. In October 1880, the city council enacted an ordinance specifically targeting organ grinders, who "shall not pursue their vocation on the public streets or sidewalks before 9 o'clock, A.M., or after 10 o'clock, P.M." An 1886 ordinance prohibited the playing of musical instruments, including hand organs, on public streets or highways within a radius of three hundred feet of any church or place of public worship.

In New York organs were purchased by individuals who hired people to play them. These organ grinders, usually Italian and often itinerate, sometimes simultaneously peddled statuettes. Although Hearn alludes to Italians ("olivaceous complexioned"), his image appears to be of a black man. The 1880 census of New Orleans lists only a few organ grinders and includes French, German, and black or mulatto Louisianians as well as Italians. Those listed appear to have supported their families through their grinding, and none seem to have lived in squalid tenement houses like those described by observers of the residents of New York's Five Corners, although such places probably never appeared in census records.

The organ grinder has completely faded from the streets of New Orleans, but some current residents recall seeing an Italian organ grinder in the French Quarter as late as the mid-1940s.

Sources: Forester, *The Italian Emigration of Our Times*, 324–25; Hearn, "Concerning the Barrel Organ," *City Item*, January 20, 1879 (collected in *Literary Essays*); Hearn, "A Musical Compliment," *City Item*, July 2, 1880. See introduction for definition of *charivari*. For charivari and drums, see N.S. 427, Arts. 170, 172, in Jewell, *Jewell's Digest*, 340; for organ grinders on public streets, see A.S. 6677 (Oct. 1880), Arts. 166–67, in Jewell, *Jewell's Digest*, 339; for grinders and places of worship, see Ord. 1765, in Jewell, *Jewell's Digest*, rev. ed., 325. Tenth U.S. Census, 1880.

ILLUSTRATED LETTERS FROM THE PEOPLE: MY OFFICE IN MY HAT

In July 1880 the city council passed ordinances authorizing the Administrator of Commerce to "see and require that all produce, wares, goods and other articles landed on the wharves or levees by any vessel or other water-craft, shall be laid as near as possible to the paved part of the levee approaching the street, so that the bank of the river and wharves be neither obstructed nor encumbered thereby," and to confiscate goods that were not removed within forty-five hours after cargo was unloaded.

Source: A.S. 6572, Arts. 146–50, in Jewell, *Jewell's Digest*, rev. ed., 146–47.

HANCOCK AND ENGLISH

Winfield S. Hancock, a Union general who was engaged in the Battle of Gettysburg, was briefly commandant of the Federal Reconstruction government's Fifth Military District—Louisiana and Texas—and hence headquartered in New Orleans. A Democrat sympathetic with the conquered South, he won the favor of whites when he issued General Order No. 40, which reconfirmed some provisions of home rule and established a changed attitude of Reconstruction government in that district. He was given a standing ovation when he attended a performance at a New Orleans opera house.

William Hayden English was an Indiana lawyer who served in the U.S. House of Representatives from 1853 to 1861.

Source: Dawson, *Army Generals,* 69–70.

MORNING CALLS—VERY EARLY

Children without a father, children without a mother!
What do you do for money?
We'll go to the other side to find potatoes,
We'll go back to the bayou to fish for sunfish,
And that's what we'll do for money.

Children without a father, children without a mother,
What do you do for money?
We'll go into the woods to dig palmetto,
We'll sell the roots to scrub floors,
And that's what we'll do for money.

Children without a father, children without a mother,
What do you do for money?
To make tea we'll dig sassafras,
To make ink we'll bring pokeweed seeds,
And that's what we'll do for money.

Children without a father, children without a mother,
What do you do for money?
We'll go into the woods to gather cancos berries,
With our cages we'll catch birds,
And that's what we'll do for money.

Children without a father, children without a mother,
What do you do for money?
We'll go tonight to Miss Maroto's,
In St. Anne Street, we'll gamble at keno,
And that's what we'll do for money.
—translation by Tom Klingler

Source: Hearn's source for this song was probably George Washington Cable, who included it in his *Creoles and Cajuns: Stories of Old Louisiana.* It is included in Hall, *Africans in Colonial Louisiana,* 201.

THE GO-AT

The city council in 1881 passed ordinances declaring "goats running at large in the streets and other public places within the limits of the city" to be a nuisance and providing that roaming goats should be picked up and taken to a pound. However, fencing goats was problematic, and animal control ordinances were not well enforced. Many goats grazed in Assumption Square throughout the 1880s. In fact, a New Orleans newspaper regretted the moving of the Clay statue from its place at the intersection of Canal and St. Charles/Royal Streets to one of the "shabby goat-pastures we facetiously call 'squares.'"

Sources: A.S. 7045, Arts. 15–22 (May 1881), in Jewell, *Jewell's Digest,* rev. ed., 533–53; *Picayune,* December 29, 1880.

OAKLAND PARK SCENERY

George L. Bright, attorney and owner of Oakland Riding Park, "has, among other peculiarities, an intense horror of policemen. That certain recent events should have inspired such a fantasy may seem natural enough, but that this fantastic hatred for the police should assume the form of enmity to the whole police force and even to such of the public as desire to secure the services of policemen, certainly evidences an abnormal condition of mind. When we accuse Mr. Bright—God bless him! We bear him no ill will—of hatred to anything possessing the appearance of a policeman we do so upon logical grounds only."

A German organization held a picnic at the park, but the "roughs," knowing Bright did not allow policemen in the park, entered the park "armed cap-a-pie." Fighting broke out, and several policemen, despite the injunction against their presence, arrived to try to restore order and narrowly escaped with their lives. The German organization threatened to sue Bright for damages. Hearn suggests alternative action: "We would suggest that the bums and the b'hoys should monopolize Oakland Park themselves, where they can shoot and cut and kill and bite and gouge and swear and vomit as much as they please. After a few 'bum picnics' there would be fewer bums, and the community might be saved the trouble of organizing a vigilance committee." The question remained, however, as to Bright's legal right to prevent policemen from performing their duties or to make a public nuisance of his property.

The article "Forty Fights to a Dance," which describes a recent picnic held at the park, was published on an inside page several days later (July 12), accompanied by the same woodcut.

Source: Hearn, "The Oakland Park Farce," *City Item,* July 7, 1880.

CITIZEN-EXECUTIONER SHERMAN

A fight had taken place among the "country Republicans" and the "Customhouse magnates" over pledges for the presidential nomination. The former were for Grant; the latter were obligated to support their boss, Treasury Secretary John Sherman. P. B. S. Pinchback, who is possibly represented by the man in the guillotine, shifted his support to Grant.

Source: City Item, May 20, 1880.

ILLUSTRATED LETTERS FROM THE PEOPLE (JULY 12)

There were passed in 1879 ordinances addressing loitering in front of public places, including "any coffee house bar room or beer saloon," but a policeman was required to give a warning before making an arrest.

Source: A.S. 5046, in Jewell, *Jewell's Digest,* rev. ed., 486–89.

THE WOLFISH DOG

The male figure in this woodcut appears to be a self-portrait. The text is similar to a passage by Hearn in his satirical journal of his Cincinnati days, *Ye Giglampz:* "Persons desiring information regarding the condition of Constantinopolitan streets after dark, should take a midnight stroll in the east end of Cincinnati during the sultry season, armed with a heavy club, and observe the fierce loves and ruthless wars of the wolfish dogs, innumerable, that infest the quarter alluded to." Hearn may have reflected again on Constantinople after discovering the New Orleans street by that name.

Until 1879 there were few laws controlling the local dog population. In September 1879, ordinances were passed that provided for licensing dogs, impounding strays, and muzzling vicious dogs, but they were not well enforced. Six weeks earlier the *Picayune* had commented on the licensing of dogs. "New Orleans has now an ordinance requiring owners of dogs to pay licenses in order to retain the pet canines, but it does not seem as if the people were in great haste to enrich the city finances in this manner. One gentleman states that he has the paid assent of the city to his keeping three dogs; but when his neighbors allow their unlicensed prowlers to run at large, inciting his pets to riot, he does not see what benefit he derives by his contributing to the municipal treasury. He asks that the law be fully enforced or allowed to remain a dead letter."

Sources: Ye Giglampz 1, no. 5 (July 19, 1874), collected in Henry Farny and Lafcadio Hearn, *Ye Giglampz*; Ord. 6491, in Jewell, *Jewell's Digest*, rev. ed., 532–33; *Picayune*, May 30, 1880.

ILLUSTRATED LETTERS FROM THE PEOPLE: STREET CAR NUISANCES

Appearing the previous day was the article "Men and Mules," in which Hearn writes: "Perhaps it may seem a terrible thing to say,—but it is none the less true, that certain classes of workmen are worse treated than animals can be. Take for instance the lot of car drivers in most of our great cities, and especially, perhaps, in our own. They are really worse off than the mules they drive." The first street railways with "horse-cars" began in early 1835. It was not until 1893 that they began to be supplanted by electric cars.

Sources: City Item, July 15, 1880; Blain, *A Near Century,* 7, 15, 32–33.

ULTRA-CANAL

Ultra-Canal is the name the French newspaper *L'Abeille* gave to a neighborhood of the Irish Canal section of the city.

Source: A typographical error occurred in Hutson, ed., *Creole Sketches*; the title was incorrectly printed as "An Ultra-Canal Talk," rather than "Tale."

DR. TANNER (JULY 18)

Most of Hearn's reflections on the Tanner sensation were satiric, but several days before this first illustrated column on the fanatical doctor, Hearn wrote in "The American Yoghi": "It has been claimed by some that the experiment of Tanner has a scientific value. This is a mistake. The power of man to live without food or water has been thoroughly tested; and even if the experiment in this case should prove successful, and that the doctor should be able to live without eating or drinking for forty days, he will not have

accomplished anything new, or have even arrived at the point of endurance possessed by the fakirs of India."
Source: Hearn, *City Item,* July 14, 1880.

DR. TANNER (JULY 20)

H. J. Hearsey of the *States* criticized the *New Orleans Times* and *Democrat* for taking Tanner's fast too seriously. "Dr. Tanner is a worthless sensationalist, and his fasting show fit only to fill vacant space in the sensational columns of the newspapers of the period and excite the curiosity and wonder of that vast number of people the press has educated to a ravenous appetite for profitless drivel. This tendency of the press is one of the social curses of the time." Noting that before Dr. Tanner's fast nobody wanted to live forty days without eating, he added, "Indeed the great end of the exertions of men heretofore has been to get enough to eat." But he also predicted that the attention to Dr. Tanner would contribute to an epidemic of fasting matches.
Source: Hearsey, "Profitless Sensationalism," *States,* July 19, 1880.

ILLUSTRATED LETTERS FROM THE PEOPLE: MISCHIEVOUS BOYS

A subtle pun is implied in the description of the broken picture: among the most popular works of French genre and portrait painter Jean-Baptiste Greuze (1725–1805) are *The Wicked Son Punished* and *The Broken Pitcher.*

In January 1881, the New Orleans City Council prohibited the possession of slingshots: "That it shall be unlawful for any person or persons, to use or have in their possession, an instrument for propelling missiles known as 'nigger shooters.'"
Source: Ord. 6865, in Jewell, *Jewell's Digest,* rev. ed., 541–42.

ILLUSTRATED LETTERS FROM THE PEOPLE (JULY 22)

It has long been customary for residents of the French Quarter and other New Orleans neighborhoods to sit on their front stoops. Even today it is common to see people and pets overflowing onto the sidewalks in front of houses. A decline of the custom in recent years in the Quarter is due to an increase of crime and air-conditioning and a decrease of full-time, native residents.

ILLUSTRATED LETTERS FROM THE PEOPLE: THE BANANA CURSE

An ordinance prohibiting the tossing of refuse into the gutters was in existence in 1880, and individual property owners were responsible for the repair of the "banquettes" (sidewalks) in front of their places, but no local laws required property owners to clean them or prohibited the public from littering them. The next day an editorial by Hearn called "Good!" praised New York's new law that banned tossing fruit peels on sidewalks and said New Orleans ought to pass a similar one. "There is no place in the United States where more bananas are eaten, and more fruit-peels flung upon the streets; and many severe accidents have been caused by them. This law is really a necessity of civilizations. London and Paris long since adopted police regulations to prevent this lazy, filthy, and criminal practice." But it was not until 1885 that it became unlawful for people in New Orleans "to lay, place or throw upon any of the banquettes or footways within the limit of the city any banana, orange, fruit peelings, or other substance whereby pedestrians, by stepping thereon, may be injured." Due to lack of law enforcement, littering is an ongoing problem in the city.

Sources: *City Item*, July 24, 1880; Ord. 1399, in Jewell, *Jewell's Digest*, rev. ed., 330.

DR. TANNER (JULY 24)

Hearn defended the doctor against correspondents' "exhorting him to turn from wickedness and embrace religion, and turn his thoughts to the awful subjects of damnation and the grave." Even though Dr. Tanner was setting a bad example, he said, it was unjust to "treat him as an unregenerate monster of iniquity in danger of eternal torments."

Source: Hearn, "An Ancient Nuisance," *City Item*, July 23, 1880.

THE KNIFE-GRINDER

Only a few knife grinders are listed in the census records of 1880, most of them natives of France. The butchers of New Orleans, also almost invariably French, were a close-knit trade group who had formed the Butchers' Benevolent Society. Tool sharpeners and scissors grinders also served the city's many tailors, seamstresses, and dressmakers. An 1895 photograph of a knife grinder, who also made keys, shows that he announced his presence with a modern bell mounted on a collapsible grinder treadle, which he carried over his shoulder.

Sources: Tenth U.S. Census, 1880; Huber, *New Orleans*, 200.

DR. TANNER'S PRESENT ASPECT

When asked why he had left his wife, Tanner said, "Take an old man's advice and never marry a woman who indulges in pork and cabbage, morning, noon and night." In spite of his failing health, Tanner continued fasting, but was forced to take alcoholic vapor baths.

Sources: "Why Tanner Left His Wife," *States*, July 28, 1880 (reprinted from the *Cincinnati Times-Star*); *City Item*, August 2, 1980.

ATTENTION, ROWDIES!

In his article "Eternal Vigilance Is the Price of Liberty," of the same date, Hearn remarks on increased lynchings throughout the country.

> It is true that lynchings are now increasing in proportion to the increase of crimes, but it is also true that they have been becoming more frequent during a decade in proportion as the laws have been gradually neglected or maladministered. The curse of political corruption has been paralyzing justice throughout the country, and the American people will always take law into their own hands when they can not—or, at least, when they fancy they can not—obtain it in any other way. We say, fancy; because they have received the power of self-government, and it is partly their own fault if they do not govern themselves better. Yet partly also the fault of certain bad laws. Judges must cease to be political creatures; and life-terms must be substituted in our judicial system for the terms of two, three, or four years.

He further observes that vigilance committees would continue to be formed by honest men until the judicial system became effectual again, and warns, "Epidemics travel. If our dangerous classes are not careful they need not be astonished to find that Judge Lynch knows how to find his way to New Orleans."

Source: City Item, July 30, 1880.

TAXPAYERS' CATECHISM

Law required weekly settlements of city tax collections, but notorious irregularities in procedures had never been revised. Civil sheriff Gautreaux failed to turn in taxes he had collected, estimated at over $150,000 due the state and not less than $100,000 to the city. Even though it had been ten months since he had submitted receipts to the state, and five months to the city, government officials had yet to demand accountability. City authorities claimed to have been ignorant of the thefts, popularly known as "Gautreaux's defalcation," and were slow to take action, at first trying to scapegoat the clerk, as the sheriff had done.

Penalties on delinquent taxes had been suspended but would be reinstated on January 1, after which tax collectors were instructed to enforce immediate payment in compliance with the rigid provisions of the new revenue bill, Act 93, which the Taxpayers Association challenged as unconstitutional. Meanwhile, Gautreaux's term had expired and a new civil sheriff was installed, who, along with Administrator of Finance Isaacson, attempted to persuade taxpayers to pay 1880 property taxes early, based on 1879 assessments, so that the school teachers, police, and other city employees could be paid. Unsurprisingly, many citizens were reluctant to pay either their delinquent 1879 taxes or taxes for the year 1880. Gautreaux, who had fled to Louisville, pledged from his sickbed payment of some of the funds, amounting to only $12,723. He was the third consecutive civil sheriff to embezzle taxes.

Sources: City Item, October 6 and September 29, 1880; *States,* July 1, 1880; *Democrat,* September 20 and 30, 1880.

AH SIN ON THE SITUATION

Chinese laundries were located on Poydras Avenue, Baronne Street, and S. Rampart Street, in what is today the Central Business District. In this column, the Chinese laundryman complains in broken English of harassment by a black man who has appeared at night waving a lantern and chiding him for being a "Ballee-head Chinaman" with a "longh tail," who, unlike himself, doesn't have the right to vote. Both Republicans and Democrats fiercely competed for the black vote in the 1880 national presidential election. The caption of the October 30 cartoon (now lost) says, "Rumor has it that the Republican stalwarts in this city have been trying to dispose of the colored vote to the highest bidder among the local nominees." In this column the black "Melican" (American) brandishes the names "Thlantchok" (Hancock) and "Ginglish" (English), "Glah-flee" (Garfield) and "Ah-Tah" (Arthur), mixed with taunts of "Johnie Chinaman GO." Garfield's support for an increase in Chinese immigration was seized upon by Democrats and used to frighten American workers, especially blacks, with the threat of losing their jobs to Chinese, who were depicted in an illustration published by the *Democrat* (October 30, 1880) as disembarking in droves at a New Orleans river wharf.

INS AND OUTS

Infighting among "the Regulars," the conservative Democratic faction made up of overlapping rings, began as soon as Governor Wiltz called for city elections. One result of the bickering was E. A. Burke's withdrawing his support after his candidates were not nominated.

UNDER THE ELECTRIC LIGHT

Development of the resort West End Gardens, often still called New Lake End, began in 1871. It featured some of the city's first electric lights, which were a novel attraction. Developed only a year earlier, the open arc Brush lights—named after their maker, Charles F. Brush of Cleveland, Ohio—were only appropriate for outdoor use in covered galleries. During 1880, the *Democrat* announced that it was electrifying its equipment and replacing its gas lamps with electric lights. It also said that electric lighting would be a serious consideration in the city within a decade. Hearn responded that gas lamps would be supplanted more quickly. "The mere fact that the light, within six months after its invention, has been adopted in theaters, public halls, pleasure resorts, parks, and lighthouses is a certain guarantee that before another year it will be adopted for nearly all public purposes of illumination; and before two years have passed it will no doubt be used as a substitute for gas in private residences." Hearn's prediction was accurate. Installation of electric street lights began in 1881, and by 1882 there were approximately 500, concentrated in the business district, wharves, and public squares and markets.

Sources: Huber, *New Orleans,* 230; Arthur Schlesinger, *The Rise of the City,* 99; Hearn, "The Electric Light," *City Item,* July 20, 1880 (collected in Hearn, *Editorials*); Jackson, *New Orleans,* 165.

DR. TANNER: SLAMS THE DOOR ON THE UNDERTAKER'S NOSE

The *City Item* continued its criticism of Tanner's experiment, saying "the result will be that alms house soup will become thinner than ever, and charity will intermit its hospitable meals so as to provide them only once a month." At the conclusion of Dr. Tanner's fast, Hearn reprinted in his "crop column" an imagined exchange between a tramp and cook. "Tramp: Would you please give me something to eat, ma'am? I haven't had a mou'ful for fourteen days. Cook: No, get out of here; it's only been a fortnight since I gave you a slice of bread, and here you are pretending to be hungry a'ready."

Source: City Item, August 3 and July 30, 1880.

SARAH BERNHARDT

The French actress arrived in New Orleans on Saturday, February 4, 1881, just ahead of a violent storm (see "The Inundations," February 10), having traveled with her thirty-seven-member company, which included her sister, in a luxury train car from Cincinnati via Mobile. They roomed at the St. Charles Hotel, where Bernhardt and her sister "occup[ied] the best apartments in the hotel, and [had] a dining room to themselves. The Mademoiselle was pleased to say that the cuisine was the most satisfactory she had found on this side of the water." Her first appearance of the eight-day engagement in the city was on Sunday: "Sarah Bernhardt appeared last night, she was seen and she conquered. In spite of the storm the house was crowded." The play was *Frou Frou* (by Henri Meilhac and Ludovic Halévy), "which is so familiar to the playgoers of this city, both through the English version, and in the original French, that it needs no comment on its motive and story." Of Bernhardt's performance as Gilberte, the *Picayune* said "the death scene is painfully real." She died again and again, as Camille at the following Saturday matinee, when "ladies occupied all seats in the gallery, even, and there was no standing room anywhere unoccupied. This was at full night prices, and the audience represented more money than was ever in the theatre before. No one can say Bernhardt is not a success in New Orleans."

Source: *Picayune,* February 7–14 (collected in Hearn, *Editorials*); see also Hearn, "Canada vs. Bernhardt," *City Item,* December 23, 1880.

JEWELL'S DEFENCE OF GARFIELD

Jewell, former postmaster general, was chairman of the National Republican Committee.

HUNTING FOR THE HONEST EIGHT

There were eight city administrative positions to be filled: mayor and administrators of finance, accounts, improvements, commerce, police, waterworks, and assessments. The November election also included judges for the first and second recorder's courts. In a later issue, the *City Item* said that "Boss Tweed and his ring were overthrown, with millions of plunder in their hands, by a determined 'committee of seventy' honest citizens, who sacrificed a little time, a little money, and a little personal convenience, in behalf of the general good. This is the time, but where is the man, to head a similar reform movement in New Orleans?" Because a new city charter that made provisions for the elections had not been approved by the state legislature in the recent session, there were questions about the legality of the upcoming municipal elections. As a result, sitting administrators had no interest in holding elections and relinquishing their positions, despite the governor's order. The People's Democratic Association nominated a slate of reform candidates, of which their choice for mayor, Joseph Shakspeare, was the only one elected.

Source: "Wayside Notes," *City Item,* October 1, 1880.

COMING EVENTS CAST THEIR SHADOWS BEFORE

The following year there appeared in the *City Item* Hearn's translation of a letter to the editor from a "French Citizen" who advocated forming vigilance committees to curb violent crime in the city. The letter was followed by Hearn's response that a general formation of vigilance committees would be "pernicious":

"Too many cooks spoil the broth."

If a vigilance committee is to be formed at all, it should be formed for very serious business indeed;—there must be no mere bugbear nonsense about it. Whatever ought to be done should be done most thoroughly and terribly.

Please bear this fact strongly in mind.

To form such a vigilance committee, none but resolute, determined, audacious men are needed. There must be no braggadocio, no threats, no secret tattle, no intimation to the public of just what is going to be done. "Dogs that bark the loudest bite the least."

The purpose of such a vigilance committee should be to administer such a lesson to rowdyism as would be remembered in this city in the year 1980. One short sharp lesson will be enough. We should be the last to disapprove of it.

But for God's sake, let there be no farces—no gas explosions. A farce would be fatal to the cause of order and decency. If there is some ugly work to be done, let it be well considered and planned beforehand, and then most thoroughly well executed. It were better to go even too far in severity, than to fall short of what is needed.

A word to the wise ought to be appreciated.

Violent crimes began to decrease after 1880, and that some of the gangs responsible were broken up was due not to an improved police force but to vigilantism.

Sources: "Vigilance Committees," *City Item,* May 29, 1881; Kendall, "Old-Time New Orleans Police Reporters and Reporting."

QUACK! QUACK!

In an editorial several months earlier, Hearn reported that foreign journals were "full of satires in regard to American doctors" and that the American medical profession would be harmed by the scandals. "It seems that German quacks have come over to this country expressly to purchase diplomas, and then return to poison and murder their fellow-countrymen. Yet we are merely told that the government 'will try to make it discreditable for any one to do this.' Until the American government shall take at least as active an interest in medical education as the European governments, it is probable that quackery will continue to increase and multiply and flourish."

"Quack! Quack!" was prompted by the arrest the week before of Dr. E. A. Munt, a native of Prussia, who had submitted a death certificate for a child who had died of "worm spasms." Finding no record of a licensed physician named Munt, the city coroner ordered his arrest for violating two statutes regarding unlicensed practitioners. "It is very unfortunate," wrote Hearn in yet another editorial, "that there is no law against quackery,—except a section of the Revised Statutes which prescribes a fine of twenty dollars for any quack attempting to collect fees by legal process." The same fine was issued to gamblers and prostitutes and did not check the growth of their illegal activities. A bill "to prevent quackery" had just been introduced to the 1880 legislature but failed. Backed by the Board of Health, the coroner, "notwithstanding that there is no law to properly punish quacks . . . determined to unmask each and every one of them. The public will do well to note all arrests or exposures made under this reform movement."

Sources: Hearn, "American Quackery," *City Item,* May 16, 1880; "Quackery," *City Item,* August 20, 1880.

THE CHINESE VICE

On the previous day the *City Item* said it could "justly congratulate itself on its triumph in warring upon the opium dens. The Board of Health has taken measures to close up all dens of this kind." But the dens continued to operate, employing men on commission to promote them. Since "the administration of criminal justice is too imperfect," closing the dens would require more than a declaration by the Board of Health that they were a nuisance. "One must be after the police all the time with a sharp stick to make them do their duty."

To further warn young readers about the danger of the narcotic, Hearn selected for reprint an article from *Youth's Companion* called "Opium Drunkards," written after a young socialite on the East Coast died from an overdose of morphine.

> Opium drunkenness is said to be on the increase in this country, and it prevails largely among women. Very few matrons or young girls, when suffering from weakness or nervous disorders, would resort to brandy or whisky. But a dose of laudanum, or some other anodyne, they regard as harmless.
>
> Physicians, too, heedlessly prescribe something which they vaguely call "drops" to an overworked mother, or young girl exhausted by incessant dancing and flirting, when the proper remedies would be a few weeks' rest from labor and care, and a more wholesome, rational life.

Source: City Item, August 20 and November 6, 1880.

CAT-ANKAROUS

There were no city ordinances regarding control of the feral cat population of New Orleans, which Hearn compared in "Shu! Shu!—Cats!" to that of New York. There the president of the SPCA agreed to take "steps to suppress the cats of New York which afflict the people much as rats afflicted the people of Hamelin before the Pied Piper came there with his magic flute." To the relief of many concerned New Yorkers, he spoke to the mayor about the cat problem and

> observed that cats had become a source of inexpressible annoyance. He even pointed out sundry diabolical proclivities peculiar to New York cats which had never been observed by His Honor the Mayor. He showed that functionary that where tall fences were fringed with exceedingly sharp spikes, or walls covered with unutterably keen morsels of broken glass, the cats always chose by preference the spiked fences and the glass besprinkled walls wherein to hold their midnight orgies. "By all means," he said, "let them be destroyed."
>
> Why should they not be destroyed in New Orleans? The amount of human misery caused in New Orleans by these orgiastic fury of cats could not be adequately expressed even by a line of ciphers in nonpareil that would reach from here to the moon! The only useful thing about a New Orleans cat is his skin. There's millions in catskins. Will somebody take the hint?

Source: City Item, July 25, 1880; see also "Prolific Crime," in Hearn, *Editorials*.

MURDER AND VIOLENCE

The opinions "stated on another page" were those written by Hearn in an editorial called "Our Abolition of Capital Punishment," which begins, "We believe that the result of the most trustworthy statistics in Europe has proved the necessity of capital punishment to limit crimes of violence; and that its abolition has almost invariably resulted in a remarkable increase in the number of murders and attempts at assassination annually committed." The ruffians of the city had no fear of consequences for their actions, he writes. Capital punishment had not been abolished by law, but rather by custom. The last execution in memory was that of William Mumford "by Yankee Butler's orders." Three years earlier several "villains" were hanged,

> but they were not white men and had no political friends to help them. But so far as the white population of the parish of Orleans is concerned, the law regarding the death-penalty has remained a dead letter for nearly a generation. It is not wonderful therefore that murder and attempts at assassination have been steadily increased in number, and that the papers are perpetually recording horrible cutting scrapes or cold-blooded killings of inoffensive people.
>
> Probably at least sixty white men ought to have been hung in this parish during the last fifteen years. Probably at least one hundred terrible crimes of violence committed during that time have gone almost unpunished. Justice has been shamefully robbed and defrauded.

A few terrible examples were needed to get murderers under control, he concludes, stating that "if a few assassins were strung up as high as Haman, we feel assured that there would be a little more peace and good order in New Orleans."
Source: City Item, August 24, 1880.

ROWDYISM SUPPRESSED

The problem of the city's rowdy element was the focus of many editorials of the *City Item* and its contemporaries. Several days earlier Hearn published "Manufacturing Interests and Rowdyism," in which he refuted a *Democrat* editorial claiming the increase in the city's crime was linked to a lack of manufacturing businesses and low-skilled jobs. The city's condition, Hearn argued, did not create the "bummer class" of "low ruffians and aristocratic rascals." All large cities had that breed who did not make themselves useful to society, but other cities were policed better and their "local politics are not quite so rotten perhaps." The necessary changes would come when the business class had a larger influence in municipal affairs.

> They would be obliged to take strong measures to protect their property and the lives and property of their employees; they would have to see to it that the city was well policed;—they would have to take such active part in politics as to modify the present condition of affairs at elections; and in return for the benefit they would confer by their enterprise and capital the community would be compelled to aid them in such a good work. The ruffians will always be ruffians; but they would cease to ruin and bully the community as they do to-day.

Hoodlumism was a plague spreading in cities throughout the country. "Impudent and thoughtless boys, who make the name [hoodlum] a terror to all peacefully disposed persons, grow up into rough, depraved and brutal men, and having no respect for themselves or others, become a nuisance and a curse to whole communities."
Sources: Hearn, *City Item,* August 23, 1880 (collected in Hearn, *Editorials*); "Hoodlumism," *City Item,* July 8, 1880.

NOT A DREAM AT ALL

In "Rowdyism in Other Cities," Hearn offered New Orleans readers advice from New York. The answer might be, he suggested, to go back to "the good old times" when clubbing was permitted and a doctor could make fifty dollars a night treating wounded rowdies at the local jail.

> There is a great deal of truth in this. We believe that clubbing our New Orleans loafers would have a charming moral effect. But unfortunately the police do not use their clubs as much as they ought to. Of course there are people who would howl when a loafer has his scalp cut; but these are usually friends of loafers. One trouble has been that certain ruffians who obtained positions on the police force used to club weak women or inoffensive citizens, while the roughs were allowed to do as they pleased . . . What we want now are men who are not afraid to use their clubs on the heads of desperate characters; and if some of these desperate characters have their skulls broken no honest men will be sorry.

Source: Hearn, *City Item,* August 25, 1880.

OUR GHOULS

A reader apparently objected to the comparison of the city's "ghouls" to ragpickers, to which Hearn responded:

> The correspondent who abuses the "ghouls" is wrong. The "ghouls" are very useful and honest members of a community. They are human scavengers. They pick out bones, rags, paper, etc. from the dump boxes, and enable society to economize a good deal of valuable material that might otherwise be thrown away. They are not lazy, as our correspondent declares. On the contrary they are among the most energetic of the poor, like rag-pickers in all cities. We do not think that the remedy for the garbage nuisance suggested by our correspondent would greatly better the present condition of affairs.

The reader wrote again.

> *Editor City Item*—I beg your pardon, but I did not mean to abuse the "ghouls." I said plainly that I did not want to cast even a shadow on them, but, my dear sir, they can not be compared to the rag-picker, or bone-picker. In all civilized communities there exists a class of people who earn a living by gathering rags, bones, etc., which are sold to the manufacturers of paper and boneblack, whereas these ravens eat the dirt they find in the boxes. They might be scavengers, but, good God, how sickening to see them do the business, and what does the stranger think, when here on a visit, the first thing he sees in the morning is an open dirt box with a dog half lost into it, or a "ghoul" at work?

But Hearn was unconvinced the ghouls did not deserve sympathy: "Well, well! Perhaps it is even so! But we were not aware of it before. However, as the ghouls do not eat their carrion before the public gaze, we doubt whether strangers visiting the city would ever suspect the ghouls to be aught-else than rag-pickers and bone-finders. Moreover, our correspondent should have charity. Necessity sometimes forces poor people to do terrible things."

Sources: City Item, August 31, 1880; "The Ghouls," *City Item,* September 2, 1880.

WASHERWOMEN

In 1880 there were approximately two thousand washerwomen in New Orleans, 90 percent of whom were black (including mulatto, as they were differentiated in the 1880 census). About half of the white washerwomen were natives of Ireland or of Irish parentage. Several French women distinguished themselves as performing "fine washing," and one Irish male ran a "stain laundry." While laundry services were monopolized by Chinese immigrants in some U.S. cities, they were still a cottage industry in New Orleans; oftentimes a mother and daughter of a household did washing and ironing. Thirteen of the 140 prisoners incarcerated in Orleans Parish Prison were laundresses. A decade later Hearn extolled the virtues of St. Pierre's washerwomen in his essay "Les Blancisseuses."

Sources: Tenth U.S. Census, 1880; Hearn, *Two Years in the French West Indies.*

THE MILKMAN

In "Horrors of Milk-Drinking, Adulterated Milk" (1879), which drew from the "Report on Milk and Dairies in the City of New Orleans," the *City Item* said that some of the milk sold in the city was diluted with as much as thirty-four parts water. The report, results of an investigation by members of the New Orleans Medical and Surgical Association, also cited filthy dairy conditions and contaminated wells and canals, which were sources of milk-cows' drinking water, wash water for milk cans, and possibly the water added to the milk.

Sources: City Item, July 18, 1879; Jackson, *New Orleans,* 179.

CONTRABAND

Selling cigars required a license, but federal revenue collectors were usually too preoccupied with regular business—examining books and licenses, etc.—to attend to enforcement. However, later in September, "Deputy Dan Rose came across Julio Caro with a quantity of cigars in his possession which he was peddling, and as he had no license Deputy Dan arrested him and seized his stock." Since Caro lacked money for a bond, he was remanded to the parish prison.

Source: Democrat, September 24, 1880.

THE INDIGNANT DEAD

The severely flawed criminal justice system of New Orleans was the subject of numerous newspaper editorials. In February 1880, Hearn wrote about circumstances throughout the United States in which dangerous criminals had virtual immunity from justice. "Such a condition of affairs as disgraces American communities at present must sooner or later produce a violent reaction; and that reaction will manifest itself in the shape of iron laws, which money can not soften or legal cunning evade, and which will perhaps be stricter than those governing any advanced European society. The admirable administration of justice in France is sufficient to show that a republic can govern itself better than a monarchy; and that the defects in our social system may be remedied by proper legislation." He weighs the benefits of a government's being granted the powers of both Argus and Hercules as greater than the dangers for law-abiding citizens, although the success of such authoritarian powers depended on near-perfect laws and an impeccable police system.

Source: Hearn, "Wanted—Iron Laws," *City Item,* February 22, 1880.

DEAD SEA FRUIT

"Dead sea fruit" (or "dead sea apple"), a figure of speech seldom used today, refers to something whose exterior looks fine but which crumbles into dust when touched. Here it is applied somewhat literally to the sale of old fruit by produce vendors, who were mostly Italian. There were local laws requiring that produce sold in the markets be fresh and authorizing market managers to seize any not meeting set standards.

THE ALLIGATORS

Benjamin Butler, while commandant of Reconstruction's Seventh District, is said to have boasted that "in six months New Orleans should be a Union City or—a home of the Alligator." Americanized as it was in 1880, three years after the end of Reconstruction in Louisiana, New Orleans was part of the Solid South and arguably more the home of the alligator than it was a Union city. With canals and swamplands within the city limits, the alligator was not an unusual sight. Even today animal control agents are occasionally called on to capture an alligator in a New Orleans suburb.

Source: Dawson, *Army Generals,* 9.

THE VENDOR OF WISDOM

Among the bookstores Hearn patronized were Fournier's Book Shop, Royal Street near Toulouse; Julien's, Royal Street; Armand Hawkins' Book Shop, Canal Street; and Muhl's Book Shop, Exchange Alley. Hearn wrote in a letter about the bookseller depicted here:

> First my old friend Louis Bauer, the bookseller, departed very silently one dark night . . . I remember as it were yesterday, leaving the big white Thompson Dean, that had brought me (the only passenger) and 7000 bales of cotton to the New Orleans Port;—I see myself plainly walking up Canal Street in its early blaze of gold, and halting in front of Exchange Alley, attracted by the shadowy quaintness of that thoroughfare;—and I also hear again the voice of the little rosy-faced bookseller who so kindly answered my inquiry as to where I could "see the Creoles." Thus Louis was the first acquaintance I made here, and we became pretty fast friends. He was such an odd little man,—quite as odd as myself: our dual oddity crystallised—there was a queer legend in the alley that he had never been seen with his hat off, and that his employer, Goldthwaite having once attempted to unhat him, the two men never spoke again, except in case of absolute business necessity. Louis was never sick, never in bed in his life. On Monday morning the door of his room had to be broken open; and it was found that his life had gone out in the dark. He seems to have died asleep, but there was foam on his lips. I went there and saw the poor little secret of his bald head, that he had hidden so jealously for thirty years, and all the misery of his little possessions;—and I must say the city seemed to me a great deal lonelier than ever before.

Sources: Stevenson, *Lafcadio Hearn,* 120; Hearn to Page Baker, August 20, 1885, folder 3, Lafcadio Hearn Correspondence, Special Collections and Archives, Loyola University, New Orleans.

THE CURSE OF THE NEWSPAPER VENDOR

One of Hearn's crop columns included a related barb: "A North Carolina editor declares that 'the man who will read a newspaper three or four years without paying for it will pasture a goat on the grave of his grandfather.'"

Source: City Item, September 8, 1878.

CAKES AND CANDY

Many children died or were orphaned during the yellow fever epidemic of 1878. "Bon Dieu" (Good God) knew where her erstwhile small customers were.

THE PULLER OF NOSES

Two other Hearn articles on barbers have been identified, including the collected "Barbarous Barbers," from his Cincinnati years. In the illustration of "The Puller of Noses," the barber is shown gazing at the copy of the *City Item* his customer is reading, but in "An Indignant Fat Man," he (perhaps the same barber) is even less attentive to his work. "He was a sleepy, absent minded sort of a barber, too lazy to talk, with a look of bitterness in his sad, solemn face that meant an aggrieved, resentful feeling toward all mankind. He stood at his chair, listlessly rubbing the customer's face, and gazing woefully into space, without thought or heed to immediate surroundings. It was plain to be seen that his soul was not in his work. He had danced all the livelong night preceding at a shin dig in Bucktown, and his eyes were heavy." The "portly man with a bald head, mutton chop whiskers, and a mind untroubled with care" erupts in indignation after he yawns and the drowsy barber drops the lather brush into his mouth.

Sources: Collected in Hearn, *Barbarous Barbers; City Item,* September 18, 1878.

YE PILOT

Navigation between the Gulf of Mexico and the port of New Orleans via the Mississippi has required (through the present day) a bar pilot to take a vessel into the mouth of the river, and a river pilot, with experience of the Mississippi and its currents, to navigate upstream. In 1879 the *City Item* had defended the bar pilot's role and salary.

Source: "Bar Pilotage," *City Item,* November 4, 1879.

AWFUL CONSEQUENCES OF POOR SHOOTING

Hearn reported on a trip to Jersey Farm, a 640-acre plantation one mile from Arcola (near Amite), where he attended a picnic of the Louisiana Field Artillery. The entertainment included a competition of shooting bats with shotguns, hence Hearn's depiction of the haunting of a Jersey Farm resident by bats, due to poor aim.

Source: Hearn, "The Jersey Farm," *City Item,* September 20, 1880.

POLICE EFFICIENCY

On Wednesday, September 22, French native Jean Marie Bares died of injuries from kicks delivered by Corporal Driscoll. Bares, owner of a large grocery on Customhouse Street, had been a quiet and industrious man in the past but had lately begun drinking and causing disturbances for which he had been arrested several times. Recent treatment for a serious illness may have included prescribed narcotics that contributed to the violent drinking episode during which the man's wife and daughter called the police after he threw a pitcher and weight at them (because the water they gave him was not iced). Bares resisted arrest, and "in order to coax him quicker to jail, why the corporal simply kicked Bares in the stomach." Despite being seriously injured by the kicks, he did not receive medical attention and was forced to appear in court the following morning. "Bares' appearance in court was truly pitiful. He was almost bent in two; his voice was gone; only a nervous whisper could be heard issuing from his lips, and when called to the bar he had to be assisted by two officers." Bares explained that he had been hit in the abdomen and chest, but it was presumed that he was "shamming." After his wife paid his ten-dollar fine, they went home, where he complained that he was dying from his injuries. Indeed, he was virtually kicked into his grave.

Source: City Item, September 27, 1880.

THE MASTER SPIRIT

It was typical of "ward bums" to sit upon ballot boxes on election day and prevent votes being placed for the opposing party. The "Master Spirit" and his diabolical expression evoke the title character of the Italian opera *Mephistopheles,* which was performed in New Orleans the year before.

Source: See Hearn, "Mephistopheles," *City Item,* January 22, 1881; collected in Hearn, *Occidental Gleanings,* vol. 2.

ILLUSTRATED LETTERS FROM THE PEOPLE: ANOTHER CHANCE FOR REFORM

Many New Orleans public school teachers had to take their certificates of indebtedness, which they received from the city instead of payment, to brokers, who made bids as low as sixty-five percent. In 1880, Philip Werlein, owner of the Canal Street music store, initiated a relief fund to provide interest-free loans to teachers as an alternative to selling their certificates at a loss to brokers.

Source: "Relief for the School Teachers," *States,* May 24, 1880.

YOU PAYS YOUR MONEY, AND YOU TAKES YOUR CHOICE

After hearing his victim had died (see "Police Efficiency"), the arresting officer who had fatally kicked him stayed home, and "it was at once circulated in the fourth precinct that Driscoll was at home in bed, suffering from the effects of kicks received from Bares." But when the police officer was arrested on the basis of the initial report of the coroner, he was by all appearances well. Driscoll was arraigned on a charge of manslaughter and the bond set at $5,000. A charge of murder was usually made in all cases of homicide until the coroner's jury made a ruling.

Further testimonies by witnesses examined by the coroner's jury were as imaginative as they were varied:

J. M. Sabatier saw Bares lying down, an officer being on each side of him and another in front of him; Bares raised his feet, but did not kick anyone; the officer standing in front raised his foot, but witness did not see him kick—in fact saw nothing.

Madame Pierre, of 219 Customhouse street, saw Bares when between two officers, and another behind him fall flat on his back at the corner of Liberty and Customhouse streets; the officer behind Bares held his hair; she saw no one kicking on either side.

John Henry, colored, of 224 Customhouse street, saw Bares on his back kicking in the air; two officers held him, one on each side, and Corporal Driscoll was behind; no one was injured, and he certainly would have seen any damage done, for he was only forty feet away.

John Biesel, of 58 North Derbigny street, was present when Bares was made a prisoner; he saw him fall; he saw him kick the officer who was behind him, and saw the officer retaliate by kicking Bares; he does not know how many times.

The *City Item* maintained that "Bares was not a criminal; he was under the protection of the law. Yet he was killed by an executor of the law." The officer "had no right to lay hands on the deceased without an affidavit" attesting to his violation of laws.

Sources: *States,* September 27, 1880; "The Bares Case," *City Item,* September 30, 1880; *City Item,* September 28, 1880.

THE *GREAT EASTERN*

The year before, managers of the *Great Eastern* considered sending the great ship to Galveston for the cattle trade to inaugurate its entry into the commercial marines, but they were now interested in New Orleans, provided the Mississippi River and the Port of New Orleans could accommodate the ship's needs. The New Orleans Administrator of Commerce and a special city council committee began investigating the possibilities. They were assured the ship could pass through Eads' jetties (completed in late 1879) at the mouth of the Mississippi River, even if it drew thirty-one feet, and that free pilotage and towage through the jetties could easily be arranged. But offering reduced wharf fees seemed more difficult to arrange than the engineering feat.

The lessees at first said that reducing the fees would set a dangerous precedent. Newspapers promoted the benefits to the city that would come from offering generous accommodations. *L'Abeille* asked, "Shall we say to the *Great Eastern* that she was wrong to expect any abatement of wharf charges and port dues, and that so far from granting her such diminishment, we count upon her on the contrary to meet our foolish expenses and pay our debts? Should we do so we should deserve to perish, and to perish miserably!"

Later the New Orleans wharf lessees decided for legal reasons they could not offer docking at the city's wharves free of charge but they offered to contribute $1,500 toward the ship's expenses, which was enough for the *Great Eastern* to dock for several weeks. It is unknown whether or not the ship visited New Orleans earlier than 1885, when it was expected to deliver "a large portion" of the exhibits for the Cotton Centennial and World Industrial Exhibition and would "form one of the noteworthy sights for the visitor."

Sources: *City Item,* September 21, 1880; translation from *L'Abeille* by Hearn, *City Item,* September 24, 1880; *Democrat,* September 24, 1880; *Manufacturer and Builder* 13, no. 9 (January 1885).

THE WAGES OF SIN

When the new civil sheriff was installed, the former one, Gautreaux, had still not turned in tax collections to the state and city treasuries. The *City Item* asked, "What are you going to do about it, gentlemen of the Hall and State House?" "Claimants for hard-earned wages and long over due accounts are daily turned away from the treasury doors with the calmly uttered sentence, 'No money,' while month after month the funds provided to relieve their necessities are permitted unlawfully to remain in the pockets of a delinquent official. Slowly but surely is popular indignation growing greater at this great neglect of official duties and trusts; and when opportunity comes all concerned will be held to strict accountability."

Source: City Item, August 4, 1880.

THAT VERDICT

At the close of the inquiry on the death of Jean Marie Bares, the coroner's jury—made up of A. Delamore; Edward Quirk, a bar tender; P. Graham, a grocer; and E. Denekamp, keeper of a second-hand store—signed the *procès verbal:* "We find that death was caused by peritonitis. We further find that said Jean M. Bares received sufficient falls to produce peritonitis." Corporal Driscoll was to be tried before Judge Miltenberger the following week, but the finding of the coroner's jury drastically weakened the case against him.

Source: "The Bares Case," *City Item,* September 30, 1880.

PONEY UP!

One of the streets on which prostitutes—"courtesans" as they were called in the census—worked was Dauphine Street.

Source: Tenth U.S. Census, 1880.

329

James A. Garfield, as U.S. representative, played an important role in the disputed 1876 presidential race between Republican Rutherford B. Hayes and Democrat Samuel Jones Tilden. An electoral commission created by Congress decided to give Hayes all the electoral votes of Louisiana that were in question, making him the victor by one vote, even though Tilden had won the popular vote. With such charges as intimidation and illegal conduction of elections, the Returning Board of Louisiana (dubbed the "Overturning Board" by the *Picayune*) threw out only 1,831 Republican votes and 6,631 Democratic votes, including all those of East Feliciana Parish, hence the appearance of the name Feliciana in Hearn's cartoon. After the passage of the Compromise Bill, which gave the presidency to Hayes, a congressional hearing revealed that the president and other members of the Louisiana Board of Returns had accepted bribes from Washington Republicans to falsify, in favor of Republican candidates, the returns of some of Louisiana's parishes. As a result, Garfield was particularly unpopular among Louisiana Democrats.

The number 329 refers to the amount of a loan by Garfield from Oakes Ames. Several days after this illustration was published, the *Times* of New Orleans reprinted an article from the *Chicago Times* that explained "The 329 Craze."

Everywhere the mystic figures spring into being like magic; they become literally the handwriting on the wall. All the Irish-Americans who sat down to save their country at Saratoga had $329 in gigantic chalk marks staring at them from their desks. All through the New England towns $329 is marked on the sidewalks and fences. People go to rest at night never dreaming of what is before them, and in the morning their eyes light upon 329 chalked everywhere. The houses of Republican politicians have been covered with the sign. Democratic politicians make their bets $329. Portraits of Garfield are decorated with $329.

Sources: Picayune, November 14 and December 7, 1876; *Times,* October 6, 1880.

STATEMENT OF A VICTIM

Elsewhere, Hearn wrote of the cowardice of police brutality against women, saying, "we believe that any policeman who has manhood and courage enough to club a real rowdy, will have too much manhood to strike or abuse women or unoffending citizens. If there has been a great outcry here about police brutality it has been perhaps partly owing to the fact that clubs have been used in a most cowardly manner upon the unfortunate women and people who never violate the laws. However low a woman may be, the man who strikes her is a brute and a coward, and such people are not wanted on our police force."

Source: Hearn, "Rowdyism in Other Cities," *City Item,* August 25, 1880.

IMPROVED POLICE IDEAS

Until December 1891, New Orleans firefighters were volunteers organized as the Firemen's Charitable Association (F.C.A.), which operated under contract with the city. Because of the city's financial crisis, the F.C.A. had agreed to accept considerably less than its annual $140,000 for the years 1879 and 1880 (with the right to collect the balance at a later date). This meant having to forego updating the twenty-year-old Fire Alarm Telegraph system, which included eighty-two boxes—most of them the old crank-style—that transmitted signals from points throughout the city to the engine houses within thirty seconds. The badly worn internal workings of the boxes could cause delays and transmission errors.

Apparently, the alarm worked sufficiently in the case depicted here and described further in Hearn's article "Almost a Riot, the Fire Department Summoned to the Scene." A policeman in need of immediate backup resorted to the use of a fire box to summon assistance from firemen rather than his fellow police officers. "Between three and four hundred of the 'brethren and sisteren,' headlights in the Mount Zion Society, being moved by the spirit of the Lord, congregated to attend *en masse* the funerals of some of their departed members to their last resting place, in the St. Vincent De Paul Cemetery, on Louisa street." Perhaps more than one funeral procession was passing at Elmira and Rampart Streets, for a number of squares were blocked when the funeral marshals refused to allow vehicles to pass. The police officer tried to take control but was beaten by the mob and "advised by the Sisters never again to interfere with respectable colored people's funerals, and if he attempted to take any of the faithful to limbo they would tear him to pieces, limb by limb." The mob turned on the lone officer, and it appeared a riot might ensue, so he turned in an alarm from the fire department's box at the corner of Rampart and Louisa Streets. Firemen arrived promptly and restored order.

Sources: O'Conner, *History of the Fire Department,* 226, 524–26; *City Item,* October 6, 1880.

BLACKMAILING

Police captains and sergeants wore winter and summer uniforms of double-breasted coats with double rows of brass buttons. Corporals and patrolmen wore single-breasted coats with silver buttons. The following month Hearn wrote that prostitutes should be taxed and policemen should have nothing to do with collection of the taxes.

> Not only is it a shame upon the city, upon public morals, upon the manhood of public officials, to obtain money illegally from so indecent a source; but it aggravates a public nuisance. So long as these women pay, little attention is paid to what they do otherwise. They are permitted altogether too much liberty on the strength of their contributions to the secret fund of the police. Were they regularly taxed by the city, and compelled to pay revenue only to authorized city officials,—then we might expect that they would be obliged to act decently. It would also be right and proper that they should be protected against violence and brutality, which they are not at present.

Sources: Waring and Cable, *History and Present Condition of New Orleans,* 292; Hearn, "Aggravation in the Mask of Reform," *City Item,* January 20, 1881.

SCOURGED TO THE BALLOT

In Indiana's statewide election of October 1880, twenty to thirty thousand fraudulent votes were cast for Republican candidates by professional repeaters and blacks brought in from the South. "Thus has public opinion of a great State been falsified," said the *City Item,* "and thus were the people deprived of the privilege of self-government. But the game is too gross to be played a second time." Neither the South in general nor Louisiana had a monopoly on voting fraud.

Sources: Democrat, October 18, 1880; *City Item,* October 18, 1880.

AÏDA

The 1878 presentation of *Aïda* at the French Opera House, the first U.S. performance of Verdi's 1871 opera, was outdone by the spectacular 1880 production. Weeks later Hearn summarized the story in poetic prose for *City Item* readers. "The footsteps of the priests, the sacred hymn, die away. Alone in the darkness above, at the feet of the silent gods, there is a sound as of a woman's weeping. It is Amneris, the daughter of the king. Below in the everlasting gloom the lovers are united at once in love and death. And Osiris, forever impassible, gazes into the infinite night with tearless eyes of stone." The *Democrat* featured a half-page illustration of the spectacular set of the double scene in the last act with the grand duo between Aïda and Radames. The performances for the full house were reportedly superb, the scenery magnificent. Beauplan's meticulous attention to every detail included having eight Egyptian trumpets reproduced in Paris after an authentic original.

Sources: Hearn, "Aïda," *City Item,* January 17, 1881 (collected in *Fantastics*); *Democrat,* December 17, 1880.

NOT 329 BUT 350

This title is an allusion to the "329 Craze." (See "329.") Patrick Meallie, administrator of police, scandalized the city by misappropriating $350.

JOURNALISTIC DISSECTION

The "professor" portrayed in this cut is E. A. Burke, publisher and managing editor of the *Democrat,* also Louisiana state treasurer and one of the most powerful figures in business and politics of Louisiana and New Orleans. Candidate for city administrator of improvements John Fitzpatrick stated during a rally in Algiers that the *Democrat* had been trying, along with the "ring combination," to influence the nomination of municipal candidates. The *Democrat* refuted the claim, stating that Burke, as managing editor, had avoided any connection with the local factions and declaring that it was the *Times* that was guilty of nefarious ring activities. In its October 21 morning edition, the *Democrat* said the quarrel between the papers had begun when it said that the *Times,* a Republican paper, never lost an opportunity to injure the Democratic party when it was safe and profitable to do so. The four-column exposé surveyed the political history of Charles Clinton, manager and principal proprietor of the *Times.* According to the article, Clinton, as state auditor during Reconstruction, diverted tax funds, which he admitted in court to having used to defray the cost of "whipping those rebel skunks." Clinton filed a lawsuit against the *Democrat* for libel. But, as H. J. Hearsey had learned when he lost that paper because of his antilottery stance, making Burke or any of his interests an editorial target was journalistic suicide. The following year, Burke bought out the *Times* and quickly made the *Times-Democrat* one of the most formidable newspaper enterprises in the South. (He also hired Hearn away from the *City Item* shortly after the acquisition.)

Burke distinguished himself by his leadership in the World Industrial Exposition but later was discovered to be arguably the greatest and craftiest scoundrel in Louisiana political history. In a scheme that began in 1880, he allowed bonds to continue circulating and paying interest. Ultimately, he stole as much as $1,777,000 from the state treasury and never faced the nineteen charges of embezzlement and fraud brought against him. As the scandal broke in 1889, Burke fled to Honduras, where he lived out his days as the *gringo* with the vastest land holdings, exercising much influence on national political affairs.

Source: Jackson, *New Orleans,* 42.

SPANISH MOSS

In this poem, the only signed piece of the series, Hearn takes poetic license in writing about Spanish moss. However, a commentary in the *City Item* remarked: "In some comments on the moss industry of Louisiana, our neighbor the *Democrat* speaks of the Spanish moss as 'a parasitic growth.' This is incorrect. The moss is an air plant, drawing none of its sustenance from the tree to which it clings. This fact may be verified by seeing its healthy development on old posts which are wholly sapless. We for a year or two witnessed the growth of healthy moss on an abandoned lamp post near the Bayou St. John Bridge." Spanish moss was gathered and dried for use as stuffing for mattresses and upholstered furniture.

Source: City Item, December 2, 1880.

FIRE!

The following note regarding telephone use appeared in the *City Item* (December 7, 1880): "The value of the telephone in recent cases of fire has been proved beyond all cavil. Through a circuit of wires instantaneous information is given to the various alarm stations, and before the bell can toll out so much of the Arabic alphabet as to indicate the location of the fire the story of the danger has been told. We are living in an age of marvels, and the telephone is by no means the least of these marvels."

ALL SAINTS!

The city's streetcars going to the Metairie Ridge cemeteries on All Saints' Day were crowded. The Firemen's, Greenwood, St. Patrick's, Metairie, St. Vincent de Paul, Lafayette No. 1, St. Joseph's, and Girod Street Cemeteries were decorated throughout, and one of the graves at Potter's Field had a wreath on its headboard.

Soldiers of the Orleans Artillery mounted guard stood at the gates of St. Louis Cemetery No. 1, arms at rest. Inside, memorial tablets were framed in garlands of evergreens and flowers. The tomb of the New Orleans Italian Mutual Benevolent Society, built in 1857, was draped with crape, decorated with Italian and American flags at its corners, and a Garibaldian ensign leaned against the statue on the dome. Nearby, the tomb of the Portuguese Benevolent Association was draped in mourning and hung with national flags, their folds gathered up with crape bands. Also festooned with crape, the tomb of the Cazadores d'Orleans was hung with Spanish and American flags. Muskets were stacked in the corners of the lot of the tomb of the Regiment (formerly Battalion) of Orleans Artillery, which was draped with American, French, Spanish, Austrian, and Battalion flags, and sentries marched back and forth before it. The tomb of the Société Française de Bienfaisance et d'Assistance Mutuelle was draped with the society's flags, and wreaths and other emblems were hung on the vault tablets. Tapers burned at many of the tombs, before which loved ones knelt.

Hearn documented in his woodcut a now-lost tradition: troops of flambeau carriers who marched around cemeteries lighting the long tapers visitors brought to their family tombs.

Source: Democrat, November 2, 1880.

THE CHINESE POISON

A month earlier Hearn had praised the Board of Health for declaring the proliferation of opium dens a nuisance but questioned the inaction of the city council. "Since we first called attention to the subject the opium dens have increased in number. There are, we believe, no less than five in the Second District alone. Daily, early at sunrise, men and women may be seen staggering out of them into the street, drunk with the venomous fumes of the narcotic, and hideous with the pallor of the hideous debauch. The dens are patronized by hundreds and hundreds. It is bad enough that we should have morphine eaters and opium eaters; the spread of opium smoking is a far more alarming evil."

In October the *City Item* boasted that it had caused the closing of two opium dens in the Vieux Carré: "Another victory for *The Item*. Our articles have at last had the good effect of causing the proprietors of the opium dens on Customhouse street and Dauphine street to fold the tent and move away. And with that astute secrecy so peculiarly Chinese, they have moved away so silently that nobody knows where they have gone to. The habitués of these dens have held an indignation meeting, it is said, and there is a sound of wailing and tribulation. We shall keep a good lookout, however, on the movements of the departed."

In spite of these claims, editorials alone did not shut down these dens. Harry S. Michel, at the time city editor, later recounted that he instructed reporter Peter Kiernan to go to the den he called "Tucker's joint" (on Dauphine, between Conti and St. Louis Streets), smoke a pipe of opium, and afterwards file an affidavit. Judge Miltenberger issued a warrant for the arrest of the owners and seizure of the opium. However, since there were still neither state nor local laws prohibiting opium possession or use, the case was thrown out. Later opium cases were tried based on violation of laws regulating the use of poisons. Not until several years later did a New Orleans city council outlaw opium use and the "opium joints."

Sources: Hearn, "The Opium Dens," *City Item,* October 5, 1880 (collected in *The New Radiance*); *City Item,* October 19, 1880; *Item-Tribune,* New Orleans, June 26, 1927; Ord. 750, in Jewell, *Jewell's Digest,* rev. ed., 75–76, 539.

GLADNESS IN THE GRANITE BUILDING

Political appointees of the customhouse, especially the "magnates," were jubilant over the election of the Republican candidate Garfield.

FRENCH OPERA

The 1880–81 opera season in New Orleans featured the U.S. première of *Carmen* at the French Opera House, which for decades stood regally on Bourbon Street (lakeside) at Toulouse, its Greek Revival–style edifice of pilasters and colonnades towering above surrounding buildings. The evenings of opera performances, when its opulent white, red, and gold interior received some of the city's wealthiest citizens, provided a pleasant spectacle for neighborhood residents, as well as subject matter for visual and prose studies by some, including Lafcadio Hearn, who lived less than a block away on the river side of Bourbon, near St. Louis Street. In 1879 Hearn published an untitled sketch of a scene that also inspired his woodcut created a year later.

> The lighted windows of the Opera House, the deep hum arisen from the handsomely dressed crowd pouring up the double stairways, and the splendid array of carriages, hacks, coupes, and buggies marshalled along Bourbon street, suggest to the one who observed the spectacle from a balcony the other evening, remembrances of an epoch when the pretty theatre was the focus of artistic pleasure in the South,—when the name of New Orleans suggested a tropical Paris, and when the fashionable world of the South dreamed in a thousand prosperous plantations of musical delights during a winter trip to the Crescent City. The windows seemed to glow again with the brightness of other days; and it did not require much imagination to rehabilitate the neighborhood of Bourbon and Toulouse streets with the asperse of twenty odd years ago. Hundreds seem inspired by the same thought, and knots of old French residents on the illumined street, could be heard exchanging reminiscences of the past.

So central was the French Opera House to New Orleans residents that to give up the theater for Lent was considered *une pénitence de Carmélite,* self-deprivation of a most severe order. Therefore, it was especially tragic when on December 2, 1919, shortly after it was purchased and donated to Tulane University, it was destroyed by fire.

Sources: *City Item*, November 28, 1879; Huber, *Creole Collage*, 102.

RECOLLECTIONS OF THE THEATRICAL SEASON

Hearn later elaborated on his complaint about the millinery nuisance in an editorial called "Broad-Brims at the Theatre."

> A disheartened theatre manager declares his business can never be made to pay until the tyrant fashion again condescends to permit women to go to the theatre without bonnets. In the best of days of the theatre in this city the ladies wore only nubias, or some article easily removable, and then those who sat in the front row did not hide the stage from the rest of the audience. The present fashion of head gear for the fair sex is abominable, though so long as the wearers can be made to believe it is "becoming" there will be no use to rail at it. Man can only get even by looking for amusement where broad-brimmed, crumpled bonnets can not intrude.

Source: *City Item*, November 25, 1880.

THE BONE OF CONTENTION

When Mayor-elect Joseph Shakspeare appeared on November 15 to take office, outgoing mayor Isaac W. Patton refused to surrender his office, claiming the election for city administrators was null because the new city charter, which had been written as ordered by the Louisiana Constitution of 1879, had not been approved by the legislature; therefore no valid provision existed for a local election. Shakspeare had no choice but to await the courts' rulings. The only officer to surrender his office was Administrator of Improvements Col. Joseph Collins; however, Patton declared that office vacant and appointed someone else. Both the district court and the Louisiana State Supreme Court decided against Patton. The new administration was not installed until December 14, a month behind schedule.

Source: Kendall, *History of New Orleans*, 1:424.

THE PELICAN'S GHOST

The emblem on the official flag of Louisiana is an image from ancient mythology of the female brown pelican, the state bird, piercing her own breast to feed her young. Andrew Jackson (1767–1845) was a national war hero and has long been considered a patron saint of the city for leading troops in an 1815 victory over the British in the Battle of New Orleans.

SOMETHING TO BE PROUD OF

New Orleans "banquettes" (sidewalks) were about ten to twelve feet wide and, depending on the section of the city, paved with various materials. Streets where the upper classes lived tended to be wider and paved with what was called "German flags" or "Schillinger pavement," an artificial stone. In most of the business sections a material known as "North River blue-stone flags" was used, and sidewalks in lower-class residential areas were typically brick. Narrow wooden sidewalks in the newer sections were the most problematic, with boards loosening and rotting after a short time. The sidewalks of Schillinger pavement were very durable; many not demolished can be found today in some sections of the city.

Maintenance was the responsibility of the owner of the property in front of which the sidewalk ran. Neglect by property owners and lack of enforcement were constant problems and the cause of many complaints. In January, Hearn described the sidewalks in wet weather: "It is impossible to distinguish where the sidewalk ends and the gutter begins, or where the submerged and narrow bridges over the said gutters have their local habitation. The water rushes furiously. Slip! and you either go up to your middle or roll at full length in the stream. No one has any sympathy for you. A burst of mocking laughter hails your misfortune."

Sources: Waring and Cable, *History and Present Condition of New Orleans*, 272; Hearn, "Awful Weather, Ain't It?" *City Item*, January 21, 1881.

THE MAN SOCIALLY LOVED

On November 3, the day after elections, the editor of the *North Louisiana Republican*, Dr. W. B. Jones, was murdered. The paper's publisher, B. H. Lanier—deputy collector of internal revenue of the upper Louisiana parishes and unsuccessful candidate for Congress—claimed in a dispatch from Lake Providence, Louisiana, that the death had been a political assassination and that both he and Jones had received death threats. Incredulous, the *City Item* suggested it was the dissemination of an assassination theory that was politically motivated and that being a tax collector was reason enough to make Lanier the target of public hatred.

Source: "The Lanier Case," *City Item*, November 21, 1880.

"OFT IN THE STILLY NIGHT," ETC.

A popular tune at the time, this Scotch air is from Thomas Moore's collection *National Airs* (1815), of which the first stanza follows.

> Oft, in the stilly night,
>   Ere Slumber's chain has bound me,
> Fond Memory brings the light
>   Of other days around me;
>   The smiles, the tears,
>   Of boyhood's years,
>   The words of love then spoken;
>   The eyes that shone,
>   Now dimmed and gone,
>   The cheerful hearts now broken!
> Thus, in the stilly night,
>   Ere Slumber's chain has bound me,
> Sad Memory brings the light
>   Of other days around me.

Source: Moore, *The Poetical Works of Thomas Moore*, 351.

UGH!!

The following month Hearn wrote of the flooded streets: "The sidewalks are covered, the street is a canal. Canal street is a lagoon. There are Rialtos enough; but no bridges. And where the horses are plodding up to their bellies in water, there are strong currents of soup-colored water."

George W. Waring and George Washington Cable in their 1880 report said the drainage of New Orleans "is of the most ineffective and simple character, adapted solely to the removal of surface water from the streets and house-lots." The drainage system was a "rude adoption of the Polder system of Holland," made up of street gutters, protective levees, a couple of canals, and three old steam-driven Dutch paddle-wheel pumps placed at different points at the rear of the city that revolved vertically, forcing water from one canal to another, ultimately draining into Lake Pontchartrain. The pumps usually had to work "only intermittently and moderately except during storms, when the full force is not adequate." When there were storms or days of steady rain, the water backed up into the city. This would have been bad enough in itself, but many of the streets, particularly unpaved ones, were impassable for wagons, making garbage collection impossible. Furthermore, the filthy condition of the open gutters, which received household liquid wastewater, as well as leakage from privy vaults and toxic discharges from factories, meant that flood waters were extremely rank as well as a health threat.

An organization formed in the months of late 1879 and early 1880, the Auxiliary Sanitary Association (A.S.A.), raised money for a gutter-flushing system, which involved a steam pump for lifting water from the Mississippi River and use of the city's water hydrants. The condition of the gutters was improved, but the system proved to be more effective for streets perpendicular to the river; the parallel streets tended to remain in a foul condition.

Sources: Hearn, "The Weather," *City Item,* March 18, 1881; Waring and Cable, *History and Present Condition of New Orleans,* 272.

MORAL EDIFICATION

One of the cases brought before the board of police commissioners the night before was considered by the public one of the most infamous in the history of New Orleans police: three officers were accused of stealing a watch from a corpse. Officer J. W. Potter was found guilty based on the testimony of a witness who claimed to have seen him in possession of a timepiece bearing the initials of the victim. But, as it was observed, "when thieves fall out just men get their dues." Potter in turn claimed that one of the other two officers accused of the crime, D. J. Muller, had taken the watch from the body of the dead man and had it in his pocket. The watch was found, and both officers were arrested and dismissed from the police force.

Source: Democrat, November 30, 1880.

"WET ENOUGH FOR YOU?"

The text speaks of the extreme weather, but the image implies criticism of the Department of Improvements, which was responsible for street repairs. Street conditions had not been this bad since the 1840s. Because of the city's financial crisis, few funds existed for improvements. The flushing of the gutters by the Auxiliary Sanitary Association was expected to improve the condition of the streets considerably, but corruption in the Department of Improvements continued because of a contractors' ring, which cornered the contracts for street improvements by underbidding honest competitors. They often used scant materials or did not do the work at all. "Contracts have been made for shell pavement of a thickness of eight or nine inches; and hardly enough shells have been laid down to cover the surface. Shell heaps have been measured over and over again and paid for, and then carted off and dumped somewhere else and measured again. Lumber has been contracted for, and measured and remeasured. When the appropriations have been exhausted, it is found that the city has paid a great deal of money for nothing, and that nobody has been benefited but the contractors, and still the work goes on." Proving these allegations was not easy, "for every ring knows how to cover up its own dirt cat-fashion."

Sources: Jackson, *New Orleans,* 60; Hearn, "Our Streets," *City Item,* May 19, 1881.

TANTALIZING

Overcast skies and inclement weather dominated the winter into spring. Hearn noted a correlation between the increased number of suicides in the city and the dreary weather. "The mind, mirroring its surroundings through the senses, assumes the colorlessness and sluggishness of the atmosphere. In bright, clear weather, the mind is also sunny, and it fancies light as the fleecy clouds which float in the blue immensity of day without dimming it. In such times as these our dreams are somber and gloomy; and those who need hope can not feed its flame in this season of mental and material dampness. The sacred lamp sputters and flickers, and too often finally goes out forever."

Source: Hearn, "The Weather," *City Item,* March 18, 1881.

A MILLER WHO COULDN'T MILL

E. C. "Kid" Miller was a "bunko steerer" or "roper"—one who lured unsuspecting tourists into gambling halls with fixed devices and persuaded them to place bets in a game they had no chance of winning. Every morning Kid Miller, notorious among locals, headed into town from the Mobile train depot with "grip sack in hand, overcoat slung over his shoulder, and umbrella in the other hand, with an oafish air as if he were a stranger." His mistake the day before was in trying to rope in Dr. George Little, an elderly gentleman in town for the National Sanitary Conference. The doctor, according to one report, claimed to have never been taken in by Miller, but only pretended to be in order to prove his suspicions. When Miller approached him, Dr. Little asked for directions to the cars so he could visit the lakeside resorts. Miller, attempting to ingratiate himself to a visitor he believed might be easy prey, persuaded the doctor to accompany him to a nearby saloon, where he immediately won a game. But when he asked the doctor to play, the latter let his suspicions be known by raising his cane and threatening to beat both bunko men, who fled the scene. Dr. Little reported the incident to police, and Miller was eventually apprehended. He was arraigned on a vagrancy charge the day this column appeared. Unable to pay the $500 bond, he was remanded to Orleans Parish Prison.

The following week the *City Item* reported an "Examination of a Bunko Establishment."

In examining a room which had recently been employed as a bunko gambling establishment, a party of gentlemen yesterday stumbled on a mechanical device which serves to explain how the milk gets unwittingly into the coacoanut. Beneath the floor, on the spot where the roulette formerly stood, were found trap doors with machinery designed to effect the issues of the game in ways that are dark. In fact, the machinery was employed in what is technically known as "the brace game," and the brace, operated by pedal action, always resulted disastrously to the betters against the bank, except in cases where a sprat is thrown away to catch a larger fish. The little jiggers were curiously inspected by the uninitiated.

The *Picayune* told readers "it would be well for the many strangers in the city to be very, very cautious."

Such schemes have survived in New Orleans into the twenty-first century. In recent years an investigation of a bunko establishment in the French Quarter resulted in the arrest of the owners, who had bilked tourists out of untold sums over the years, and several New Orleans policemen who had been paid off to ignore the scam.

Source: Picayune, December 9 and 10, 1880.

THE INUNDATIONS

After seven weeks without an illustrated column, Hearn crowned his series with one last woodcut. On Sunday, February 6, 1881, a violent storm passed over the city, filling the drainage canals with rainwater and flooding some areas. As the *Democrat* described the catastrophe, it was not until the sustained winds blew in the following night that conditions drastically worsened: "The wind is from that direction always looked upon as dangerous, as it drives the waters of the sound through the Rigolets into Lake Pontchartrain and backs them up into the New and Old Basins, threatening the city." Levees overflowed, pumps stopped working, and waters rose steadily, covering an increasingly vast area. A break in the Old Basin Canal levee caused further flooding in the Tremé neighborhood. The deluge covered the entire rear of the city and worsened as winds from the east strengthened. For days people—including many of the city's poorest—were stranded without food and water. People in makeshift skiffs floated through flooded streets looking for provisions. It was, according to the *Democrat,* the highest storm water ever known to have deluged the city. "Many families have had to take refuge in the second stories, or, where buildings are only one story, in the lofts, and even on the roofs, and we have no words to convey to our readers the extent and character of the suffering which is at this moment being endured within a stone's throw of the very centre of this great city."

Sarah Bernhardt, who was performing in the city at the time, visited the stricken areas. She was "altogether delighted with the situation, but could not understand how the people managed to live in the city with water all about them." Despite the storm and the flood, the public packed the theater to see her performances.

As the floodwaters slowly receded, the *City Item* published articles on how to prevent similar catastrophes in the future, including Hearn's editorial "Excelsior!"—of the same day as his last woodcut—which recommends that houses beyond Rampart Street be elevated above possible flood levels:

> We may not be able to do like Chicago, raise our whole city; but we might raise our dwellings in the future above flood level, and even above the level of those rain-floods which often compel people to wade home who do not live more than two or

NOTES ON COLUMNS, PAGE 130

three squares above Rampart. Should the project of raising the ground level be ever seriously entertained, the elevation of houses hereafter constructed would aid the execution project greatly. With wise and well enforced laws on the subject, all the cottages and small dwellings of the district recently inundated might be raised above the highest flood level before the expiration of twenty-five years.

In this last woodcut, Hearn depicts Mayor Joseph Shakspeare being ferried through a street on the back of a black man. Shakspeare's victory in November had been largely due to the black vote. Blacks definitely carried him to his second mayoral victory when he ran again in 1888.

Sources: Democrat, February 6–10, 1881; *City Item,* February 10, 1881; Hearn, "Excelsior!" *City Item,* February 10, 1881.

BIBLIOGRAPHY

UNCOLLECTED ARTICLES BY LAFCADIO HEARN
FROM THE *DAILY CITY ITEM*

"Aggravation in the Mask of Reform," January 20, 1881.
"Almost a Riot: The Fire Department Summoned to the Scene," October 6, 1880.
"American Quackery," May 16, 1880.
"An Ancient Nuisance," July 23, 1880.
"An Astrological Ass," February 19, 1881.
"Awful Weather, Ain't It?" January 21, 1881.
"Condoning Crime," May 24, 1880.
"(The Death of Cham)," September 14, 1879.
"Eternal Vigilance Is the Price of Liberty," July 30, 1880.
"Excelsior!" February 10, 1881.
"The Ghouls," September 2, 1880.
"Illustrated Newspapers," September 13, 1878.
"An Indignant Fat Man," September 18, 1878.
"The Jersey Farm," September 20, 1880.
"Laughter and Woe," August 17, 1880.
"Midnight in New Orleans: Whistling for a Policeman Who Does Not Answer," August 1, 1880.
"Quackery," August 20, 1880.
"The Most Remarkable Schoolhouse in the World," October 20, 1879.
"A Musical Compliment," July 2, 1880.
"The Oakland Park Farce," July 7, 1880.
"Orleans Regiment Artillery: Sambola's Little Gun Created Mischief But Gains Popularity," August 28, 1880.
"Our Streets," May 19, 1881.
"Our Telephone," November 16, 1881.
"(Paris of America)," October 3, 1879.
"The Parish Prison and Dr. Jones," September 5, 1880.
"(Roses of Gullistan)," January 18, 1881.
"Rowdyism in Other Cities," August 25, 1880.
"A Study of Cartoons," November 18, 1878.
"Sunday Amusements," October 19, 1880.
"Sunday Recreations," July 17, 1880.
"Vigilance Committees," May 29, 1881.
"Wanted—Iron Laws," February 22, 1880.
"The Weather," March 18, 1881.

BOOKS AND ARTICLES

Allen, Edison B., ed. *Of Time and Chase.* New Orleans: Habersham Corporation, 1969.

Bisland, Elizabeth. *Life and Letters of Lafcadio Hearn: The Writings of Lafcadio Hearn in Sixteen Volumes*. Vol. 1. Boston: Houghton Mifflin, 1923.

Blain, Hugh Mercer. *A Near Century of Public Service in New Orleans*. New Orleans: New Orleans Public Service, Inc., 1927.

Bronner, Milton, ed. *Letters from the Raven, Being the Correspondence of Lafcadio Hearn with Henry Watkin*. New York: Brentano's, 1907.

Buchanan-Brown, John, ed. *The Illustrations of William Makepeace Thackeray*. London: David and Charles, 1979.

Bulwer-Lytton, Edward. *A Strange Story and the Haunted and the Haunters*. Philadelphia: J. B. Lippincott and Co., 1881.

Cott, Jonathan. *Wandering Ghost: The Odyssey of Lafcadio Hearn*. New York: Knopf, 1991.

Dawson, Joseph G., III. *Army Generals and Reconstruction: Louisiana, 1862–1877*. Baton Rouge: Louisiana State University Press, 1982.

———. *The Louisiana Governors: From Iberville to Edwards*. Baton Rouge: Louisiana State University Press, 1990.

Dryden, John. *Essays of John Dryden*. 2 vols. Ed. W. P. Ker. New York: Russell and Russell, 1961.

Elliott, Robert C. *Satire: Magic, Ritual, Art*. Princeton: Princeton University Press, 1960.

Emerson, Ralph Waldo. *Ralph Waldo Emerson: Essays and Lectures*. New York: Library of America, 1983.

Farny, Henry, and Lafcadio Hearn, eds. *Ye Giglampz: A Weekly Illustrated Journal Devoted to Art, Literature and Satire*. Cincinnati: Crossroads Books, with the Public Library of Cincinnati and Hamilton County, 1983.

Forester, Robert F. *The Italian Emigration of Our Times*. Cambridge: Harvard University Press, 1919.

Gayarré, Charles. *History of Louisiana*. 4 vols. New Orleans: F. F. Hansell and Bro., 1903.

Grant, Richard. *Théophile Gautier*. Boston: Twayne, 1975.

Hall, Gwendolyn Midlo. *Africans in Colonial Louisiana: The Development of Afro-Creole Culture in the Eighteenth Century*. Baton Rouge: Louisiana State University Press, 1992.

Hearn, Lafcadio. *Barbarous Barbers and Other Stories: Lafcadio Hearn's American Articles*. Ed. Ichiro Nishizaki. Tokyo: Hokuseido, 1939.

———. *Creole Sketches*. Ed. Charles Woodward Hutson. Boston: Houghton Mifflin, 1924.

———. *Editorials by Lafcadio Hearn*. Ed. Charles Woodward Hutson. Boston: Houghton Mifflin, 1926.

———. *Fantastics and Other Fancies by Lafcadio Hearn*. Ed. Charles Woodward Hutson. Boston: Houghton Mifflin, 1914.

———. *Gombo Zhèbes: Little Dictionary of Creole Proverbs in Six Dialects*. New York: W. H. Coleman, 1885.

———. *Inventing New Orleans: Writings of Lafcadio Hearn*. Ed. S. Frederick Starr. Jackson: University Press of Mississippi, 2001.

———. *Lectures on Shakespeare by Lafcadio Hearn*. Ed. Iwao Inagaki. Tokyo: Hokuseido, 1928.

———. *Literary Sketches: Lafcadio Hearn's American Articles*. Ed. Ichiro Nishizaki. Tokyo: Hokuseido, 1939.

———. *The New Radiance and Other Sketches: Lafcadio Hearn's American Articles*. Ed. Ichiro Nishizaki. Tokyo: Hokuseido, 1939.

———. *Occidental Gleanings of Lafcadio Hearn: Sketches and Essays Now First Collected*. 2 vols. Ed. Albert Mordell. New York: Dodd, Mead, and Co., 1925.

———. *Two Years in the French West Indies*. New York: Harper and Brothers, 1890.

Hess, Stephen, and Milton Kaplan. *The Ungentlemanly Art: A History of American Political Cartoons*. New York: Macmillan, 1968.

Huber, Leonard V. *Creole Collage: Reflections on the Colorful Customs of Latter-Day New Orleans Creoles*. Lafayette: Center for Louisiana Studies, University of Louisiana, 1980.

———. *New Orleans: A Pictorial History*. New York: Crown, 1971.

Hughes, Jon Christopher, ed. *Period of the Gruesome: Selected Cincinnati Journalism of Lafcadio Hearn*. Lanham, MD: University Press of America, 1990.

Jackson, Joy J. *New Orleans in the Gilded Age: Politics and Urban Progress, 1880–1896*. Baton Rouge: Louisiana State University Press, 1969.

Jewell, Edwin L., comp. *Jewell's Digest of the City Ordinances, Together with the Constitutional Provisions and Acts of the General Assembly, Relative to the Government of the City of New Orleans*. 1882; rev. ed. New Orleans: Edwin L. Jewell, 1887.

Kendall, John Smith. *History of New Orleans*. 3 vols. Chicago: Lewis Pub. Co., 1922.

———. "New Orleans Newspapermen of Yesterday." *Louisiana Historical Quarterly* 29, no. 3 (July 1946): 771–90.

———. "Old-Time New Orleans Police Reporters and Reporting." *Louisiana Historical Quarterly* 26, no. 3 (January 1946): 44–58.

———. "Sarah Bernhardt in New Orleans." *Louisiana Historical Quarterly* 26, no. 3 (July 1943): 770–82.

Kennard, Nina H. *Lafcadio Hearn*. New York: Appleton and Co., 1912.

Kernan, Alvin B. *The Cankered Muse: Satire of the English Renaissance*. New Haven: Yale University Press, 1959.

Lafargue, André. "Opera in New Orleans in Days of Yore." *Louisiana Historical Quarterly* 29, no. 3 (July 1946): 660–78.

Lévi-Strauss, Claude. *The Raw and the Cooked*. Trans. John Weightman and Doreen Weightman. Chicago: University of Chicago Press, 1964.

McWilliams, Vera. *Lafcadio Hearn*. Boston: Houghton Mifflin, 1946.

Mencken, H. L. *The Impossible H. L. Mencken: A Selection of His Best Newspaper Stories*. Ed. Marion Elizabeth Rodgers. New York: Doubleday, 1991.

Mercier, Vivian. *The Irish Comic Tradition*. Oxford: Oxford University Press, 1962.

Moore, Thomas. *The Poetical Works of Thomas Moore.* Boston: Phillips and Sampson, 1849.

Mordell, Albert, ed. *An American Miscellany.* 2 vols. New York: Dodd, Mead, and Co., 1924.

O'Connor, Thomas. *History of the Fire Department of New Orleans from the Earliest Days to the Present Time; Including the Original Volunteer Department, the Firemen's Charitable Association, and the Paid Department Down to 1895.* New Orleans: n.p. listed, 1895.

Oswald, John Clyde. *A History of Printing: Its Development Through Five Hundred Years.* New York: Appleton and Co., 1928.

Perkins, P. D., and Ione Perkins. *Lafcadio Hearn: A Bibliography of His Writings.* Boston: Houghton Mifflin, 1934.

Poe, Edgar Allan. *Collected Works.* 2 vols. Ed. Thomas Ollive Mabbott. Cambridge, MA: Belknap, 1969.

Pope, Alexander. *Selected Works.* Ed. Louis Kronenberger. New York: Random House, 1948.

Press, Charles. *The Political Cartoon.* London: Associated University Presses, 1981.

Rabelais, François. *Gargantua and Pantagruel.* Trans. Sir Thomas Urquhart and Peter Le Motteaux. London: D. Nutt, 1900.

Schlesinger, Arthur Meier. *The Rise of the City, 1878–1898: A History of American Life.* New York: MacMillan, 1933.

Seidel, Michael. *Satiric Inheritance.* Princeton: Princeton University Press, 1979.

Somers, Dale A. *The Rise of Sports in New Orleans, 1850–1900.* Baton Rouge: Louisiana State University, 1972.

Stevenson, Elizabeth. *Lafcadio Hearn.* New York: Macmillan, 1961.

Tinker, Edward Larocque. *Bibliography of the French Newspapers and Periodicals of Louisiana.* Worcester, MA: American Antiquarian Society, 1933.

———. *Lafcadio Hearn's American Days.* New York: Dodd, Mead and Co., 1924.

———. *Two-Gun Journalism in New Orleans.* Worcester, MA: American Antiquarian Society, 1952.

Turner, Arlin. *George W. Cable: A Biography.* Baton Rouge: Louisiana State University Press, 1966.

Waring, George E., and George W. Cable. *History and Present Condition of New Orleans, Louisiana, from Report on Social Statistics of Cities, 10th Census of the U.S.* Washington, D.C.: U.S. Department of the Interior, 1881.

Watson, John F. "Notitia of Incidents at New Orleans in 1804 and 1805." *American Pioneer: A Monthly Periodical Devoted to the Object of the Logan Historical Society* (Chillicothe, Ohio: Jno. S. Williams), 2 (1842): 227–37.

Wilds, John. *Afternoon Story: A Century of the "New Orleans States-Item."* Baton Rouge: Louisiana State University Press, 1976.

Worcester, David. "Selections from *The Art of Satire.*" In *Modern Satire,* ed. Alvin B. Kernan. New York: Harcourt Brace Jovanovich, 1962.

Wright, Thomas. *A History of Caricature and Grotesque in Literature and Art.* 1865. Reprint, New York: Frederick Ungar, 1968.

MANUSCRIPTS

Lafcadio Hearn Correspondence, Special Collections and Archives, Monroe Library, Loyola University, New Orleans.

GOVERNMENT RECORDS

Tenth Census of the United States, 1880.

PERIODICALS

Daily City Item (New Orleans), 1879–81. The woodcut images were drawn from copies in the archives of Tulane University Libraries, Special Collections, and from microfilm copies.
Daily Picayune (New Orleans), 1880–81.
Daily States (New Orleans), 1880–81.
Democrat of New Orleans, 1880–81.
Harper's New Monthly Magazine, 1861.
Item-Tribune (New Orleans), 1927.
Le Charivari Louisianais. New Orleans, 1846. Louisiana Collection, Special Collections, Tulane University Libraries. Tulane possesses the only known originals of this journal.
Manufacturer and Builder. Western and Company, 1885.
Times of New Orleans, 1880–81.

www.ingramcontent.com/pod-product-compliance
Lightning Source LLC
Chambersburg PA
CBHW020814230426
43666CB00007B/1010